Rights under Trial, Rights Reflections

POLITICAL AND SOCIAL CHANGE

Edited by Martin Bak Jørgensen and Óscar García Agustín

VOLUME 8

Zu Qualitätssicherung und Peer Review der vorliegenden Publikation

Die Qualität der in dieser Reihe erscheinenden Arbeiten wird vor der Publikation durch einen Herausgeber der Reihe sowie durch einen externen, von der Herausgeberschaft ernannten Gutachter im Blind-Verfahren geprüft. Dabei ist der Autor der Arbeit dem Gutachter während der Prüfung namentlich nicht bekannt.

Notes on the quality assurance and peer review of this publication

Prior to publication, the quality of the work published in this series is reviewed by one of the editors of the series and blind reviewed by an external referee appointed by the editorship. The referee is not aware of the author's name when performing the review.

Ben Dorfman

Rights under Trial, Rights Reflections

13 Further Acts of Academic Journalism
and Historical Commentary on Human Rights

Bibliographic Information published by the Deutsche Nationalbibliothek
The Deutsche Nationalbibliothek lists this publication in the Deutsche Nationalbibliografie; detailed bibliographic data is available in the internet at http://dnb.d-nb.de.

Library of Congress Cataloging-in-Publication Data
A CIP catalog record for this book has been applied for at the Library of Congress.

Cover Image: @ Akarawut/shutterstock.com

ISSN 2198-8595
ISBN 978-3-631-79938-3 (Print)
E-ISBN 978-3-631-80607-4 (E-PDF)
E-ISBN 978-3-631-80608-1 (EPUB)
E-ISBN 978-3-631-80609-8 (MOBI)
DOI 10.3726/b16314

© Peter Lang GmbH
Internationaler Verlag der Wissenschaften
Berlin 2020
All rights reserved.
Peter Lang Edition is an Imprint of Peter Lang GmbH.

Peter Lang – Berlin · Bern · Bruxelles · New York ·
Oxford · Warszawa · Wien

All parts of this publication are protected by copyright. Any utilisation outside the strict limits of the copyright law, without the permission of the publisher, is forbidden and liable to prosecution. This applies in particular to reproductions, translations, microfilming, and storage and processing in electronic retrieval systems.
This publication has been peer reviewed.

www.peterlang.com

To my students and children. Thank you.

Acknowledgments

This is the second of two volumes exploring a range of issues in human rights vis-à-vis history, politics, culture, international relations, and aesthetics – a range of elements contributing to the human rights lifeworld. This comes at a moment when the discourses of humanitarianism, if not rights themselves, are under strain. In the context of this situation, it is imperative that those committed to rights beliefs, behaviors, and mindsets speak up – that they articulate their understandings of the world around them and attempt to make those understandings as accessible and grounded as possible. This volume – indeed, both volumes involved in this project – are efforts in that direction. They hope to stand as occasions for discussion, chances for those both in academia and outside of it to explore and follow-up on particular lines of thought, and as an invitation for all to express their views on the state of rights issues both closer to home and more afar as well as concerning problems both highly tangible and more conceptual in nature. This book hopes that we will be ourselves in the face of such issues – that we will explain our perspectives and claim them as our own. These are imperfect volumes. They are also nonetheless volumes that will hopefully provoke.

The number of people involved in making this project possible has been innumerable. The History of Ideas division at Gothenburg University hosted me for an invaluable stay and set of seminars in 2017 that provided excellent food for thought for many aspects of this book. Close colleagues and friends like Marie Aquilino, Kalle Pihlainen, and Agnieszka Pantuchowicz provided invaluable discussion on many the central points in the essays presented here. Annette, thank you for all you are and the many provocative trips to places like Nuremberg. The students in the Language and International Studies Program at Aalborg University have often been the initial point of discussion for many of the ideas across these volumes, and they have my deepest gratitude and respect. The Department of Culture and Global Studies at Aalborg University has been highly supportive of this project and was willing to stand behind it at key moments. And, of course, series editors Óscar Garcia Agustín and Martin Bak Jørgensen deserve thanks for being willing to go out on a limb for something so adventurous and for maintaining a commitment to styles of communication working outside the norm. They've produced a provocative series of benefit to a world of academics and activists alike. Finally, I would like to thank my Ph.D. supervisor,

Benjamin C. Sax, from the Department of History at the University of Kansas. Ben, who recently passed, contributed much to the thinking across not only this volume, but an entire career. For his friendship and intellectual companionship, I will always be grateful. – *B.D., New York, New York, May 2019*

Contents

Introduction: The Fate of Rights in a Time of Trial: The Long Road Back 11

May 4, 2019

Mother May I: When We Lose Even When You Win 31

June 9, 2017

Dog Whistles You Can Hear: The White House and Social Strife 47

August 24, 2017

Codas of Anger and Silence: Finding Resolution from the Yugoslav '90s 67

December 12, 2017

Art, Being, and Human Rights: A Hamburg Exhibition 87

February 2, 2018

Justice and the Confrontation: Human Rights and Social Politics 101

February 12, 2018

Trespassing the Untrespassable: Poland and Its Holocaust Speech Law 121

March 21, 2018

Shirtless on a Horse: The Revenge of the Vozhd 139
March 29, 2018

The Turning Point: When Will It Stop in Israel/Palestine? 153
April 18, 2018

Tossin' Bombs and Sayin' "Uncle Tom": Where Michelle Wolf Got it Wrong 169
April 30, 2018

June in Singapore: When Militant Authoritarians Make Peace 181
May 15, 2018

When It Goes Too Far: Venezuela 195
May 23, 2018

Nuremberg: The Center of the Vortex 217
September 17, 2018

Khashoggi: A Tragedy and a Wrong 241
October 22, 2018

Introduction: The Fate of Rights in a Time of Trial
The Long Road Back
(May 4, 2019)

I would love to say that these are perilous times for human rights – however, when are they not? In my lifetime, the moment that seemed to hold the most human rights "promise" was the period in which the Berlin Wall came down and the Soviet Union moved to close its doors – not because the Soviet system was inherently anti-human rights, but because it seemed that a liberal consensus might have been on the cusp of emerging in which it was understood that democracy and inclusion were important and that peace might be the *raison d'être* of the new world order. Of course, it took little time before the cracks in that façade showed as Yugoslavia quickly descended into Europe's worst violence since the Second World War and genocide broke out in places like Rwanda.[1] Still, as momentum around the role of international institutions seemed to grow and there appeared to be a heightened willingness on the part of key actors to at least *refer* to the discourses of human rights, the health of what I've called the human rights "lifeworld" often seemed to be good. The human rights "lifeworld" refers to the notion of rights as points of reference for high politics and grass-roots social movements; the subject of empirical research as well as a source for the imaginations of fiction and film. I.e., in the post-Cold War world, it often felt as though human rights were simply "there." We might not always realize them, and they might be hard to effect. Still, there appeared to be a notion that one had to at least give *lip-service* to them, and, whether one was watching a film like *The Interpreter*

---

1 See Catherine Baker, *The Yugoslav Wars of the 1990s* (London: Palgrave, 2015); Linda Melvern, *Conspiracy to Murder: The Rwandan Genocide* (London: Verso, 2004). For a sense of the way in which a range of issues were being thought come the end of the Cold War period, see Michael J. Hogan, ed., *The End of the Cold War: Its Meanings and Implications* (Cambridge: Cambridge University Press, 1992). Of course, perhaps the decisive statement of post-Cold War optimism was Francis Fukuyama, *The End of History and the Last Man* (London: Penguin, 1992).

(2005) or reading a graphic novel like *Persepolis* (2000), the idea might at least inspire us.[2]

Indeed, I would say that the human rights "lifeworld" enjoyed relatively good health until relatively recently – sometime after 2015, to be exact. Now, yes, the U.S.' use of waterboarding, black sites, and "stress positions" vis-à-vis interrogations in the "War on Terror" seemed to mark a challenge to rights concepts and a "U-turn" in what should have been an era of increasing concord. However, such practices came under widespread criticism and, come the Obama era, they had essentially been rebuked.[3] For sure, countries like Denmark engaged in immigration politics that raised rights organizations' eyebrows.[4] Still, there seemed to be enough momentum for a Europe based on free movement and transnational identities that it wasn't clear that such attitudes wouldn't become the exception as opposed to the norm. Regimes from Turkey to Syria to Saudi Arabia clearly reeked of strongman politics. Still, the smell of Arab Spring

---

2   On the notion of the human rights "lifeworld," see Ben Dorfman, "A Human Rights Life-World? Politics, Society and Representation at the Start of the Twenty-First Century," *Academic Quarter* 5 (2012): 153–72.

3   See Peter Baker, "Obama's War Over Terror," *The New York Times*, January 4, 2010, https://www.nytimes.com/2010/01/17/magazine/17Terror-t.html. It's true that Obama didn't close Guantanamo Bay, as promised, nor did the harsh interrogation techniques borrowed from the Bush years that went into events like the killing of Osama bin Laden just disappear. It's also the case that the Bush, Jr. administration had taken moves against its own practices. Still, Obama tried to embody an attitude that displayed more interest in international rights standards and it had meaning that among his first acts in office was signing an executive order indicating the *intention* to close Guantanamo and stop waterboarding. I.e., he captured a public attitude that frowned on such violations and a political culture which had begun to do so as well. See also David P. Forsythe, "US Foreign Policy and Human Rights: Situating Obama," *Human Rights Quarterly* 33, no. 3 (2011): 767–89.

4   See Chris Bowlby, "Do Denmark's Immigration Laws Breach Human Rights?" *BBC News*, February 10, 2011, https://www.bbc.com/news/world-europe-12366676; Harriet Agerholm, "Denmark Uses Controversial 'Jewelry Law' to Seize Assets from Refugees for the First Time," *The Independent*, July 1, 2016, https://www.independent.co.uk/news/world/europe/denmark-jewellery-law-migrants-refugees-asylum-seekers-unhr-united-nations-a7113056.html; Rachael Kennedy, "A 'European Race to the Bottom': Human Rights Defenders Criticise Denmark's New Immigration Bill," *EuroNews*, February 22, 2019, https://www.euronews.com/2019/02/22/a-european-race-to-the-bottom-human-rights-defenders-criticise-denmark-s-new-immigration-b.

was in the air, even if results were hard to predict.⁵ The turning point? The 2015 European migration crisis and the 2016 election of Donald Trump. I.e., it's never been the case that human rights have *only* been advanced by the nations of the North or the "West." *Ranges* of countries have advocated for human rights' presence and contributed to their inculcation on regional as well as global scales.⁶ Still, the cultures of leading states seem to have become increasingly pervaded by attitudes that what matters is "mine" and "ours" and notions that particular territories are marked off only for particular people – that as opposed to referring to *broader* human inheritances, or the idea that one group's trials shouldn't necessarily be marked as of any less value than the trials of anyone else.⁷

Of course, there's a lot to unpack here. Vis-à-vis America's leadership on the world stage or the growth of institutions such as the EU: has it ever been the case that such things were *ever* more than the growth of a "new imperialism," as it's been put, or that "human rights" were *ever* more than the powers of the West dictating that their standards had to be the standards of everyone else? I'm not sure. Tensions between culture and rights are well-documented by now, and it's also well-known that great powers can become preachy about rights while

---

5   See Paul Danhar, *The New Middle East: The World after the Arab Spring* (London: Bloomsbury, 2013).
6   See Johannes Morsink, *The Universal Declaration of Human Rights: Origins, Drafting & Intent* (Philadelphia: University of Pennsylvania Press, 1999); Susan Waltz, "Universalizing Human Rights: The Role of Small States in Constructing the Universal Declaration of Human Rights," *Human Rights Quarterly* 23, no. 1 (2001): 44–72.
7   See Philip Alston, "The Populist Challenge to Human Rights," *Journal of Human Rights Practice* 9, no. 1 (2017): 1–15; Emir Yazici, "Nationalism and Human Rights," *Political Research Quarterly* 72, no. 1 (2019): 147–61; Glenda Sluga, *Internationalism in the Age of Nationalism* (Philadelphia: University of Philadelphia Press, 2013); Steve Carroll, "Nationalism is Back," *The Economist*, November 13, 2014, https://www.economist.com/news/2014/11/13/nationalism-is-back; The Economist, "The New Nationalism," November 19, 2016, https://www.economist.com/leaders/2016/11/19/the-new-nationalism; Christina Pazzanese, "In Europe, Nationalism Rising," *The Harvard Gazette*, February 27, 2017, https://news.harvard.edu/gazette/story/2017/02/in-europe-nationalisms-rising/; Bruce Stokes, "Populist Views in Europe: It's Not Just about the Economy," *Pew Research Center*, July 19, 2018, https://www.pewresearch.org/fact-tank/2018/07/19/populist-views-in-europe-its-not-just-the-economy/; Fernando López-Alves and Diane E. Johnson, eds., *Populist Nationalism in Europe and the Americas* (London: Routledge, 2018); Erin K. Jenne, "Is Nationalism or Ethnopopulism on the Rise Today?" *Ethnopolitics* 17, no. 5 (2018): 546–52.

sometimes falling short on rights standards themselves.[8] It's hard to know if interventions from Somalia to Yugoslavia or the *lack* of intervention in Rwanda were handled in precisely the right way; they're often described as bungled, and such arguments have often made out of rights perspectives themselves.[9] Still, be it from NATO actions in Kosovo to debates over how to handle the Syrian crisis' "red line," it's been interesting to hear *considerations* of the right response to situations and notions that that response should be handled at least *partially* by way of principle as opposed to pure national interest or victory in a *realpolitikal* competition.[10] It's also true that political projects such as the EU have been *economic* projects and, be it Europe's free-trade zone or that of North America (NAFTA), the growth of transnational capital has posed serious challenges to working classes and deepened senses of global "precarity."[11] Still, that hasn't been *absent* the realization that development might be an essential human right, nor without the response of global social movements who have argued that issues from the environment to the rights of indigenous peoples have to be taken into account (and organizations like the World Economic Forum pricking their ears up in response).[12] And, indeed, is this *really* the first time we've heard this or

---

8   See David Harvey, *The New Imperialism:* Oxford: Oxford University Press, 2003); Makau Matua, *Human Rights: A Political and Cultural Critique* (Philadelphia: University of Pennsylvania Press, 2002). See also Michael Hardt and Antonio Negri, *Empire* (Cambridge, MA: Harvard University Press, 2000).
9   See Ray Murphy, *UN Peacekeeping in Lebanon, Somalia and Kosovo: Operational and Legal Issues in Practice* (Cambridge: Cambridge University Press, 2007); Michael C. Davis, et al., eds., *International Intervention in the Post-Cold War World: Moral Responsibility and Power Politics* (London: Routledge, 2015).
10 See Chih-Hann Chang, *Ethical Foreign Policy?: US Humanitarian Interventions* (Farnham: Ashgate, 2011); John Shattuck, *Freedom on Fire: Human Rights Wars and America's Response* (Cambridge, MA: Harvard University Press, 2003); Forsyth, "US Foreign Policy;" Simon Chesterman, "The Responsibility to Protect, the Obama Doctrine, and Humanitarian Intervention after Libya," *Ethics & International Affairs* 25, no. 3 (2011): 279–85; Rodger Shanahan, "Syria Intervention: Obama's Unpopular Choices," *Australian Broadcasting Corporation News*, August 30, 2013, https://www.abc.net.au/news/2013-08-30/shanahan-syria-intervention/4923942.
11 See Matthew Johnson, ed., *Precariat: Labour, Work and Politics* (London: Routledge, 2015); Donatella della Porta, Tiina Silvasti, Sakari Hänninen and Martti Siisiäinen, eds., *The New Social Division: Making and Unmaking Precariousness* (New York: Palgrave MacMillan, 2015).
12 Jeffery F. Addicott, Md. Jahid Hossain Bhuiyan and Tareq M.R. Chowdhury, *Globalization, International Law, and Human Rights* (Oxford: Oxford University Press, 2013); Jorge E. Viñuales, *The Rio Declaration on Environment and Development: A*

that nation "first!" No. Ideas of American exceptionalism are well-recognized by now, and the skepticism of European states towards the EU *qua* project as well as doubts about multiculturalism in general are long-term parts of the continent's politics. Nonetheless, it's clear that, for many years, the momentum was towards international organizations' expansion and that the general tendency of such organizations was towards an interest in rights. As the Human Rights Watch 2017 World Report put it, we might be witnessing a global attack on human rights "values." We may today be experiencing subtle attacks on *concepts* of humanitarianism as well as the idea that, whether one lives in Paris or Dar es Salaam, we're all in this together.[13]

This book doesn't address all of these topics – though it addresses some of them, either directly or in implicit form. This book also isn't a treatise on rights nor a history of them, though it invokes notions of what rights should *do* and attempts to illustrate what a range of issues look like from a human rights-positive frame of mind. What this book *does*, like its sister volume from 2017, is pick-up thirteen topics from a subjectively-oriented cognitive space concerning international political and cultural affairs and offer *reactions* to those issues which blend dimensions of rights scholarship, dashes of international law, lines of thought concerning historiographical, aesthetic, and cultural concerns, and

---

Commentary (Oxford: Oxford University Press, 2015); Tahmina Karimova, *Human Rights and Development in International Law* (London: Routledge, 2016). Indeed, one of the major international rights declarations, the Vienna Declaration and Programme of Action (1993) might be seen as a direct response to such so-called "third generation" human rights issues. See Michael Posner, "Reflections on the Vienna Conference on Human Rights," *Proceedings of the Annual Meeting (American Society of International Law)* 91 (1997): 317–21; United Nations, "Vienna Declaration and Programme of Action" (1993), https://www.ohchr.org/en/professionalinterest/pages/vienna.aspx. It is also extremely telling, reading the World Economic Forum "Agenda" page. While the organization has been subject to extensive protest by groups looking for economic and climate justice (and often seen as representative of a "rich man's" club seen to be running the global economy via organizations such as the IMF or World Bank), the organization, as other international financial/monetary/economic organizations are, is at least attempting to indicate that it's *interested* in such issues by way of picking up precisely the vocabularies of protestors themselves. See, e.g., Natalie Pearce, "It's Not Just the Protests: Here's How Young People are Helping the Planet," World Economic Forum (Agenda), April 18, 2019, https://www.weforum.org/agenda/2019/04/its-not-just-the-protests-heres-how-young-people-are-fighting-for-the-planet/.

13   Human Rights Watch, "World Report 2017" (2017), https://www.hrw.org/sites/default/files/world_report_download/wr2017-web.pdf.

wrap the whole thing in a package in which the form is opinion pieces and a kind of journalistic writing, yet opinionating and journalism with a modicum of academic undergirding and a chunk of historiographical awareness. I.e., as with its predecessor volume, composed between 2014 and '16, many of this book's pieces refer to items prominent in the news while some pieces present more personal reflections, engaging artistic or historical sites. By the time this book comes out, the "apex" of the moment at which many of the pieces were written will have gone by, standing a year or two in the past. Nonetheless, the point is to indicate that human rights aren't just a matter of policy debate but that rights are a framework for approaching world affairs and a mode of thinking narratives we might ascribe to the past. Rights are a mindset and a mode of thought; they're a variety of philosophy and a meeting point for the "spirit" as well as the "letter" of the law. Again, aesthetically, the point has been to fuse a kind of *feuilleton*-esque writing style with reference to more "scholarly" arguments such that one creates entreaties to discuss the nature of rights ideas by offering the views on such issues one has *oneself*. The idea is to present one's own views *as* one's own views as opposed to determined matters of "science" or "truth." The point has also been to write in the flow of events elucidating thoughtways that might emerge as one encounters cultural and political scenes and approaches them with a general humanist's eye. Again, I seek to do nothing more than offer a *gestalt* sense of international justice, history of ideas, political theory, social change, and the history of arts and culture in the context of a maw for goings-on. The hope is to do nothing more than repel down into the lifeworld of a political concept and shine the light a bit around. That's at the same time that I'd like to suggest that one needn't repel to far because that lifeworld is around us, available, right there, on the surface.

Now, in this context, a few questions emerge. A few problems poke their heads up vis-à-vis what in some ways is a clearly academic book, yet also not. There's a question of what to do with a book that operates in *view* of scholarship, yet sometimes downplays "science" in favor of colloquialism and the invocation of subjective voice. What does one get from such writing – writing that happens at the interstices, or between the spaces of the intellectual and the academic, and vis-à-vis a vocabulary which should be simultaneously plain-spoken yet informed by an involvement with cultural theory and political philosophy?[14] What does one

---

14 It doesn't specifically use the vocabulary of "writing at the interstices" – that comes from a reviewer of the first volume of these books. However, I'd like to nod to Dahlia K, Remler, Don J. Waisanen and Andrea Gabor for their "Academic Journalism: A Modest Proposal," *Journalism Studies* 15, no. 4 (2013): 357–73. Though it didn't specifically

get out of the "*gestalt* perspective" – something generalistic and oriented towards "thoughts," or towards opening as opposed to *ending* debates, or having the last word in rights and international affairs?

In part, this book is concerned to say that not all academic communications need be about the "knowledge gap" and not *everything* need concern the "state of the art." It's concerned to assert that we need a *diversity* of academic communications, and there might be room for but reflection, showing the academic as *musing*, or magnifying the thoughts in which many of us are engaged. Indeed, that's central to this project: suggesting that "intellectuals are ordinary," or that, in the same way that a plumber might have a specific set of tools or lines of attack to address a stopped-up sink, so too might someone who's spent time in grad school, with history books, in cultural studies conferences, and talking with students about political issues in college classrooms have a set of wrenches available to them regarding socio-political concerns and the culturo-political tensions of the day.[15] I.e., we all look at and see the world; we all have thoughts about it. Many of us have socio-political awareness, and for most of us – indeed, I'd say all of us – when we read the newspaper or catch the news regarding an election or terrorist attack, the lights go on and a range of thoughts and observations come to mind. That raises the question, though, as to *what* observations come to mind, and, if one is asked to *say* something about those observations, what one might say. *What* does one seek to articulate, and what are the lines of thought involved? All, or at least many of us, enter into political and philosophical discourse with one another. Certain of us may have taken some history, philosophy, or political science courses. However, there is no "great conversation;" there's no one with whom we *have to* talk. There's only *the* conversation – a larger discourse in which all of us are involved. That's by way of being present for the world and having the capacity to react to it – which, it seems, we do.

Now, throughout this book, as well as its sister volume, I try to be careful about getting into exhaustive accountings of philosophical "schools" or name-dropping arrays of theoretical perspectives. I seek to take a plain-language approach, and that means not talking *only* in ways one has to have gone to grad school to understand. Still, I'd like to take a moment to name-check the late-nineteenth-century

---

influence this project – I discovered the article late in the writing process – Remler and company's proposal is not drastically distinct from mine: bridging the spaces of academic and journalistic writing, in part out of concern with the accessibility and relevance of the aesthetics of not a small amount of academic literature.

15 Stefan Collini, *Absent Minds: Intellectuals in Britain* (Oxford: Oxford University Press, 2006), 505.

philosopher Wilhelm Dilthey. Part of a philosophical movement that was concerned to establish rigorous modes of human scientific analysis yet which also recognized the enormous subjectivity of human life, Dilthey wrote about what he termed the "lived experience of time," or existence as we have it in a mundane way. "The ship of our life," Dilthey argued, "is…carried forward on a constantly moving stream." "The present," he put forward, is "wherever we are on those waves." There was an "interconnectedness," the philosopher proposed, to what appears before the mind.[16] Now, I'd also like to name-check a contemporary of Dilthey's from a similar philosophical school – the sociologist Georg Simmel. The relation between historical reality, Simmel wrote – history in its entirety, which simply can't be known – and what one perceives and emerges for one as one moves through space and time, is "no different from the relation between…the landscape painting and the complete reality it portrays." A "spontaneous functioning of personal subjective synthesis" is required to understand our surroundings, and phenomena can only be comprehended from their "focal point."[17] Winnowed down, we move through the world. *As* we move through the world, we bring certain information with us – information we've accumulated over time and which contributes to who we are. Out of that "base of information," or perspective, as such, we may see the truth of a thing, or we may not. We may have things as they are, or just imaginations of them. However, as we encounter the world, *massive* circuits of connections go off, senses of historical reality swing into play, convictions about ethics and morality are set into motion, understandings of logic and reason enter the framework, and we deploy ideas of social change and notions of what's "natural" and what's "not." We engage in a "descriptive psychology," as another theorist has called it, embarking on sense-making and establishing stories that in fact allow *gestalt* senses of a situation and its attendant concepts.[18] Indeed, as we're social creatures, we're likely to communicate those senses. Our narratives might be comprehensible to- or shared by- others; that's the nature of living in society. Because knowledge has to exist for *someone*, however, at the moment that one generates a story or an understanding, that story or understanding is fully *ours*; it's property of one's own.

---

16 Wilhelm Dilthey, "Awareness, Reality: Time: From 'Draft for a Critique of Historical Reason'" in *The Hermeneutics Reader*, ed. Kurt Mueller-Vollmer (New York: Continuum, 2002), 149–50.
17 Georg Simmel, *The Problems of the Philosophy of History: An Epistemological Essay*, trans. Guy Oakes (New York: Free Press, 1977), 82, 85.
18 Edmund Husserl, *Logical Investigations*, trans. J.N. Findlay (London: Routledge, 2001), 175.

This book is but an attempt to capture the thoughtways and chains of associations that have gone off for a specific individual in relation to a range of continuing socio-cultural sceneries and unfolding political events. The attempt has been to catalog a range of thoughts, experiences, and ideas emerging vis-à-vis particular historical and contemporary scenarios for *one person* and in relation to their "base of information." However, the point here is that that's been done because *that's what we do*. One can work in one's studio like Caravaggio, crafting the details of a particular study. Or, one can take one's paints into the field like Van Gogh and offer an impression. One can work on a portrait like Gainsborough; or, one can try to capture the moment of the rising sun, like Monet. I'd hardly claim that we've got Van Gogh- or Monet-like essays here. Still, I have wanted to load my paints into my backpack, stick the easel on the back of the bike, and go to the shore. That's to capture something of the moment one sees something, or provide the panoply of, when one looks at the sky, what comes into view.

Of course, that raises the question of to *what* sky one has looked at or to *which* shoreline one has gone – what fields has one tried to paint, or the impressions of *what* sceneries has one tried to convey? *Why* has one chosen the subjects one has, and is one on the terrain of the intentional, or the fully random? I.e., to the extent that we have a *range* of experiences and it's difficult to break the categories of experience off from one another, there are *millions of* issues one could have picked up to provide the kinds of analyses put forward here, or provide insight into the spaces in which human rights enter our lifeworld. As the historian Carlo Ginzberg argued in his *The Cheese and the Worms* (1976) – something of the historian's attempt to capture the immediate lifeworld of a subject – it's remarkable the number of things that can be compacted into small moments, what can feed into particular encounters with people, or what it takes to create a specific idea or thought. The "levels" of culture, Ginzberg asserted, are vast, and the "complex of attitudes, beliefs [and] codes of behavior" we maintain are labyrinthine. Many tributaries can flow into a river or stream, and there's by no means one path to get to the sea.[19] *Has* the approach here been like a gameshow contestant grabbing dollar bills in one of those "booths where they blow them around," as it was described in volume one, or has there been an *explicit* attempt to elucidate the multiple registers in which human rights play-out – a world of high politics,

---

19 Carlo Ginzberg, *The Cheese and the Worms: The Cosmos of a Sixteenth-Century Miller*, trans. John and Anne Tedeschi (Baltimore: Johns Hopkins University Press, 1980), xxi-ii.

combative cultural situations, encounters with art, architecture, and history, and goings-on in multiple geographical locales? *Has* there been an attempt to capture human rights as both "literal" and "figurative," or is it simply the case that such a thing has fallen into place?[20] Has there been *no* calculation involved – only stream of consciousness – or has there been an attempt to put a few stones and pebbles somewhere such that the stream goes *somewhere*, and enough brookside gardens get at least some of the water they're supposed to have?

I'd be lying if I said there wasn't some deliberation here. I.e., the pieces themselves should be impressionistic and the content an act of politicological "descriptive psychology." There is meditation on political-philosophical questions, and that in relation to a spectrum of events. Still, the point of departure for this book has been the idea that, as one historian puts it, human rights represent our "highest moral precepts and political ideals."[21] Even if rights standards have been dinged lately – and many of the essays attempt to convey that they have – it's *still* rights standards we tend to invoke as the measure of what's good and what's not, what we should be moving towards, and to provide a sense of what we're looking at when we look at a cultural or historical scene over and above obvious issues of political affairs. Invoking a point made by a number of scholars, human rights have a kind of ideological ascendancy today – they're the gold standard of global politics. However, it isn't just in the political realm that human rights play out. They also make their presence felt when we interpret the human story *generally*, and we look at a world of not only legislation and international relations,

---

20 I draw the vocabulary of "literal' and "figurative" from Edmund Husserl, *Ideas Pertaining to a Pure Phenomenology and to a Phenomenological Philosophy, First Book*, trans. F. Kersten (Dordrecht: Kluwer, 1983), 51. Husserl wasn't discussing human rights – at least not specifically. His notion of "literal" and "figurative" included *all* things, from mundane varieties of experience to concepts of society, the arts, rights, and law. The significance of Husserl's vocabulary, however, came in laying out the range of modes of existence for concepts and objects of consciousness in terms of their ability to appear tangible as well as more theoretical and intuitive. And, indeed, in later work, Husserl bordered on discussing how such ideas in fact touched specifically on readings of the political and ethical worlds. See Husserl, "Philosophy and the Crisis of European Man" in *Phenomenology and the Crisis of Philosophy*, trans. Quentin Lauer (New York: Harper Collins, 1965), 149–92.

21 Samuel Moyn, *The Last Utopia: Human Rights in History* (Cambridge, MA: Harvard Belknap, 2010), 1.

but spaces involving the arts and architecture, or locations involving historical memory.[22]

That has been important for me to capture. Historically, we often mark our world through high politics. Elections, summits, concords, treaties, major social upheavals – that's the stuff of history books, and for good reason. Firstly, not everything can be chronicled. There are choices to be made regarding our narratives, as sometimes we lack the material to fill them in. History, it's been argued, is occasionally driven by the form of narrative, or the idea that, come hell or high water, we have to get from point A to B.[23] Secondly, in the absence of being able to chronicle everything, we need events we feel are emblematic of larger atmospheres and might have significance vis-à-vis the run of the past. The "plot" has to be driven forward somehow, and that's sometimes at the level of "on the surface" affairs.[24] That's at the same time, though, that social history *does* exist. The arts and aesthetics are *part* of atmospheres we encounter. Memorialization, signification of the past, and the landscapes of cities are things we see and are part of a world we invest with meaning too. Any attempt to capture a "lifeworld," if not the lifeworld of a political concept, has to reflect this. It might not be *histoire totale*, as a group of historians once called it; it might not be an attempt to offer a *comprehensive* look at a historical scene or affair. It also might not be "grand history," as it's also been monikered, or an attempt to provide a unifying arc above everything else.[25] It might be something of a sampler

---

22 See Lynn Hunt, *Inventing Human Rights: A History* (New York: W.W. Norton, 2007); Costas Douzinas, *The End of Human Rights* (Portland: Hart, 2000); Stephen Hopgood, *The Endtimes of Human Rights* (Cornell: Cornell University Press, 2013); Daniel Levy and Natan Sznalder, *Human Rights and Memory* (University Park: Penn State University Press, 2010); Joseph Slaughter, *Human Rights, Inc.: The World Novel, Narrative Form, and International Law* (New York: Fordham University Press, 2007); Dorfman, "Are Human Rights a Philosophy of History?: The Case for the Defense," *International Social Science Review* 89, no. 1 (2012): 1–35.
23 See, e.g., Hayden White, "The Value of Narrativity in the Representation of Reality" in *The Content of the Form* (Baltimore: Johns Hopkins University Press, 1987), 1–25.
24 Ibid. White makes the wonderful point in this essay that in medieval chronicles in which important events from sets of years are noted, some years will be noted as simply "empty," waiting for another event of some kind of significance.
25 The notion of *histoire totale* was advanced by the so-called "Annales School" of historians, which attempted to address the "totality of the field of social force" – i.e. offer an exhausting, comprehensive reading of historical problems, from their most mundane, everyday and even environmental dimensions to the world of high political decision making. See J.H. Hexter, "Fernand Braudel and the *Monde Braudellien*" in *The Annales School: Critical Assessments, vol. III*, ed. Stuart Clark (London: Routledge,

plate, however, in which one gets a sense that rights ideas have at least a *possible* presence in looking at elections and international relations, but such things also make appearances in historical interpretation or even locations like literature and art. *Qua* idea, human rights have "triumphed on the world stage," it's been written. One finds them invoked by the "minister and the rebel" and from the "developing world [to] Hampstead and Manhattan." They're at least *among* the most referred to ideas in our "global culture."[26] The question is thus whether one captures this only by way of discussing figures like Trump and Putin, or if one can find other locations where rights ideals might wend their way in, helping us to understand our atmospheres.

Still, this book doesn't just describe where or how one finds rights in our "atmosphere" – how one might discuss events from Charlottesville to Caracas through a human rights lens. This book also *advocates* for rights and *criticizes* Nicolás Maduro, Donald Trump, and Vladimir Putin for not living *up* to them. It finds it *regrettable* when Theresa May announces on the eve of an election that she's skeptical of rights standards, and thinks it's *wrong* when Israelis and Palestinians do battle with each other and, especially, when Israel opens fire. The book doesn't *want* us to have regimes like those that built "party rally grounds" at Nuremberg (the Nazis), and it's *glad* the international community developed standards of international law it might use to indict inhumane, abusive regimes. This book is *glad* when an artist like Wolfgang Tillmans might offer us a sense of the rights subject, and it thinks we should pause and think for a moment about events like the end of major trials at the criminal court established to investigate war crimes in the former Yugoslavia. As was the case with volume one, we don't just have here an *analysis*, or explanation, of rights; we have arguments *for* them and an attempt to say that if one *isn't* living up to rights standards, it's a problem.

I need to make it clear that a third book will need to be part of this series. Firstly, if one wants a world organized around human rights standards, what would that look like and how would that happen? *How* does one constitute the "better society," as I sometimes put it, and how does one do that regardless of frontiers? *What* is likely to create a world of "freedom, justice and peace," as human rights phrase it, and what kind of political systems are likely to assure that people are accorded the dignity they're supposed to have?[27] In the most

---

    1999), 56. On the notion of "grand history," see Kerwin Lee Klein, *From History to Theory* (Berkeley: University of California Press, 2011), 91.
26 See Douzinas, *The End of Human Rights*, 1.
27 United Nations, "Universal Declaration of Human Rights" (1948, preamble), https://www.un.org/en/universal-declaration-human-rights/index.html. Hereafter UDHR.

direct sense, these are answers I *don't* provide in this book. I *don't* theorize global governance, nor global governance by way of human rights. I *don't* discuss the nature of a global social contract, nor do I discuss how one or the other state, group, or individual should be handled when they *violate* that contract or become involved in behavior we've said they shouldn't. I haven't discussed what the administrative units of a "human rights global system" would look like – do we maintain nation-states, for example? – and I also haven't presented a theory of what justice or fairness is, or what the "dignity" is that all are supposed to have. I.e., as these are shorter, impressionistic pieces, volumes one and two should be followed up by a piece of rights theory. There should be a longer work discussing the human rights lifeworld as not just a cultural or intellectual atmosphere, but an actually manifestable political practice in which rights form the basis of globally effective law.[28]

Still, there are indicators in this book that point in that direction. There are signposts about what the positions would be in a larger work of rights theory and an attempt to outline an effective space of rights politics. Firstly, I often point to the idea that one need recognize *both* essential varieties of human rights: civil and political, and social, economic and cultural rights. I know – there are discussions of other "generations" of rights exceeding some of the classically discussed rights terrain of the nineteenth and twentieth centuries. There have been criticisms that those approaches to rights are too informed by the classic standpoints of liberalism and socialism, without opening up for the possibilities of either a "third

---

28 Of course, human rights are, and well can be, "effective law." Concrete court decisions and politics are concretely our of human rights, and rights law is effective at both national and international levels. The question is how to *further* rights regimes, however, and have them as a yet, deeper, less-questioned dimension of global governance – i.e., a theory of what a system of global governance delivering universal justice would look like, yet tied to an elucidation of *why* human rights, and human rights as largely iterated today in major rights conventions, would be that point of reference. For a broad-lensed look at international human rights law, see Mashood A. Baderin and Manisuli Ssenyonjo, eds., *International Human Rights Law: Six Decades after the UDHR and Beyond* (London: Routledge, 2010). See also David Weissbrodt and Connie de la Vega, *International Human Rights Law: An Introduction* (Philadelphia: University of Pennsylvania Press, 2007). For the closest works to the concept I have in mind I've been able to so far find, see Daniele Archibugi, *The Commonwealth of Global Citizens: Towards Cosmopolitan Democracy* (Princeton: Princeton University Press, 2008); Janna Thompson, *Justice and World Order: A Philosophical Inquiry* (London: Routledge, 1992); Janie Leatherman and Julie A. Webber, eds., *Charting Transnational Democracy: Beyond Global Arrogance* (New York: Palgrave, 2005).

way," or potentially something else. There is sometimes a concern that the first two generations of rights derive from social movements that aren't contemporary enough, not embracing the asymmetries and postmodernisms of contemporary activism.[29] I tend to focus on civil and political rights and socio-economic rights, however, because I think they get at issues supremely fundamental: the idea that politics need address both our material lives and the life of the mind, thought, and "soul." Politics need involve foodstuffs and doctors, yet also what we could potentially write and say. I.e., in volume one of this project, I occasionally used the terms "material" and "intellectual" rights, and that has relevance here. If we don't keep the human being physically alive, we've got problems. Free speech and democracy mean little absent something to eat. However, human rights aren't the excuse for concentration camps. *Just* getting a bowl of porridge so your body makes it through the day is no human rights world. A world in which we *do* have democracy and free speech is.[30]

To that extent, I often suggest that while both socio-economic rights and civil and political rights need be upheld, it *is* a world in which the human being is able to pursue free thought and his or her potentials that's *really* what human rights envision. The "full" development of the human personality is a phrase I often pull out, and to me, it defines the teleology of rights.[31] In other words, there are highly concrete issues as to how we distribute global wealth and, *offhand*, I can't see why that's not done equally. *Offhand*, I can't see why somebody working ungodly long hours in lord-knows-what kind of conditions in the developing world should have to do that while someone who simply *inherited* money should be able to

---

29 This is to some extent addressed in footnote 12. I am also not trying to dismiss claims to further "generations" of rights. I am, though, asserting that, regardless of "generation," the categories of civil and political rights and socio-economic rights hold preeminence, and to some extent should, because there is an ultimate question of caring for both the material and intellectual individual – something no generation of rights wouldn't claim to do. See Darren Kew, Malcolm Russell-Einhorn and Adriana Rincón Villegas, "Rise of Global Human Rights Regimes: Challenging Power with Humanity" in *Interdisciplinary Approaches to Human Rights: History, Politics, Practice*, ed. Rajini Srikanth and Elora Halim Chowdhury (London: Routledge, 2018), 34–49; Jim Ife, *Human Rights from Below: Achieving Rights Through Community Development* (Cambridge: Cambridge University Press, 2009).

30 This point will come up several times over the course of the essays in this book. However, a touchstone for the notion that physical minimums don't equate with human rights standards comes from Giorgio Agamben, *Homo Sacer: Sovereign Power and Bare Life*, trans. Daniel Heller-Roazen (Stanford: Stanford University Press, 1995).

31 See UDHR, article 26.

live in luxury. I don't get why any laborer in the "first world" who is providing an essential service would make anything less than someone who's *not*. I also don't get why anyone living in any kind of world in between would *necessarily* see their labor as valued differently than someone else's, even if their work has less "prestige."[32] It doesn't seem to me, however, that rights envision a world of automatons. They *don't* provide for material sustenance simply to assure everyone goes home and sits in silence, prays to a "great leader," or doesn't make a critical remark or say something new. Rights suggest that we should be present for the world, and that that means *us*, as we are. One is supposed to be able to engage in reflection and share with others what one has thought. One is supposed to be able to say something about what one and others might do, and how things might be organized such that that "doing" might get done. Some would say this is "prioritizing" civil and political rights; that it's leaving material concerns aside in favor of the "spiritual." It's not. It's simply saying that rights aren't supposed to be about minimums. They're supposed to be about *realizing* human potential and theoretically *maximum* guarantees.[33]

And, here, a particular *epistemology* of rights comes into play. I suggest a particular *justification* for the rights ideal – human rights ideal – that I think *grounds* the plea for rights standards, or at least the demand that we notice that they're there. There's a particular *theory* of rights at work here, or at least the ethics around them, suggesting why human rights are a must. In other words, *though* this isn't the thorough, systematic going through of the political theory behind rights, or at least the political theory I'd like to advance, there are particular theoretical perspectives from which I'm departing that have politicological consequences.

Now, I almost don't at all use the vocabulary through the essays in this book. I come close a couple of times, but never quite get there. However, generally, one might call mine a "historical phenomenology" of rights. I.e., in contradistinction to human rights *themselves*, I *don't* see human rights as natural, and I see the human being as having *no* essence. I *don't* maintain a belief in a subject that's

---

32 Here, I obviously develop not only a roughly Marxist sense of the value of labor, yet also draw from notions of "social capital" in which the question is not just the financial valuation of labor, but also the understanding and valuation of social actors. See Richard Howson, *The Sociology of Postmarxism* (London: Routledge, 2017).
33 Of course, "spiritual" here is meant in the *intellectual*, not religious, sense – as related to the German notion of *Geist*. See Barbara Cassin, et al., eds., *Dictionary of Untranslatables: A Philosophical Lexicon* (Princeton: Princeton University Press, 2014), 368–73.

necessarily universal, and I prescribe no requirements to how human experience plays out. I *don't* find any necessary meaning in concepts like "mind" or "body," nor am I fully sure of what the one person needs as opposed to someone else. I'm *not* sure of the state into which human beings are "born," and I couldn't tell anyone what the end of history looks like. I have no idea about the teleology of law, nor can I prove who or how someone is supposed to have influence on how law is made. What I find interesting though, is that, in fact, we *do* have assertions about such things. For whatever reasons, it seems that *we* have decided that human rights are how we want to talk about justice and that, for whatever reason, "human rights" is not only what activists and do-gooders want to appeal to, but sometimes scoundrels, racists, and anti-Semites too (that we shouldn't forget *they* also have rights). We *have* created human rights acts at the national level – say, those of Britain and Canada. However, *more* convincingly, we have *massive* numbers of declarations, conventions, and laws at the *international* level. We *have* organizations like the UN, the European Court of Human Rights, the Inter-American Court of Human Rights, and the rights declarations of the League of Arab Nations. We have human rights declarations from organizations from the African Union to ASEAN, and, of course, many – indeed, most – major human rights conventions are ratified into the laws of states. Few regional organizations *haven't* published human rights standards or laws and, of course, massive numbers of *non*-governmental organizations are active on the human rights front.[34] Again, while this book posits neither a metaphysical need nor existential grounding for rights – that there's nothing about "God" or "Nature" demanding that "human rights" are something we have – it takes as highly noticeable that *we* seem to be saying there are things about God and Nature that have that effect, and that *we* might decide if we'd be interested to follow the pathways we've laid out to the "better society" or not.[35] Rephrased, the question for human rights isn't the standards we *might* invoke. It's rather the standards we *do*.

Now, I understand – that's a complex picture. Have all nations entered the human rights compact willingly? Perhaps not. Maybe human rights *are* something one has to pay lip-service to if one wants to be part of the "international community." Maybe they're a catechism one has to utter to assure that one won't

---

34 See, e.g., Dinah L. Shelton and Paola G. Carozza, *The Regional Protection of Human Rights* (Oxford: Oxford University Press, 2013); Claude E. Welch, Jr., ed., *NGOs and Human Rights: Promise and Performance* (Philadelphia: University of Pennsylvania Press, 2001); Jean H. Quataert, *Advocating Dignity: Human Rights Mobilizations in Global Politics* (Philadelphia: University of Pennsylvania Press, 2009).
35 See Morsink, *The Universal Declaration*, 284.

be badmouthed by the Americans or Europeans. Perhaps human rights are a mode of social control. Maybe they're a way of dividing the world up into good nations and bad and insisting certain places are "virtuous" while others are clear villains. And, how many people could tell you precisely what their human rights are whether you walk down the street in New Delhi, Mexico City, or a small town in Idaho? I don't pretend people walk around with the Universal Declaration of Human Rights (1948) in their hands like Mao's Little Red Book in Beijing in 1966. And, even if they did, they wouldn't be holding a legally binding document. Human rights *have* legal effect, and that need be noted. It can often well be their moral authority that holds sway, however, or again, that place where ideals and practicable law meet.[36]

Nonetheless, I also wouldn't be surprised if most people in Boise and Minsk have heard of human rights and in fact, it need be noted that we're *not* only talking about an idea. We *are* talking about a world of some quite concrete principles and indeed often law or, at the very least, a substantive body of discourses to which the social and political worlds refer. We're talking about an idea that actually has a body, and not small numbers of actors connected to a wide variety of institutions and movements have taken extensive time to systematize. That's meaningful and, as with volume one, that plays a central role in this book – making it concrete where our rights ideas are or putting it out there that when we talk about issues from free speech to equal pay for equal work, there's some codification of such things and a codification which is relatively accessible. In terms of the central positions of this book, however – its "epistemology" – more to the point is that, *because* we've put them out there, we may have a choice. Because we've institutionalized rights ideas at political and legal levels, there are questions of what those institutionalized ideas *say*. Do we *not* think that "everyone has the right to life, liberty and security of person," and do we not think that people deserve "freedom of thought?" Do we *not* think that "slavery and servitude" are problems (indeed, should be outlawed), or that no one should be "subjected to torture," or be free of "degrading treatment of punishment?" Are we *not* in agreement that people should have a "fair and public hearing," or that we should be treated equally before the law? Do we

---

36 Of course, vis-à-vis the current American government, whether or not nations live up to rights standards may be of little consequence. That point is made in a couple of the essays. However, emblematic of this is the U.S.' withdrawal from the UN Human Rights Council. See BBC, "US Quits 'Biased' Human Rights Council," June 20, 2018, https://www.bbc.com/news/44537372. See also, e.g., Thomas Risse, Stephen C. Ropp and Kathryn Sikkink, *The Power of Human Rights: International Norms and Domestic Change* (Cambridge: Cambridge University Press, 1999).

not agree that "food, clothing, housing and medical care" are necessities, and do we think that anyone *doesn't* deserve not to be discriminated against because of their gender? Indeed, are any of us *not* looking for "freedom, justice and peace" in the world, and do any of us *want* our societies built off of "barbarous acts?" Is a world in which we abrogate our "equal and inalienable" worth a world we're looking *for*, and is releasing the forces of "tyranny" and "oppression" something we seek? In other words, I don't care how human rights got "made." Maybe some slow "mobility of [our] epistemological arrangement[s]" explains how we moved from a world where we didn't believe in human rights to one in which we do.[37] It may also be the case that not everyone spends oodles of time on the UN website or that international law sometimes has amorphous authority. Many of us have *asked* for rights standards, however; enormous numbers of us have petitioned for recognition out of human rights arguments. Broad-based social movements have been established based on rights ideas and important politicians and cultural voices point to such concepts and promote their worth. We've *in fact* created institutions – many of them – to promote and support human rights, and those institutions haven't only been influenced by a cabal of university-educated elites, but wide swathes of citizens over many decades indicating they'd like justice too. One can accuse rights of being imperialistic or sometimes not taking all views of the human being into account. One *can* deconstruct rights or demonstrate their historicity, suggesting that potentially, the "age of rights" will disappear. In our day and age, however – in times we have made – we have to carefully ask if universal dignity is not a concept we believe in, and if we *don't* think that everyone should be dealt with in certain fundamental ways, somebody has to explain why.[38]

Those, then, are the concerns that animate this book. Those are the concepts, that though in different ways and vis-à-vis multiple places in our political and cultural lifeworlds, I seek to advance. Those are the philosophies I seek to promote, and those are the positions on which I attempt to stand. At large, we own our rights futures. The "better society," as such, is up to us. *If* we're interested in thinking through and promoting political standards, we need to deal with a concept we've

---

37 Michel Foucault, *The Order of Things* (New York: Vintage, 1994), 217. In essence, Foucault's argument was that what's understood as "real," "obvious," "transcendental" or "empirical" – in essence, true – was contingent upon the ordering of knowledge and an era's particular epistemological arrangements. This included political concepts. See also Foucault, *Discipline and Punish: The Birth of the Prison*, trans. Alan Sheridan (New York: Vintage, 1979). This involved a critique of rights: realizing them as historically contingent as opposed to transcendental truth.
38 The quoted rights principles are from UDHR, articles 3, 18, 4, 5, 10, 25, preamble.

put out there, and in which governments, social groups and movements, individual citizens, the young and the old, and in many places and many locales around the world, have said they have interest. Again, the most important question may not be *why*, but whether or not we *don't* think that the larger bulk of ideas represented in major rights declarations and covenants *in fact* represent the vision of the kind of societies in which we'd like to live. The most important question is whether, roughly, when we point to, say, the broad range of ideas indicated in a document like the Universal Declaration of Human Rights, we *haven't* got our hands on something that looks like what we want and whether or not, if that *is* the case, it shouldn't be pointed out when we fall short, or how meaningful and prevalent those ideas are. Again, "human rights" can't be accepted uncritically – rights are supposed to encourage free thought, which involves their own criticism. One wants to see what in rights ideas can be dangerous because dangerous isn't how rights are supposed to be.[39] Still, the issue is comprehending how we *do* talk about justice, having a sense of what it means to us, entering into discourse with one another about such things, and letting the issue somehow breathe. It's laying our standards before us, letting them have a life with us, and saying something about how that life goes. That's again because it seems like, to more than a few of us, it's relatively important: that we find societies of recognition, that we feel a level of fairness, and that we feel seen as human beings. Maybe human rights have taken a hit. Maybe this isn't their best moment; maybe there's an aggressive tack in today's politics making us wonder where rights ideas have gone. There *is* a way back though: offering our *own* reflections on rights issues, engaging rights' charges ourselves, and discussing what about them that *we* see as important. It's positioning ourselves vis-à-vis ideas we find meaningful and trying to find *some* way to indicate why we see them that way. Over thirteen essays, from the results of the British elections in 2017 to personal moments of cultural reflection to the death of Jamal Khashoggi, that's what I've tried to do: offer my take on a portion of a moving world of rights issues and scenarios and my sense of the dimensions of the idea. It's done a bit randomly and a touch haphazardly; it's somehow an imperfect project. That's the world of perception and commentary, however – fast-moving, full, and occasionally incomplete.

---

39 Indeed, this emerges as a theme in several of the essays: that one need be careful that rights aren't addressed without consciousness of the idea that they *can* discipline and be mechanisms used to box individuals into standards which *are* socially arrived at. Agamben (see footnote 30) and Foucault (see footnote 37) are often invoked as touchstones for this idea. Again, though, the question is whether this is what rights *can* do, or are *intended* to do.

Mother May I
When We Lose Even When You Win
(June 9, 2017)

Abstract: *The UK held elections last night, and, in the wake of recent terrorist attacks, security was on the agenda. That's while Labour did better than expected. At the end of the electoral cycle, Theresa May offered deep criticisms of human rights. That's disappointing given the historical importance of British liberalism to rights theory as well as its importance the history of democratic thought at large.*

Clearly, the whole thing was noticeably more of a nail-biter than it should have been. On May 10th, *The Guardian* newspaper noted a poll gap between Jeremy Corbyn, the left-leaning Labour Party leader, and Theresa May, his opposite number in the Conservatives, of roughly 16% – the recipe for what would be a pretty thorough trouncing if the numbers held good. Of course, that was after a *disastrous* set of local elections on May 4th in which a party that's been one of the UK's main staples since the 1920s (Labour) managed to gain barely more than a quarter of the vote.[1] When the final results came in, however, much of the electoral furniture had been rearranged, even if the tables hadn't been completely turned. The Tories, expected to keep a stranglehold on their parliamentary majority if not make a few gains, did no such thing. Rather than pushing forward or at least holding onto the preponderance of MPs, May's Conservatives *lost* twelve seats – that

"The United Kingdom or Union Jack grunge flag" @PHOTOCREO Michal Bednarek/shutterstock.com 205060654

---

1 See The Guardian, "Councilor Gains and Losses," May 5, 2017, https://www.theguardian.com/politics/ng-interactive/2017/may/04/local-and-mayoral-elections-2017-live-results-tracker; Toby Helm, "Trust in Theresa May Raises Tory Hopes in Labour's Northern Heartlands," *The Guardian*, May 6, 2017, https://www.theguardian.com/politics/2017/may/06/poll-shows-tories-holding-election-advantage-with-five-weeks-to-go.

while Corbyn's Labour gained a stunning thirty-one. A party that had been left for dead had suddenly come roaring back to life. Not since Bernie Sanders lifted his arms in victory after the February 2016 New Hampshire Democratic primary have I seen a politician look as positively invigorated as did Mr. Corbyn come last night.[2]

Of course, it's an election with much behind it. The UK is involved in Brexit negotiations – something with significant consequences for the Eurosphere – and the UK's path has meaning *beyond* Europe as the country stands as perhaps the U.S.' closest ally, it maintains one of the world's eight or nine nuclear arsenals (it's not just social programs at stake when Britain votes), it stands as one of the top handful of nations in terms of generalized military might *regardless* of how one measures such things, and London will continue as a world financial center regardless of the particular agreement the country happens to come to with the EU.[3] That's at the same time that Britain finds itself in the midst of a revitalized "War on Terror," or, even if that vocabulary isn't *de rigueur*, dealing with the consequences of a recent string of incendiary attacks prosecuted on national shores.[4] The first of those attacks, lest it be forgotten, was committed by a self-described British "patriot": the 2016 murder of Jo Cox – Cox being a Labour parliamentarian who was dedicated to intercultural outreach and who maintained sympathy for especially the plight of Syrian refugees.[5] According to her attacker,

---

2 For an iconic photo of Sanders after his New Hampshire win, see Molly Ball, "Sanders Wins New Hampshire," *The Atlantic*, February 9, 2016, https://www.theatlantic.com/politics/archive/2016/02/bernie-sanders-new-hampshire/462105/.

3 On Britain in the world economy, see Bernard W.E. Alford, *Britain in the World Economy since 1880* (London: Routledge, 1996). Of course, it can be that the final deal reached with the EU *will* have economic impact on the UK; that's part of the idea that there should be a deal with the bloc as opposed to a "hard" exit in which the UK simply leaves. Still, a long history of Britain as a global financial center will not be easy to undo. See also Financial Times, "What Brexit Means for the UK Economy," March 2, 2016, https://www.ft.com/content/1465ef50-da34-11e5-98fd-06d75973fe09.

4 On the "War on Terror" vocabulary, see Oliver Burkeman, "Obama Administration Says Goodbye to 'War on Terror,'" *The Guardian*, March 25, 2009, https://www.theguardian.com/world/2009/mar/25/obama-war-terror-overseas-contingency-operations.

5 See Holly Yan and Jo Sterling, "Jo Cox: Mother, Humanitarian, Politician Killed by an Attacker," *CNN*, June 17, 2016, http://www.cnn.com/2016/06/16/europe/jo-cox-profile/index.html; The Guardian, "The Guardian View on Jo Cox: An Attack on Humanity, Idealism and Democracy," June 16, 2016, https://www.theguardian.com/commentisfree/2016/jun/16/the-guardian-view-on-jo-cox-an-attack-on-humanity-idealism-and-democracy.

Cox had not put "Britain first" – a phrase he yelled as he committed his dastardly act, and which represented a regrettable articulation of the hyper-nationalistic sentiment that's seeped into the politics of more than a few European states.[6] The three further attacks, however, fit, for better or worse, into a more stereotyped view of how the terrorist attack should look. On March 22nd, Khalid Masood, though himself a British passport holder, drove a car into a group of pedestrians on Westminster Bridge, killing five and injuring fifty; that before making his way towards the Houses of Parliament, where he was summarily shot. The grounds for the attack were thought to emerge from the kind of jihadism inspiring groups like Al-Qaeda and Islamic State – though authorities found no direct connection between Masood and IS.[7] On May 22nd – within the space of the recent electoral cycle – *twenty-two* people were killed and over *one hundred* were injured as a bomb exploded at a pop concert in Manchester's largest arena. The bomber was Salmen Abedi, and, *à la* Masood, his motives were *also* thought to be connected to the extremism preached by organizations like Al Qaeda and IS (though, again, precise connections turned out to be less-than-easy to make).[8] Then, but days before the national election (June 3rd), *eight* people were killed, and *dozens* were injured in something of a repetition of March 22 – only this time with *London Bridge* as the target and terrorists going after people in local shops once they found themselves afoot.[9] Predictably, expressions of outrage and assurances of

---

6   Robert Booth, Vikram Dodd and Nazia Parveen, "Labour MP Jo Cox Dies after Being Shot and Stabbed," *The Guardian*, June 16, 2016, https://www.theguardian.com/uk-news/2016/jun/16/labour-mp-jo-cox-shot-in-west-yorkshire. See also *The Economist*, "The New Nationalism," November 19, 2016, http://www.economist.com/news/leaders/21710249-his-call-put-america-first-donald-trump-latest-recruit-dangerous.
7   See Griff Witte, "No Evidence London Attacker Was Linked to Islamic State, Police Say," *The Washington Post*, March 27, 2017, https://www.washingtonpost.com/world/europe/no-evidence-london-attacker-was-linked-to-islamic-state-police-say/2017/03/27/28791d48-130c-11e7-bb16-269934184168_story.html?utm_term=.23d448a988ad.
8   Esther Addley, Nazia Parveen, Jamie Grierson and Steven Morris, "Salmen Abedi: From Hot-Headed Party Lover to Suicide Bomber," The Guardian, May 26, 2017, https://www.theguardian.com/uk-news/2017/may/26/salman-abedi-manchester-arena-attack-partying-suicide-bomber.
9   See Steven Erlanger, "Another Terrorist Attack Strikes the Heart of London," *The New York Times*, June 3, 2017, https://www.nytimes.com/2017/06/03/world/europe/london-bridge-van.html?mcubz=1&_r=0; Yonette Joseph, "London Bridge Attack: The Implements of Terror," *The New York Times*, June 11, 2017, https://www.nytimes.com/2017/06/11/world/europe/london-bridge-attack-knives-fake-suicide-vests-van.html?mcubz=1.

increased security followed each of these events.[10] It was an "evil act," proclaimed Manchester mayor Andy Burnham in reaction to May 22; the city and the national government would do everything in their power to make sure such things never happened again.[11] The June 3rd attack, however, received a particularly vociferous response. In what's tough to see as anything but an attempt to project a face of force before the national electorate, Theresa May suggested that if human rights laws were "getting in the way" of preventing terrorist attacks – if they didn't allow law enforcement to act quickly enough, or if they allowed people to stay in the country who were suspected of harboring terrorist-sympathetic views – then the country's relation with human rights law should be changed. At issue seems to have been the UK's relation with the European Convention on Human Rights (1950) and the nation's 1998 Human Rights Act. Both are oft-indicated landmarks in the attempt to deepen global attachment to essential freedoms and privileges on national as well as global scales.[12]

Of course, it's not the first time that human rights have been identified as problematic regarding "security" or maintaining the defense of states. In the U.S., e.g., the Bush, Jr. administration was willing to push the boundaries of treaties like the UN's Convention against Torture and Other Cruel, Inhuman or Degrading Treatment or Punishment (1984) and the Geneva Conventions (1949) in the

---

10 See Lianna Brinded, "Theresa May: 'Tomorrow Morning, Parliament Will Meet as Normal. We Will Come Together as Normal. And Londoners and Others around the World Will Get Up and Go about Their Day as Normal,'" *Business Insider*, March 22, 2017, http://www.businessinsider.com/theresa-may-speech-westminster-london-attacks-terrorism-suspect-victims-2017-3?r=UK&IR=T; BBC News, "Manchester Attack: Theresa May Terror Threat Speech in Full," May 23, 2017, http://www.bbc.com/news/uk-40023457.
11 Esther Addley, et al., "Manchester in Shock as Families Search Desperately for Missing Victims," *The Guardian*, May 23, 2017, https://www.theguardian.com/uk-news/2017/may/23/manchester-attack-city-shock-search-victims-continues.
12 Rowena Mason and Vikram Dodd, "May: I'll Rip Up Human Rights Laws That Impede New Terror Legislation," *The Guardian*, June 6, 2017, https://www.theguardian.com/politics/2017/jun/06/theresa-may-rip-up-human-rights-laws-impede-new-terror-legislation. See also Ed Bates, *The Evolution of the European Convention on Human Rights: From Its Inception to the Creation of a Permanent Court of Human Rights* (Oxford: Oxford University Press, 2010); Dinah Shelton and Paolo G. Carozza, *Regional Protection of Human Rights, vol. 1* (New York: Oxford University Press, 2013); David Hoffman and John Rowe, *Human Rights in the UK: An Introduction to the Human Rights Act 1998* (Harlow: Pearson, 2010).

name of gaining information on groups like Al-Qaeda and the Taliban; the use of waterboarding and stress positions at black sites and places like Guantanamo Bay is by now a well-documented affair.[13] Turkey, to turn to but another example, has but *feasted* on the idea of eroding the soft edges of rights – that in the name of defending the "people" and especially since the July 2016 coup that attempted to bring the Erdoğan government down.[14] Of course, the Cold War as an entire historical *period* featured extensive surveillance efforts by supposedly democratic governments – that though it was in the name of values like free speech and the right to critique authority that democratic regimes *existed*, and in whose name it was justified to take the fight to the communist "enemy" so hard.[15] Still, hearing criticisms of rights ideals coming from the lips of a sitting PM was jolting. Sometimes, the U.S. and France are posited as human rights' historical seat. That's due to the meaning of figures like Rousseau, Voltaire, and Jefferson, and the significance of documents like the Declaration of the Rights of Man and Citizen (France, 1789) and the U.S.' Declaration of Independence (1776). Still, British intellectual history has played no less a role in basic rights' formulation as figures like Thomas Hobbes provided essential conceptions of the social contract and thinkers like John Locke argued that governments should make their first

---

13 See Matt Apuzzo, Sheri Fink and James Risen, "How U.S. Torture Left a Legacy of Damaged Minds," *The New York Times*, October 9, 2016, https://www.nytimes.com/2016/10/09/world/cia-torture-guantanamo-bay.html?mcubz=1; Tzvetan Todorov, *Torture and the War on Terror*, trans. Gila Walker (New York: Seagull, 2009); Jason Ralph, *America's War on Terror: The State of the 9/11 Exception from Bush to Obama* (Oxford: Oxford University Press, 2013).

14 See Harry Cockburn, "Turkey Coup: 2700 Judges Removed from Duty Following Failed Overthrow Attempt," *The Independent*, July 16, 2016, http://www.independent.co.uk/news/world/europe/turkey-coup-latest-news-erdogan-istanbul-judges-removed-from-duty-failed-government-overthrow-a7140661.html; Rod Nordland, "Turkey's Free Press Withers as Erdogan Jails 120 Journalists," *The New York Times*, November 17, 2016, https://www.nytimes.com/2016/11/18/world/europe/turkey-press-erdogan-coup.html?mcubz=1.

15 See, e.g., Seth Rosenfeld, *Subversives: The FBI's War on Student Radicals, and Reagan's Rise to Power* (New York: Farrar, Strauss and Giroux, 2010); Luca Prono, "Cointelpro" in *Encyclopedia of Intelligence and Counterintelligence*, ed. Paul F. Kisak and Rodney P. Carlisle (London: Routledge, 2005), 146–7; David C. Engerman, "Ideology and the Cold War, 1917–1962" in *The Cambridge History of the Cold War, vol. 1: Origins*, ed. Melvyn P. Leffler and Odd Arne Westad (Cambridge: Cambridge University Press, 2010), 20–43; James Smith, *British Writers and MI5 Surveillance, 1930-1960* (Cambridge: Cambridge University Press, 2013).

principle the recognition of the individual's naturally free state.[16] One thus wonders what May was up to – that again as many view Great Britain, along with powers like America and France, as among those nations most likely to *speak up* for rights' sustenance and to push for their institutionalization on the terrain of both national and international law.[17]

Now, for sure: such issues are complex, and rights – perhaps especially "abstractly universal" *human* rights – *can* be difficult to comprehend ("abstract universality" being the vocabulary one historian uses to describe the nature of rights ideals and commitments to fundamental freedoms).[18] "Freedom versus security" balances *can* be difficult to work out, and there is something highfalutin' when one gets overly philosophical about rights' "nature," or the "essence" of principle in the space of international affairs. I'll take the former point first. Human rights *themselves* assert one of their primary goals as "freedom from fear."[19] One shouldn't live one's life in a state of existential threat, and the rule of law should reign. Now, a problem for rights is that they sometimes focus on "bare life." Rights *can* define *minimally* satisfactory lives as opposed to addressing richer visions of what the human being might do. If one guarantees, say, the right to life (a fundamental rights principle), that doesn't indicate what *kind* of life one might lead or if the kind of life one prescribes for others is the kind of life one might like to lead *oneself* (it's been argued that even concentration camps kept people alive – something hardly standing as a mark in human rights' favor). This is part of an intense critique of rights – the idea that rights sometimes appear but rhetorical, and that they can be used to get away with behavior that doesn't

---

16 See Jonathan Gorman, *Rights and Reason: An Introduction to the Philosophy of Rights* (New York: Routledge, 2014).
17 Observers of UK politics will note that it's not the first time May has said such things. As Home Secretary, she made deep criticisms of rights conventions in relation the Abu Hamza case – the controversial Finsbury Park imam now in prison in the U.S. Still, if one wasn't aware of that, that any PM would take her stance is startling, and it caught many by surprise anyway as it's been hard to know how seriously to take her rights criticisms. See Anushka Asthana and Rowena Mason, "UK Must Leave the European Convention on Human Rights, Says Theresa May," *The Guardian*, April 25, 2016, https://www.theguardian.com/politics/2016/apr/25/uk-must-leave-european-convention-on-human-rights-theresa-may-eu-referendum.
18 Lynn Hunt, *Inventing Human Rights: A History* (New York: W.W. Norton, 2007), 153.
19 United Nations, "The Universal Declaration of Human Rights" (1948, preamble), http://www.un.org/en/universal-declaration-human-rights/index.html. Hereafter UDHR.

seem rights-oriented.[20] That's at the same time that it remains difficult to argue about what *kind* of life individuals might lead if individuals aren't allowed to *exist* – wherein providing elemental security might be a concept with more than elemental importance. Rights versus security? Security may come first. Making sure a stroll across London Bridge remains just that might be the duty of any responsible public servant.

And, indeed, I attach the term "abstract" to human rights (and place the "human" in italics) because, when one *is* talking about rights – rights in their broadest sense (what the "human" is intended to designate) – one *is* talking about regimes that should have few physical borders and *aren't* supposed to be rooted in specific geographical space. One *is* discussing ideas that should pertain to broad populations and which should flow over and under the boundaries of states.[21] The conventions in question in the UK – again, the European Convention on Human Rights and the British Human Rights Act (it's hard to know what else they would be) – are examples of this.[22] Both are inspired by the UN rights regime, or the range of global socio-political standards established

---

20 Largely, I'm drawing arguments here from Giorgio Agamben, *Homo Sacer: Sovereign Power and Bare Life*, trans. Daniel Heller-Roazen (Stanford: Stanford University Press, 1995). In fact, Agamben's thesis is a touch more complex than I suggest. He maintained a distinction, e.g., between "bare life" and "political life" – the raw person versus the citizen, wherein the creation of citizens became the purpose of modern political systems. Still, the idea of "creating citizens" is ironic – should not democracies *reflect* citizens as opposed to creating them? – and, as one commentator on Agamben's work has noted, human rights in their minimalism may have sometimes allowed modern states to avoid taking a holistic view of the person; rights minimalism may allow people to be viewed as "undifferentiated biological units" – an idea with a distinctly un-rights sounding ring. See James Tunstead Burtchaell, Review of *Homo Sacer: Sovereign Power and Bare Life* by Giorgio Agamben, *The Review of Politics* 34, no. 6 (2006), 625. Many would also see this as connected to the view of politics provided by Michel Foucault in works such as *Discipline and Punish: The Birth of the Prison*, trans. Alan Sheridan (New York: Vintage, 1979).
21 In the words of Kofi Annan, former UN Secretary General, human rights should "cross any border, climb any wall, defy any force." See Annan, "Message by the United Nations Secretary-General," in *Reflections on the Universal Declaration of Human Rights: A Fiftieth Anniversary Anthology*, ed. Barend van der Heijden and Bahia Tahzib-Lie (The Hague: Martinus Nijhoff, 1998), 18
22 The normative power of the broadest human rights conventions – those housed in the UN – was likely not May's target; that is dangerous territory indeed. However, yet again, she has criticized the European Convention in the past, and (again) when human rights are discussed in the UK, it in fact tends to be through the 1998 Human

by the international community in the years following the Second World War. Discussing the European Convention, e.g., one might note the treaty as designed in "consider[ation] of the Universal Declaration [of Human Rights]," and intended to secure the "universal and effective recognition…of the Rights…declared therein" (broad ranges of civil liberties and social privileges).[23] UN rights should be *Europe's* rights too, and *European* nations should play a role in promoting the ideas and concepts of justice advanced by the *global* community of states. Britain's 1998 Human Rights Act "give[s] further effect to the rights and freedoms guaranteed under the *European* Convention on Human Rights." *UK* law should further *Europe's* rights ideas, wherein the UK should be in tune with *UN* concepts of justice.[24] Now, intentions behind speech can be hard to figure out. As it's difficult to determine what an artist means when they paint, one can't always be sure what's in someone's head when they utter a statement or phrase. Still, one might see May as appealing to something that one sometimes finds in popular reaction to European governance from Brussels or, in American contexts, arguments for the devolution of federal power to individual states: namely, that what's happening in faraway places like Washington or the EU capital may not have much to do with the circumstances in which most people *live*. Never mind institutions with amorphous authority like the UN offices on First Avenue in New York. When it comes to international law or the authority invested in regimes involved in *collectivities* of states, wow, are we talking about ideas and concepts generated in faraway places and perhaps not formulated by the everyday woman or man. As one-time First Lady Eleanor Roosevelt put it, it might be nice to have a "Magna Carta" for all of humankind; statements of universal principle are absolutely good.[25] If Magna Cartas don't speak to the circumstances in which most people *live*, however, what's the point? May might have been playing to that idea – that one can comprehend *national* politics, perhaps, or maybe events on a local scale. Anything larger is dubitable, however, as

---

Rights Act. See also Conor Gearty, *On Fantasy Island: Britain, Europe, and Human Rights* (Oxford: Oxford University Press, 2016).
23 Council of Europe, "European Convention on Human rights" (1950, preamble), http://www.echr.coe.int/Documents/Convention_ENG.pdf. Hereafter ECHR.
24 See The National Archives, "Human Rights Act 1998" (1998, introduction), http://www.legislation.gov.uk/ukpga/1998/42/introduction.
25 "Magna Carta" for humankind was how Roosevelt termed the Universal Declaration of Human Rights. See Micheline R. Ishay, *The History of Human Rights: From Ancient Times to the Globalization Era* (Berkeley: University of California Press, 2004), 218.

it's unclear what it has to do with regular people and the range of experiences regular people have.[26]

I take this to mean a few things. Firstly, there's such a thing as common sense. People live in places, and lives aren't theoretico-legal tracts. The philosopher Alasdair MacIntyre once made the point that justice need be thought in relation to communities and that communities are grounded *somewhere* – not in the ether of theoretical air.[27] True enough; Brussels and Washington are far away, and perhaps New York further still. Still, drawing back from principles one has subscribed to on the basis that they *in fact* concern standards to which all should subscribe can set a dangerous precedent; pulling back from ideas that *should* pertain to everyone can put us on a slippery slope. Yes: rights treaties often have "derogation" clauses via which rights can be suspended. The UN's International Covenant on Civil and Political Rights (1966) notes that, "in time of public emergency which threatens the life of the nation…the State Parties [to rights conventions] may take measures derogating from their obligations to the extent…required by the exigencies of the situation."[28] Have a situation bad enough, and one *can* turn down the volume on rights discourse and law. The *European* Convention notes that, "in time of war or other public emergency threatening the life of the nation, any High Contracting Party may take measures derogating from its obligations [in the Convention]…to the extent strictly required by the exigencies of the situation, provided that such measures are not inconsistent with its other obligations under international law."[29] Again, if the reason's good enough, one might walk *some* distance away from certain rights practices. Still, that's *only* "provided that such measures are not inconsistent with [states'] other obligations under international law" and that they "do *not* involve discrimination…on the ground of race, colour, sex, language, religion or social origin" (my italics).[30] It's *only* provided that one won't engage in social

---

26 It's been well-noted that such sentiments connect themselves to the contemporary right-populist wave in politics. See, e.g., Pippa Norris and Ronald Inglehart, *Cultural Backlash: Trump, Brexit, and Authoritarian Populism* (Cambridge: Cambridge University Press, 2018) and Roger Eatwell and Matthew Goodwin, *National Populism: The Revolt against Liberal Democracy* (London: Pelican, 2018).
27 Alasdair MacIntyre, *Is Patriotism a Virtue?* (Lawrence: University of Kansas Department of Philosophy, 1984).
28 United Nations, "International Covenant on Civil and Political Rights" (1966, article 4), http://www.ohchr.org/en/professionalinterest/pages/ccpr.aspx. Hereafter ICCPR.
29 ECHR, article 15.
30 Ibid.

stigmatization and that civil liberties won't be *fully* ruined as one tightens-up borders or beefs-up surveillance.[31] Do terrorist attacks have meaning? Yes. In a post-9/11 world, many are on edge and times can seem violent. Bombings from London to Madrid to Brussels have felt sudden, and it can feel there *is* a "clash of civilizations" via which it's hard for us to get along. Still, it's noticeable that the attack on *Jo Cox* didn't provoke discussion of reneging on rights agreements, and there are more than a few arguments suggesting that reacting drastically to perceived emergencies can in fact make them worse.[32] Rights' spirit concerns the idea that "everyone is entitled to a social and international order in which [their] rights and freedoms…can be fully realized." Fundamental liberties rely on the idea that "peace, justice and freedom in the world" are possible *because* we insist on larger arcs for human behavior, not because we withdraw from them.[33] One *can* derogate from rights; one *can* engage the "state of exception." It's not what rights *want*, however, and one wonders what the Eleanor Roosevelts and John Lockes of the world would have thought had *they* heard May's proclamations in June 2017.[34]

And, indeed, what of the image of the nation that one seeks to project? Even if we say that national life *is* the issue, there's a question of how one understands one's *own* history, and the sense of one's *own* past that one seeks to transmit. What kind of *Britain* does May seek to convey, and what relations with her *own* country's past does she hope to impart? Is Britain *about* something? Or is it just

---

31 See Evan J. Criddle, ed. *Human Rights in Emergencies* (Cambridge: Cambridge University Press, 2016).

32 See, e.g., Tore Bjørgo, *Strategies for Preventing Terrorism* (London: Palgrave Pivot, 2013); Amachai Magen, "Fighting Terrorism: The Democracy Advantage," *Journal of Democracy* 29, no. 1 (2018): 111–25. See also Maria Norris, "A Far-Right Terrorist Murdered Jo Cox. So When is Cobra Meeting?" *The New Statesman*, November 24, 2016, https://www.newstatesman.com/politics/staggers/2016/11/far-right-terrorist-murdered-jo-cox-so-when-cobra-meeting.

33 UDHR, preamble, article 28.

34 "A state of liberty," wrote Locke, is not a "state of licence [sic.]." No one should harm others. However, the solution to unjust harm is not the authoritarian state – it's the state which preserves rights themselves; guaranteeing each other's' liberty as opposed to depriving it. John Locke, *Second Treatise of Government*, ed. Richard Cox (Indianapolis: Hackett, 1982), 4. On the notion of the "state of exception," see Agamben, *State of Exception*, trans. Kevin Attell (Chicago: University of Chicago Pres, 2005); Tugba Basaran, *Security, Law and Borders: At the Limits of Liberties* (London: Routledge, 2011).

another country looking out for its "own" – that without much of a discussion of what its "own" might be?³⁵

Histories of liberalism are not the same. Taking the U.S. and UK as examples, notions of individual freedom have evolved in different ways and the socio-legal histories of the two states don't always line up. Social democratic concepts have had *much* more play in the UK than the U.S., e.g., and British common law lacks the singular point of reference that the American Constitution provides. The UK as no equivalent to the office of President, and one doesn't put administrations together the same way.³⁶ Still, the concept of government deriving its power from the will of the people and the idea that space need be preserved such that people might consider what their wills *are*, are legacies British and American life share. "The freedom…of man, and liberty of acting according to his own will, is grounded on his having reason, which is able to instruct him in that law he is to govern himself by," wrote John Locke – and such a belief in rational freedom had much to do with *Jefferson* and his colleagues deciding that the pursuit of "life, liberty, and happiness" should stand as the foundation of *American* life.³⁷ Or John Stuart Mill: "judgment is given to men that they may use it." We have the capacity to decide for ourselves and, because of that, we should.³⁸ Under the

---

35 I simply indicate here that the claim to national right – the claim of national peoples to self-determination and sovereignty – emerges from a *universal* claim to both individual and collective self-determination. Herein, though universal right and national right can sometimes find themselves at odds, one doesn't arrive at the right to national self-determination without a sense of *human* rights. See Thomas Christiano, "Self-Determination and the Human Right to Democracy" in *Philosophical Foundations of Human Rights*, ed. Rowan Crufy, S. Matthew Liao and Massimo Rezo (Oxford: Oxford University Press, 2015), 459–80. See also Hunt, *Inventing Human Rights*.
36 See Seymour Lipset and Gary Marks, *It Didn't Happen Here: Why Socialism Failed in the United States* (New York: W.W. Norton & Co., 2000); Mark Bevir, *The Making of British Socialism* (Princeton: Princeton University Press, 2011); T.R.S. Allen, "Constitutional Right and Common Law," *Oxford Journal of Legal Studies* 11, no. 4 (1991): 453–80. Obviously, these aren't the only distinctions between American and British legal and political systems (as much as, in fact, they have in common). The point, however, is to simply indicate that close though they may be, like any two national systems, one will find differences and particularities.
37 See Locke, *Second Treatise*, 37; National Archives, "Declaration of Independence: A Transcript" (2017), https://www.archives.gov/founding-docs/declaration-transcript. See also Allan Jayne, *Jefferson's Declaration of Independence: Origins, Philosophy, and Theology* (Lexington: University of Kentucky Press, 1998).
38 Of course, Mill wrote after the composition of documents like the American Declaration of Independence or the U.S. Constitution. However, he expounded ideas indicative of

influence of such ideas, impinging on civil rights has often been a tough row to hoe in American and British life; strikes against things like speech, the space to think, and the accoutrements of thought (e.g., a free press and the public flow of information), though, yes, sometimes present, have also been taken as erosions of democratic life.[39] Now, May didn't say *what* rights she'd curtail. She didn't propose specific surveillance programs or the end of due process. May didn't advocate press restrictions or put an ethnic group under the microscope (I'm looking at you, Mr. Trump).[40] In the past, however, rights-for-security tradeoffs *have* involved such things (monitoring people or changing their path through the justice system), and anti-terrorism legislation has landed in some awkward

---

the liberal spirit involved in both American and British law. See John Stuart Mill, *On Liberty*, ed. David Bromwich and George Kateb (New Haven: Yale University Press, 2003), 89; Dale Carpenter, "Autonomy (Of Individual and Private Associations)" in *The Oxford Handbook of the U.S. Constitution*, ed. Mart Tushnet et al. (Oxford: Oxford University Press, 2015), 565–86.

39 Philosopher Thomas Christiano notes that it's tough to have democracy without "the citizen attempt[ing] to advance justice and the common good according to her lights." A good point. Of course, that depends on the citizen, or simply *person*, having "lights" (ideas) at all – wherein they need time, space, and freedom to consider their thoughts. See Christiano, *The Constitution of Equality: Democratic Authority and Its Limits* (Oxford: Oxford University Press, 2008), 3.

I also don't mean to be starry-eyed here about British or American democracy. Certainly, both states have been involved with all manner of civil rights violations. Still, for every impingement on civil liberties, there have been major victories: the 1971 Supreme Court ruling that allowed publication of the Pentagon Papers, the 1959 ruling that prevented Alabama from shutting down the activities of the NAACP, or even striking down anti-terrorism laws like 2005 Prevention of Terrorism Act (UK). Liberal governments aren't paradises. However, one can well argue that progress in American and British society has come *by way of* subscription to democratic legal principles and the enshrinement of theoretical rights – not despite it. See Chris Moores, *Civil Liberties and Human Rights in Twentieth-Century Britain* (Cambridge: Cambridge University Press, 2017); Ella Dzelzainis and Ruth Livesey, eds., *The American Experiment and the Idea of Democracy in British Culture: 1776-1914* (Farnham: Ashgate, 2013); Paul L. Norton, *World War I and the Origin of Civil Liberties in the United States* (New York: W.W. Norton, 1979).

40 Of course, we know Trump began his campaign for the American presidency by asking for a complete ban on all Muslim immigration to the United States – something he didn't quite follow through on, though he instituted travel bans against an array of Muslim-majority countries. That's a startling tone for someone attempting to work as a mainstream politician. See Ben Dorfman, "Grappling with the Phenomenon: Donald Trump and Human Rights" in *13 Acts of Academic Journalism and Historical*

places vis-à-vis civil rights law.⁴¹ If May goes too far, she could damage the democratic edifice; she could chip away at principles that have traditionally grounded national life. She could make her nation a touch less liberal than it's often been wont, and she could imbue the UK's past with a meaning different than many take it to have. Britain has generally posed itself as a rights state over and above a security state. A change on such fronts would be a significant turn indeed.⁴²

To me, that adds up to this: as elated as Jeremy Corbyn was last night, it *was* Theresa May who won. Though she got by by the skin of her teeth, the skin of one's teeth is sometimes all one needs (ask George Bush in 2000, or Donald Trump last year). Thirty-one seats *is* a big gain. It didn't take back Parliament's lower house, however, and the Tories remain the UK's foremost party. In the face of the fact that May *did* win, however, the Conservative leader's statements on rights could mark a turning point; they might represent a moment at which the UK made some decisions about its path. Does one of the historical seats of liberal thought and democratic law turn, if ever so slightly, *away* from such legacies, suggesting that security is the new governing principle? Or, does the nation turn *back* from such suggestions such that it might *continue* as an example of promoting the freedoms that all should have? Does Britain say that non-derogability

---

Commentary on Human Rights: Opinions, Interventions and the Torsions of Politics (Frankfurt am Main: Peter Lang, 2017), 167–82.

41 Again, legislation like the 2005 Prevention of Terrorism Act was repealed on precisely these grounds. There have also been a number of findings concerning the dimensions of the American Patriot Act. See Edgar Tembo, *US-UK Counter-Terrorism after 9/11* (London: Routledge, 2014). See also Susan N. Herman, *Taking Liberties: The War on Terror and the Erosion of American Democracy* (Oxford: Oxford University Press, 2011); Andrea Bianchi and Alexis Keller, eds., *Counterterrorism: Democracy's Challenge* (Portland: Hart, 2008); Alison Brysk and Gershon Shafir, eds., *National Insecurity and Human Rights: Democracies Debate Counterterrorism* (Berkeley: University of California Press, 2007); Andrew Morgan, "The Patriot Act and Civil Liberties," *Jurist*, July 20, 2013, https://www.jurist.org/archives/feature/the-patriot-act-and-civil-liberties/.

42 See Robert Eccleshall, *British Liberalism: Liberal Thought from the 1640s to 1980s* (Harlow: Longman, 1988); Matt Cole, *Democracy in Britain* (Edinburgh: Edinburgh University Press, 2006). I would note that over-securitization has long been a theme in the literature on British society and politics; especially public surveillance has been a long-standing issue. Still, there's something ominous about the nation's political leader speaking *directly* against human rights and seeming to not even feel compelled to pay them lip service. On surveillance, see Benjamin J. Gould, *CCTV and Policing: Public Area Surveillance and Police Practices in Britain* (Oxford: Oxford University Press, 2004).

is what rights states stand for, even when the chips are down? Or does it say, "an agenda organized around hyper-securitization? – that's us; count us in!" It's hard to know what May's voters think – events happened so quickly come the end of the electoral cycle that there was nary time for polls on all the issues in the political air. Many items were at stake in this election, and May's comments came rather last minute. Still, last night's results suggest that at least *some* Britons might have doubts about her approach; *some* may wonder if May's on the right path. Jeremy Corbyn, e.g., immediately said he wouldn't be involved with "ripping up our rights and democracy," and more than a few in the press raised an eyebrow or two. Some of Britain's allies shot the UK a worried glance, and rights organizations argued that May's comments should be damned. More than a few newspaper editorials came out relatively quickly against May, and the Prime Minister's proclamations were featured on TV news.[43] Indeed, given the large number of *non*-Conservative voters last night, one wonders if May *didn't* create waves last minute and throw results more Corbyn's way. It's a comforting thought. One can be in the EU or out, and one can ally with whoever one wants. One can have a large military or a small one, and one can involve oneself minimally or extensively with social democratic ideas. One can tone rights; one has to think about what it means if societies have long-held religious traditions or customs around worldview that might provide different relations with justice. I'm

---

43 See, e.g., Jack Maidment, "Labour Refuses to Back Theresa May's Plans to Tear Up Human Rights Laws to Fight Terror," *The Telegraph*, June 7, 2017, https://www.telegraph.co.uk/news/2017/06/07/labour-refuses-back-theresa-mays-plans-tear-human-rights-laws/; Marian Norris and Jillian Terry, "Theresa May's Latest Response to Terror Has Shown Us How Much She Detests Human Rights," *The New Statesman*, June 6, 2017, https://www.newstatesman.com/world/2017/06/theresa-mays-latest-response-terror-has-shown-us-how-much-she-detests-human-rights; Martha Spurrier, "Theresa May Has Said She'll Rip Up Human Rights: We Should All Be Afraid," *The Guardian*, June 7, 2017, https://www.theguardian.com/commentisfree/2017/jun/07/theresa-may-human-rights-european-charter-terrorists; Rob Merrick, "Theresa May Threat to Rip Up Human Rights Laws Condemned as 'Cynical Attempt to Revive a Flagging Campaign," *The Independent*, June 7, 2017, https://www.independent.co.uk/news/uk/politics/theresa-may-human-rights-condemn-keir-starmer-general-election-2017-latest-live-london-bridge-terror-a7776496.html; Amnesty International, "Theresa May's Comments on Human Rights are 'Reckless and Misinformed,' Says Amnesty," June 6, 2017, https://www.amnesty.org.uk/press-releases/theresa-mays-comments-human-rights-are-reckless-and-misinformed-says-amnesty; BBC News, "Theresa May: 'Human Rights Laws Could Be Changed,'" June 7, 2017, https://www.youtube.com/watch?v=yXvADB_Jpyc.

not sure that's what we're talking about with the UK, however, or regarding the country's history of rights ideas. In the UK's case, we're dealing with a classic seat of liberalism and a tone-setting nation as concerns notions of democracy and freedom in international affairs. The UK is the home of *the* Magna Carta – not "a" Magna Carta – and the nation puts the "Anglo" in the concept of "Anglo-Saxon" law. In light of May's statements, it will be interesting to see if such traditions are full-throatedly maintained. Or, do we need to have an election where May *doesn't* get by the skin of her teeth for Britons to *not* have to ask, "Mother May, can we have the full range of our fundamental privileges and freedoms back"?

Dog Whistles You Can Hear
The White House and Social Strife
(August 24, 2017)

Abstract: *Racists marched on Charlottesville, Trump suggested moral equivalence between anti-racist protestors and those marching with white supremacists, and the sense of intrigue around the White House is rife. What might it all mean? Read on.*

It's been a heckuva week and a half – a *heck* of a week and a half. Now, the "week and a half" dates to the clashes in Charlottesville, Virginia, where members of a "Unite the Right" rally (read "pow-wow for groups holding some dubious racial views") decided to reenact something of a Leni Riefenstahl-esque torchlight procession through the University of Virginia campus, and a range of protestors emerged the next day to let them know, in some cases through something-less-than-peaceful means, that their views weren't appreciated not only in the university vicinity, but in American public space at-large. It was dramatic – the whole thing played out on TV – and the episode took a tragic turn as one counter-demonstrator, a legal assistant named Heather Heyer, was killed, with the specter of violence organized around issues of race becoming existential in ways perhaps not seen since the 1960s.[1] Of course, the ostensible reason for "Unite the Right" was the removal of a statue of Confederate General Robert E. Lee from Charlottesville's Emancipation Park. It's been increasingly debated in the U.S. as to whether "heritage" is enough of a reason to allow monuments for what was

"The White House in Washington D.C., the South Gate" @ kropic1/ shutterstock.com 97123109

---

1 See Maev Kennedy, "Heather Heyer, Victim of Charlottesville Car Attack, Was Civil Rights Activist," *The Guardian*, August 14, 2017, https://www.theguardian.com/us-news/2017/aug/13/woman-killed-at-white-supremacist-rally-in-charlottesville-named.

essentially a racist cause to stand (the defense of slavery in the American South), and more than a few former Confederate municipalities had begun to take them down. Emancipation Park – one can't miss the irony in the name.²

In any case, as more than a few commentators noted (present company included), the whole thing was made worse by the reactions of the American President – since January 2017, one Donald J. Trump, at that point roughly a half-year into his term. Now, that Trump would behave controversially around issues of race, if not identity at-large, was, and is, hardly news. Controversies concerning ethnicity and cultural background were staples of his campaign, and for a solid year, we had to duck news of his misadventures in the area like low-flying airplanes. Remember? At the end of May 2016, Trump made headlines by attacking a federal judge – Gonzalo Curiel – for supposedly mishandling a lawsuit against the so-called "Trump University" (a sort of business seminar school sponsored by the real estate mogul); that because he (Curiel) was of Mexican descent and, though born in the U.S. (Indiana), he would *clearly* be upset about Trump's infamous border wall proposal and take out his frustrations by perverting the course of American justice.³ What else? Earlier in the year, informed that a racist figure like former Ku Klux Klan Imperial Wizard David

---

2   See The New York Times, "Confederate Monuments Are Coming Down Across the United States. Here's a List," August 28, 2017, https://www.nytimes.com/interactive/2017/08/16/us/confederate-monuments-removed.html?mtrref=www.google.dk. Of course, there are alternative understandings of the Confederacy in popular culture – that the movement was really about states' rights, or the defense of a specific "culture." As Hugh Brogan notes, however, for nearly all scholars, it's hard to come to a conclusion about the issue other than that the Civil War was a "war about slavery;" that the question of whether to defend slavery as an institution fed fundamentally into the main streams leading to the conflict, and that it's clear that the Confederacy sought to defend the institution. One can debate Lee's specific culpability as regards the ideologies of the Confederacy. That he was the primary figure in the South's military defense, however, is not up for question, however. Indeed, that's the reason that defenders of Southern monuments sought to keep his statue in place. See Brogan, *The Penguin History of the United States of America* (New York: Penguin, 2001); Gains M. Foster, Ghosts of the Confederacy: Defeat, the Lost Cause, and the Emergence of the New South (Oxford: Oxford University Press, 1988), 23.
3   See Jenna Johnson and Philip Rucker, "In San Diego, Trump Shames 'Mexican' Judge as Protestors Storm Streets," *The Washington Post*, May 27, 2016, https://www.washingtonpost.com/news/post-politics/wp/2016/05/27/in-san-diego-trump-shames-local-mexican-judge-as-protesters-storm-streets/?utm_term=.31b2e52999a3.

Duke was enthusiastic about his campaign – that due to the candidate's oft-nativistic under-, and sometimes over-, tones – Trump declared he didn't know who Duke "was." That's with Duke as one of the most prominent figures in American racism over the past thirty or forty years, and a lot of news in the press about how ultra-rightists were among the then-candidate's most fervent supporters.[4] Of course, the one-time reality show star *began* his campaign with the proposal that all members of a particular religion (Islam) should be banned from immigrating to the United States (that until authorities could figure out what was "going on"), and the man's initial boost to political prominence came through questioning the first black president's citizenship.[5] Now in office, Trump doubled-down on such rhetoric by suggesting that, though Charlottesville's *anti-racism* demonstrations would likely have been less intense had neo-Nazis and Klansmen *not* been present in "Unite the Right," there were "egregious displays" of "racism, bigotry, and violence" on "many sides." That's right: "many sides." Apparently, anyone confronting anyone for any reason is a bigot, and all views need be brooked even if some don't even make *pretense* towards accepting all human beings as just that – human. Predictably, an outcry ensued – could one *really* suggest an equivalence between the actions of white supremacists and those taking to the streets to oppose them? Trump then engaged in one of his now not-infrequent walk-backs: the next day, he appeared to call out racists, characterizing their views as "evil" and not a part of the American fabric.[6] *Then*, however, came a meltdown of epic proportions. In a press conference held in Trump Tower ostensibly to discuss national infrastructure, Trump blasted what he called the "Alt-Left" for participating in a range of scuffles with Unite the Righters. They were also but thugs, he suggested, with their goal being to foment division in the nation. Trump then argued – vociferously – that asking for the removal of monuments celebrating Southern heritage was PC overkill and that we needed a more balanced view of the Confederate past; "when would

---

4   See Evan Osnos, "Donald Trump and the Ku Klux Klan: A History," *The New Yorker*, February 29, 2016, http://www.newyorker.com/news/news-desk/donald-trump-and-the-ku-klux-klan-a-history.
5   Michael Barbaro, "Donald Trump Clung to 'Birther' Lie for Years, and Still Isn't Apologetic," *The New York Times*, September 16, 2016, https://www.nytimes.com/2016/09/17/us/politics/donald-trump-obama-birther.html?mcubz=0&_r=0.
6   Glenn Trush, "New Outcry as Trump Rebukes Charlottesville Racists 2 Days Later," *The New York Times*, August 14, 2017, https://www.nytimes.com/2017/08/14/us/politics/trump-charlottesville-protest.html.

it stop," Trump lamented? If you couldn't celebrate Lee or Stonewall Jackson, Washington and Jefferson had to go too; the founding fathers who established principles by which slave ownership would be abolished weren't necessarily of more worth than figures who sought to establish a nation to *defend* America's "peculiar institution."[7] Trump then proclaimed that he was willing to say what few others would: that the media had turned counter-protestors into saints when they weren't, that national reporting on the event wasn't objective, and that there were "very fine" people intermingled with the neo-Nazis and white supremacists marching to "Unite the Right."[8] It was a defense of the idea that, when cultural conservatives throw their hats in the ring with folks whose beliefs encompass not only conservatism (fine) but flat-out racism (not), it's up to us to tell them apart. Then, in a strange coda to the whole affair, the Trump advisor oft-charged with pushing the President towards yet-deeper levels of ethnonationalism, Steve Bannon, was fired.[9]

---

7   To expand, it's surely true that a good number of the founding fathers were slave holders. Lest we can make no judgments at all, however, it seems meaningful draw a distinction between figures who, as flawed as they were, formulated terms through which emancipation might be *reached* (and who often had both public and private doubts about the institution) versus those who, faced with a choice between embracing such ideals and explicitly seeking to combat people's right to emancipation, choose the latter. True: racism and pro-slavery attitudes weren't only embedded in the South. Still, there may be substantive differences between societies *struggling* with racism and/or other modes of social marginalization and societies explicitly *embracing* racism and marginalization as grounding principles. For a range of perspectives on this issue, see James Oliver Horton and Lois E. Horton, eds., *Slavery and Public History: The Tough Stuff of American Memory* (New York: New Press, 2006).
8   See Rosie Gray, "Trump Defends White-Nationalist Protesters: 'Some Very Fine People on Both Sides,'" *The Atlantic*, August 15, 2017, https://www.theatlantic.com/politics/archive/2017/08/trump-defends-white-nationalist-protesters-some-very-fine-people-on-both-sides/537012/.
9   I recognize that there is a debate to be had over whether Bannon is an ethnonationalist. In an interview he gave for *The American Prospect* directly before his release by the White House, Bannon decried ethnonationalism as a "loser" position, suggesting that economic nationalism was his concern. Where this rings false is through a legacy of statements such as describing Islam as worse than the threat of fascism to Europe in the '30s, a history of radically strict views on immigration, and a long-term history on the news site he ran for years, *Breitbart*, of portraying minority and immigrant populations as threats to the nation. One can *say* one is not ethnonationalist. However, when one promotes notions of the nation in which too much diversity comes off as problematic, one would have to go further for me, anyway, in explaining how

One thing all of this does is continue an emerging legacy of relative, if not absolute, discursive and behavioral chaos within the most current iteration of the White House. I know – Richard Nixon essentially hired thugs and thieves out of the Oval Office (the odor from that still lingered when I was young), and after Reagan was shot in 1981, Alexander Haig apparently forgot the line of Presidential succession and declared he was "in control" at the White House – making many wonder who in fact was (one of my earlier political memories).[10] Did Bill Clinton's inability to control his libido contribute to national tranquility come the end of the 1990s? I'm not sure. And, man, all that Iran-Contra stuff *did* cut awfully close to the figure of Reagan himself.[11] Still, the current President spends a near-unprecedented amount of time attacking allies within his own party, uses *massive* amounts of verbal and online space to throw bombs at the press, and seems to place a *super* heavy emphasis focusing his speech near-laser-like on the culturally conservative base that forms the core of his support.[12] That's

---

ethonationalism is not part of one's worldview. See Robert Kuttner, "Steve Bannon, Unrepentant," *The American Prospect*, August 16, 2017, http://prospect.org/article/steve-bannon-unrepentant. Steve Reilly and Brad Heath, *USA Today*, "Bannon's Breitbart Tapes Raise Questions on Trump's Foreign Policy," January 31, 2017, http://www.azcentral.com/story/news/politics/nation/2017/01/31/steve-bannon-breitbart-view-radical-islam-at-war/97317230/; Michael Gerson, "Bannon's Reckless Pursuit of Ethnonationalist Greatness," *The Washington Post*, February 26, 2017, available at https://www.washingtonpost.com/opinions/bannons-reckless-pursuit-of-ethno-nationalist-greatness/2017/02/27/096fe836-fd28-11e6-8ebe-6e0dbe4f2bca_story.html. See also Maggie Haberman, Michael D. Shear and Glenn Trush, "Stephen Bannon Out at the White House after Turbulent Run," *The New York Times*, August 18, 2017, https://www.nytimes.com/2017/08/18/us/politics/steve-bannon-trump-white-house.html?mcubz=0&_r=0.

10 See Lamar Waldron, *Watergate: The Hidden History: Nixon, the Mafia, and the CIA* (Berkeley: Counterpoint, 2012); Richard V. Allen, "When Reagan Was Shot, Who was 'In Control' at the White House?" *The Washington Post*, March 25, 2011, https://www.washingtonpost.com/opinions/when-reagan-was-shot-who-was-in-control-at-the-white-house/2011/03/23/AFJlrfYB_story.html?utm_term=.42474b32069c.

11 See Malcolm Byrne, *Iran-Contra: Reagan's Scandal and the Unchecked Abuse of Presidential Power* (Lawrence: University Press of Kansas, 2014). Figures from Caspar Weinberger to Robert McFarland to, most famously, Oliver North, were subject to indictment.

12 See David A. Graham, "Trump's Shrinking, Energized Base," *The Atlantic*, September 8, 2017, https://www.theatlantic.com/politics/archive/2017/09/trumps-shrinking-impassioned-base/539160/. By way of comparison, one might consider the Obama "Beer Summit" of 2009. Barak Obama was a civil rights supporter – a position one

as opposed to finding discourses that might traverse *broader* ideological frames and at least make *overtures* towards toning down the level of confrontation in what's a starkly divided nation. It's hard to say. However, it might be telling that Trump filed his re-election papers with the Federal Election Commission on January 20th – Inauguration Day. As of now, the Trump Presidency often comes off as an at-any-costs campaign as much as a phenomenon focused particularly much on governing.[13]

With that said, however, there then really *is* that – campaign mode as opposed to what might be seen as an earnest attempt at addressing the nation as a whole. I.e., in my lifetime, I simply haven't *seen* Americans go after each other in the ways they're doing now. Now, lest we be utopic, as much as it *is* the case that the U.S. has a long (very long) tradition of peaceful transitions of power, interrupted only by the Civil War, it's not as though the U.S. has been *devoid* of Americans confronting Americans, and fellow citizens grabbing each other by the throat. Had you been a delegate to the National Women's Rights Convention in 1853 in Cleveland, for example, you would have been confronted by an angry mob; from its earliest days until the passage of the Nineteenth Amendment in 1920 (and after), you had to be a pretty hardy soul to fight for women's rights on the American tableau.[14] Of course, none of us, except maybe the "Unite the Righters" Trump appears interested to defend, are oblivious to the pictures of police dogs attacking Civil Rights protesters in the American South – and, as we know, Martin Luther King wrote perhaps

---

might consider uncontroversial. Still, though many on the left criticized the effort, when Henry Louis Gates, Jr., was arrested attempting to get into his own home – an event many saw as a result of uncured, latent racism in America's police establishment – Obama attempted to heal the divide by inviting Gates, Jr., and the arresting officer, Sgt. James Crowley, to the White House for a "beer" (indeed, they actually sat and drank beer). Schmaltzy? Perhaps. Indicative of an attempt to create consensus as opposed to division? It would seem so. See Helene Cooper and Abby Goodnough, "Over Beer, No Apologies, But Plans to Have Lunch," *The New York Times*, July 30, 2009, https://www.google.dk/url?sa=t&rct=j&q=&esrc=s&source=web&cd=1&cad=rja&uact=8&ved=0ahUKEwjwlKa1tOvYAhVF3CwKHSwcBC0QFggpMAA&url=http%3A%2F%2Fwww.nytimes.com%2F2009%2F07%2F31%2Fus%2Fpolitics%2F31obama.html&usg=AOvVaw2u1vcMqP3YzCvebZDM_pQf.

13 National Public Radio, "A Look at How Trump is Already Campaigning for 2020," August 23, 2017, http://www.npr.org/2017/08/23/545616864/a-look-at-how-trump-is-already-campaigning-for-2020.

14 Ellen Carol DuBois, *Woman Suffrage and Women's Rights* (New York: New York University Press, 1998).

his most famous work sitting in a Birmingham jail.¹⁵ The Black Panther Party packed some serious heat in the late-'60s and early '70s because they felt the society around them packed heat against *them*, and from Rodney King to Ferguson, many would say it's idealistic to locate existential social conflict only in *earlier* parts of the twentieth century, or perhaps in the spaces of the nineteenth.¹⁶ Still, today feels different. *Post*-Civil Rights, it's hard to watch Americans street fighting Americans, especially when the conflict isn't between authorities and minorities, but between two political cultures roughly evenly divided who simply can't stand each other's existence. I'd say it's like the Vietnam era except that then, there was a middle between the extremes.¹⁷ And, indeed, what makes today *particularly* dark is that I'm not sure we're really talking about "extremes." We might rather be talking about a *majority* opinion drowned out by a *minority* culture with that minority opinion trading in the idea that it's ok to take revenge on the majority because they're sure they've somehow been ignored. I.e., this isn't a minority fighting for recognition in a classic, underprivileged sense. It's rather a minority that actually represents the *majority* culture demographically as well as vis-à-vis historical privilege asserting that too much attention is being given to the historically *oppressed*. And now someone mixed in with the "very fine people" on the right

---

15 See Jonathan Rieder, *Gospel of Freedom: Martin Luther King, Jr.'s Letter from Birmingham Jail and the Struggle that Changed a Nation* (New York: Bloomsbury, 2013).
16 For a comprehensive look at the larger swathe of political and social confrontation and conflict in the American past (including many of those mentioned here), see Steven Laurence Danver, ed., *Revolts, Protests, Demonstrations, and Rebellions in American History* (Santa Barbara: ABC-Clio, 2011).
17 It is true that there were quite intense conflicts between the right and left of American society in the Vietnam years, or perhaps more precisely between the emerging counter-culture and those who saw themselves as defending traditional values. However, perhaps not unlike the conflict in Iraq, by the time the war had dragged on long enough, protest wasn't just a matter of student radicals or fringe elements on the left. It became mainstream as Americans from many walks of life began to express that the disastrous conflict should be brought to an end. Said one middle class demonstrator at one of 1969's "moratoriums" to end the Vietnam War, "it's nice to go to a demonstration and not have to swear allegiance to Chairman Mao." Average Americans could reach consensus on a moral issue. See Maurice Isserman, "Give Peace a Chance," *Dissent*, Fall 2017, https://www.dissentmagazine.org/article/ken-burns-lynn-novick-vietnam-war-review; Penny Lewis, *Hardhats, Hippies, and Hawks: The Vietnam Antiwar Movement as Myth and Memory* (Ithaca: ILR, 2013).

has killed someone. It's symbolic of the fact that the nation's worldview splits may be on the cusp of getting totally out of hand.[18]

Of course, one question this raises is whether this level of confrontation – the animosity it appears ranges of Americans feel towards one another – isn't supported by the President; that Trump may not only be playing to his base (all politicians do), but that he's intentionally seeking to keep conflict on boil – and hot enough boil to melt the pot. Now, I get it: for many, political correctness feels overcooked, and Trump's off-the-cuff speech manner forms a large part of his appeal.[19] Trump gained the Presidency through legal means – he was voted in (though we might need to discuss that Electoral College) – and, President or not, he has the right to free speech, like everyone else. Still, a calculation appears to have underlain the Trump campaign – a calculation on which Trump-as-President appears to rely again and again. This is that there *is* what Nixon termed a "silent majority" out there, or at least a large enough *minority* to bull one's way through the electoral system (again, popular majorities aren't how American presidencies are won), said majority/minority is for one or the other reason pissed-off, and, if one can keep that plurality's sensibilities on hot enough boil, there's a fragile path to another electoral win. In 2016, Trump *may* have

---

18 I want to be careful here; it is difficult to imagine the larger part of Americans in any political camp allying themselves explicitly with the views that lead to Heather Heyer's death. According to an ABC News poll taken after Charlottesville, 9 out of 10 Americans sharply disapprove of neo-Nazi views. More complex, however, is whether the so-called "Alt-Right," which merges into white nationalist politics yet also latches onto the edges of the Trump movement, is perceived as racist, or simply exercising free speech. Here, the same poll found that 21% of respondents *don't* see the Alt-Right, central in supporting "Unite the Right," as holding neo-Nazi views. I.e., many may not have articulated their presence in Charlottesville as a matter of racism, or neo-Nazism. That allowed a *de facto* mixing of simple conservatives with more radical elements – a point perhaps deserving of reflection. See Gary Langer, "1 in 10 Say It's Acceptable to Hold Neo-Nazi Views," *ABC News*, August 21, 2017, https://abcnews.go.com/Politics/28-approve-trumps-response-charlottesville-poll/story?id=49334079.

19 Ed Kilgore, "The Meaning of Trump's Cult of Political Incorrectness," *New York Magazine*, July 5, 2016, http://nymag.com/daily/intelligencer/2016/07/trumps-cult-of-political-incorrectness.html. Associated Press, "'No More Political Correctness' for Trump Supporters," April 10, 2016, https://www.pbs.org/newshour/politics/no-more-political-correctness-for-trump-supporters; Sam Altman, "I'm a Silicon Valley Liberal, and I Travelled across the Country to Interview 100 Trump Supporters – Here's What I Learned," *Business Insider*, February 23, 2017, http://www.businessinsider.fr/us/sam-altman-interview-trump-supporters-2017-2.

megaphoned what many Americans thought but weren't willing to say – that because American social norms *had* shifted, certain things *weren't* ok to say anymore, and it was insisted upon that we look critically at structures of privilege from the past. Phrased yet another way, what in American parlance are "liberal" values *had* become more centrally situated, and, worse yet, as part of maintaining its global leadership role (never mind recognizing simple demographic shifts), America was *explicitly* seeking to step closer to liberal-internationalist norms.[20] For those who felt threatened by globalization, saw multiculturalism as a code word for open borders, or thought the Obama years were too "European," Trump became a symbol of crusading for God, country, and the average Joe. Of course, when the majority *doesn't* sanction such ideas – where PC *is* anti-discrimination and God isn't a political issue except to keep religion *out* of public life – one risks a culture war. One risks a situation where wide spectrums of Americans see themselves as having to return to the barricades to fight battles they thought they had already won. Of course, *that* is then taken as evidence by conservatives that they are persecuted, and a yet harder push is needed to expunge as much social liberalism as possible from the vestiges of American life.[21]

---

20   See Robert Singh, *Barack Obama's Post-American Foreign Policy: The Limits of Engagement* (London: Bloomsbury, 2012).
21   As regards the notion that the Trump movement reflects minority views, I simply refer to the fact that when one adds Hillary Clinton's 48.18% of the 2016 presidential vote (versus Trump's 46.09%) to Bernie Sanders' 0.08% (yes, Sanders was written in by hundreds of thousands of Americans) to Jill Stein's 1.07% to Gloria La Riva's (Socialism and Liberation Party) 0.05% and one factors in a portion of the 3.72% of the vote shared by the Libertarians and Evan McMullin (the alternative Republican) (as well as the fact that more than a million remaining write-ins also featured a number of smaller socialist candidates [Socialist Worker's Party candidate Alyson Kennedy, e.g., received over 12,000 votes]), it appears fair to say that Trump's positions fall short of representing the majority of voting Americans. That's to say nothing of ongoing approval ratings hovering at 40%. The man won the Presidency. However, that's different than whether he's a majority President. See Federal Election Commission, "Official 2016 Presidential Election Results," January 30, 2017, https://transition.fec.gov/pubrec/fe2016/2016presgeresults.pdf. See also Jessica Kwong, "Trump Least Popular President Even? At This Point, Richard Nixon, Gerald Ford and LBJ Were All More Liked," *Newsweek*, November 23, 2017, http://www.newsweek.com/trump-least-popular-president-ever-point-richard-nixon-gerald-ford-and-lbj-721004. See also David A. Graham, "Why Trump Invokes 'Common Sense,'" *The Atlantic*, August 4, 2017, https://www.theatlantic.com/politics/archive/2017/08/trump-common-sense/535872/.

There are many ways to discuss this, and the amount of ink spilled on the Trump presidency is by now massive. However, I'd like to try a human rights angle on for size. Now, what I term "human rights" (broad, supposedly universal, social standards and values) are *not* necessarily a matter of *national* right. There is a long tradition of countries being quite picky about how they relate to international (and hence supposedly universal) standards of political rectitude and justice thought on global planes.²² Indeed, the U.S. *specifically* has been insistent on choosing its own ethico-legal standards, and has a tradition of maintaining its own interpretation of the norms to which the global community is supposed to adhere (the U.S. has not ratified the International Covenant on Economic, Social and Cultural Rights, e.g. [1966 (most of the world has)], and even the Obama administration, in its supposed heightened sympathy for international institutions, maintained previous administrations' policies of not joining the International Criminal Court).²³ Still, the notion of "human rights" – a phraseology through which many of us would address problems of fundamental political conduct and social justice – should lay out baselines to which we can generally assent; human rights are intended to address concepts which should help individuals in *all* of the societies in which we live. Simply put, if we look at the panoply of Trumpist behaviors around Charlottesville, there's a question as to how they line up or don't with such standards and ideals. There's a question of how not only Trump's reaction to events in Virginia, but the entire cloud of chaotic dust he kicks up, accords or doesn't with notions of basic justice and

---

22 Some of these issues are highlighted in Noha Shawki and Michaelene Cox, eds., *Negotiating Sovereignty and Human Rights: Actors and Issues in Contemporary Human Rights Politics* (Farnham: Ashgate, 2009).
23 See Michael Ignatieff, ed., *American Exceptionalism and Human Rights* (Princeton: Princeton University Press, 2005). On states which have ratified the International Covenant on Economic, Social and Cultural Rights, see United Nations Treaty Collection, "International Covenant on Economic, Social and Cultural Rights" (1966), https://treaties.un.org/Pages/ViewDetails.aspx?src=IND&mtdsg_no=IV-3&chapter=4&clang=_en. See also Mark D. Kielsgard, *Reluctant Engagement: U.S. Policy and the International Criminal Court* (Leiden: Brill, 2010); Andrea Birdsall, "The 'Monster That We Need to Slay?' Global Governance, the United States, and the International Criminal Court," *Global Governance* 16, no. 4 (2010): 451–69. This is not to say that the ICC escapes criticism. One of the most significant critiques of the ICC is that *all* of its cases and rulings, and the majority of its investigations, have involved African continent figures and conflicts; i.e., a particular prejudice may structurally pervade Court activities. Still, perhaps the U.S. could use its influence to affect such potential one-sidedness.

privileges all of us should have. When we look at what's going on with this iteration of the White House, are we on terrain we might identify as related to our "highest moral precepts and political ideals"?[24] Or have we landed somewhere else – on a terrain *abrogating* ideas of basic rights, and notions that humanity might have a higher ethical call?

Free speech returns as an issue here. I.e., if we look at documents like the Universal Declaration of Human Rights (1948), as well as more specifically targeted pacts like the International Covenant on Civil and Political Rights (1966), we see some provocative claims. "Everyone has the right to freedom of opinion and expression; this right includes freedom to hold opinions without interference and to seek, receive and impart information and ideas through any media and regardless of frontiers," the Universal Declaration asserts.[25] Expressive liberty is forwarded as a basic privilege as is the ability to think essentially as one likes. The Civil and Political Covenant says the same: "everyone [has] the right to freedom of expression; this right shall include freedom to seek, receive and impart information and ideas of all kinds, regardless of frontiers, either orally, in writing or in print, in the form of art, or through any other media of his choice."[26] In a human rights frame of mind, one has the right to voice the opinions one wants. The American Constitution echoes this, and in some ways set precedent for it. The First Amendment to the country's fundamental laws states that "Congress shall make no law…abridging the freedom of speech" – and historically, no law has meant no law, with the courts granting wide berth to speech liberties in American life.[27]

Still, things can be more nuanced. The Civil and Political Covenant, to which the U.S. is party, suggests that, yes, everyone has the right to "hold opinions without interference." One *can* think what one wants. However, "any advocacy

---

24 Samuel Moyn, *The Last Utopia: Human Rights in History* (Cambridge, MA: Harvard Belknap, 2010), 1.
25 United Nations, "The Universal Declaration of Human Rights" (1948, article 19), http://www.un.org/en/universal-declaration-human-rights/index.html. Hereafter UDHR.
26 United Nations, "International Covenant on Civil and Political Rights" (1966, article 19), http://www.ohchr.org/en/professionalinterest/pages/ccpr.aspx. Hereafter ICCPR.
27 Government Publishing Office, "Constitution of the United States" (1787–1992, First Amendment), https://www.gpo.gov/fdsys/pkg/CDOC-110hdoc50/pdf/CDOC-110hdoc50.pdf. Hereafter Constitution. See also See William B. Fisch, "Hate Speech in the Constitutional Law of the United States," *The American Journal of Comparative Law* 50 (2002): 489. See also Anthony Lewis, *Freedom for the Thought that We Hate: A Biography of the First Amendment* (New York: Basic, 2007).

of national, racial or religious hatred that constitutes incitement to discrimination, hostility or violence shall be prohibited by law."[28] Hate speech, or comfort given to it, is supposed to be out. Now, the U.S. has generally been supportive of the Civil and Political Covenant in line with the country's commitment to civil rights. Still, among the U.S.' reservations regarding its subscription to the Civil and Political Covenant is the ban on hate speech. I.e., taking a position more libertarian than states like Canada or the UK, the U.S. holds that in quashing speech which might be seen as objectionable in one context, the same rules could be used in other contexts to undermine legitimate protest or tamp down social debate. Again, this has led to some broad free speech interpretations, such as with the 1977 National Socialist Party of America v. Village of Skokie case.[29] However, that's while *that* picture can *also* be more complex. When it comes to racist *acts*, or the idea that speech might play a role in *de facto* discrimination (the concrete limitation of opportunity or keeping someone away from equal goods and services), the landscape changes. *Speech* might be protected. However, *conduct* might not. The "distinction between punishing the expression of a bigoted idea...and punishing an act because of its *motivation* in bigotry," as one scholar puts it, can be blurry; speech can sometimes be taken account of *by way of* the act to the extent that, if an act can be demonstrated to be *caused* by identity animus, we have a problem as you can't *behave* towards people in a prejudiced way; you can't keep someone from doing something they're allowed to because of a particular belief.[30] Indeed, some of the inflammatory statements made by Trump on the campaign trail *have* been taken into account in terms of at least

---

28 ICCPR articles 19, 20.
29 See Fisch, "Hate Speech." The Skokie case involved Nazis planning a march through an Illinois town with a large Jewish population, including Holocaust survivors. The city attempted to prevent the march. Though the American Civil Liberties Union generally takes up progressive causes, it defends free speech at large, and pushed the Nazi case to the Supreme Court, where the group won. The ACLU's position was simply that free speech has been important to defend for dissidents and minorities. However, if it is provided to all, it must be provided to all – even in the case of despicable ideologies. See Aryeh Neier, *Defending My Enemy: American Nazis, the Skokie Case, and the Risks of Freedom* (New York: Dutton, 1979).
30 Fisch, "Hate Speech," 489. With a conservative turn in the American court system, however (and since the initial writing of this article), this has become complex. Most famous is the "Colorado wedding cake decision," in which the Supreme Court decided that a Colorado baker (who runs a wedding cake shop) *wasn't* compelled to back a cake for a gay couple based on his religious beliefs (specifically, the ruling was that the Colorado Civil Rights Commission acted with animus towards the individual

assessing the legality of restrictions he has attempted to place on immigration to the extent that, when you place travel bans on certain Muslim majority countries after saying that you don't want Muslims to immigrate to the U.S., can you *really* say you're *not* involved in thinking of immigration in cultural or religious terms – a civil rights violation?[31] I'm no lawyer. However, it seems that there are national and international contexts suggesting that you'd be best to not just shoot your mouth off about *anything*, and that there's use in inserting the brain-mouth filter. It's good to make sure one's discourse isn't overly inflammatory, and you shouldn't make people feel shoved to the side.[32] That's without getting into the ethics of leadership or the decorum of leading one of the world's most important states.[33]

That, however, then ties itself to further issues around discrimination, or the "pushing of people to the side." I.e., if one imagines oneself as concerned with fundamental rights, one will tend to invest oneself in democratic ideals. Democratic states *usually* imagine themselves as interested in public participation in governance and they seek the participation of all in the conduct of civic life. "Everyone has the right to take part in the government of his country, directly or through freely chosen representatives," the Universal Declaration asserts; "the will of the people shall be the basis of the authority of government."[34] The Civil and Political Covenant again says the same: that every citizen has the right to take part in

---

    based on his religious beliefs). This represents a highly complex – and to my mind, dangerous – trend. There of course need be room for religious expression, including religious expression we don't approve of ourselves. However, it seems *highly* tenuous that someone's religious beliefs might limit one's access to goods and services. Again, though, this a new trend emerging with a more conservative court system bucking a longer-term trend in the opposite direction. See Ariane de Vogue, "Supreme Court Rules for Colorado Baker in Same-Sex Wedding Cake Case," *CNN*, June 4, 2018, https://edition.cnn.com/2018/06/04/politics/masterpiece-colorado-gay-marriage-cake-supreme-court/index.html.

31 Garrett Epps, "Trump's Travel Ban is Headed for a Supreme Court Showdown," *The Atlantic*, May 28, 2017, https://www.theatlantic.com/politics/archive/2017/05/trumps-travel-ban-is-headed-for-a-supreme-court-showdown/528417/.

32 See also Thomas R. Hensley, ed., *The Boundaries of Freedom of Expression & Order in American Democracy* (Kent: Kent State University Press, 2001); Michael Herz and Peter Molnar, eds., *The Content and Context of Hate Speech: Rethinking Regulation and Responses* (Cambridge: Cambridge University Press, 2012).

33 See Susan Herbst, *Rude Democracy: Civility and Incivility in American Politics* (Philadelphia: Temple University Press, 2010).

34 UDHR, article 21.

public affairs, and participate in the election of their leaders.[35] Now, here, there's no equivocation; the notion of the U.S. as a democratic society might be *the* building block of American identity, and the idea of democracy is constitutionally endorsed.[36] "The people of the several states," the Constitution asserts, shall elect their representatives.[37] Yes, in relation to the Presidential election (but one level of governance), a vote for President in Wyoming has more value than a vote for President in California. Still, even *that* is supposed to be democratic as the U.S. is a federal republic and the idea is that the citizens of Wyoming shouldn't be forgotten just because their state is small.[38] The U.S. should be a nation of citizens, and those citizens have equal rights. *All* should be seen in the political body, and Americans should feel that they can express their will.

That's at the same time that, yes, one needs the *right* to participate. Such rights should be enshrined in law; they should be "written down." However, it can be useful to *feel* that one has one's rights and have a sense that they're *supported* through the society around one. It can help to not only sense that one was given one's rights *willingly*, but that one is *accepted* in the social body to which one belongs. I.e., the Civil and Political Covenant suggests that one should promote the values which are "necessary to a democratic society."[39] One should establish atmospheres in which people's liberties are *recognized* and their relations with them made apparent. One should feel asked to *engage* one's privileges, and one should sense oneself as *requested* to take part in public affairs. It can be difficult to expect *all* people's participation in government if not all feel *welcome* to participate – in part, the basis for not only U.S.' acceptance of the Civil and Political Covenant, but legislation like the Civil Rights Act of 1964 and the Voting Rights Act of 1965.[40] In Trump's suggestion of equivalence between, if not precisely those speaking *for* discrimination, but those willing to march with

---

35 ICCPR, article 25.
36 See Richard Schneirov and Gaston A. Fernandez, *Democracy as a Way of Life in America: A History* (London: Routledge, 2014).
37 Constitution, article 1, section 2.
38 See Judith A. Best, *The Choice of the People?: Debating the Electoral College* (Lanham: Rowman & Littlefield, 1996). This is not unlike representation in the European Parliament, which is also determined via a combination of the populations of states together with recognizing the equal sovereignty of states as states.
39 ICCPR, article 22.
40 See Gary May, *Bending Toward Justice: The Voting Rights Act and the Transformation of American Democracy* (New York: Basic Books, 2013); Bernard Grofman, ed., *Legacies of the 1964 Civil Rights Act* (Charlottesville: University of Virginia Press, 2000).

those who do, and those seeking to assure that discriminatory voices are *opposed*, he signaled that one might at least not *refuse* cultures of exclusion; that there was validity in suggesting if not marginalization, then at least wild insensitivity to fellow citizens' senses of self. He suggested that one needn't make defusing neo-Nazi ideas point one and that one needn't think about whether attempts to resuscitate Third Reich-esque brownshirtism were really the best context in which to discuss the legacies of Robert E. Lee.[41] Yes, one has free speech; one *can* more or less say what one wants. We all have to ask, however, how far we're willing to go before we say we're looking at deportment of which we don't want to be a part. The imagery used in the advertising material for "Unite the Right" involved a blend of Confederate and Third Reich symbology – direct reference to anti-rights, aggressively exclusionary societies. One can see why a figure like David Duke took comfort in Trump's proclamations about Charlottesville. Trump tried to pretend he simply thought that protestors had "opinions" of equal value – but "ideas" being put in the "air." Duke knew different, however. The Trump coalition *needs* that place where cultural conservativism and ethnicized nationalism flow into one another and, given the not-so-subtle bombs so-far chucked at Mexicans, immigrants, and Muslims, one could well have seen the White House as signaling that, if white nationalists could clean up their act a bit, the President might give them cover. It was precisely what Duke had hoped for when he entered mainstream politics.[42]

---

[41] This is a complex statement; again, many who would defend the maintenance of monuments celebrating the Confederacy would be unlikely to pose themselves as doing so because they support racist worldviews. However, telling is a Winthrop University poll indicating that lacks in the South are *much* more likely to want to see monuments removed or somehow contextualized than whites – that as blacks are noticeably more likely to view the entire Confederate project as concerning oppression (which, for black Americans, it did). See Caitlyn Byrd, "Most Southerners Want Action on Confederate Monuments, but are Split over What to Do," *The Post and Courier*, December 18, 2018, https://www.postandcourier.com/politics/most-southerners-want-action-on-confederate-monuments-but-are-split/article_dac13d2a-0232-11e9-be6e-5f9b6516e7ca.html.

[42] See Greg Price, "White Supremacist David Duke Thanks Donald Trump for Slamming Antifa and Leftists at Press Conference," *Newsweek*, August 15, 2017. Over the course of the '80s, Duke transitioned out of KKK activities into a series of runs for state- and nationwide office – which included a stint in the Louisiana legislature. He remains active on the far right. See Tyler Bridges, *The Rise of David Duke* (Jackson: University of Mississippi Press, 1994).

Clearly, democratic inclusion is important. National leaders lending legitimacy to groups out to deny rights is no way to run a republic. Providing any solace to groups flying the Swastika is one heck of a way to govern. In a funny way, though, such issues may loop back to problems of consistency and stability. They may connect with the general chaos with which the Trump White House is involved – the hirings, the firings, the lack of clarity, the bellowing and yelling, and the difficulty in telling what the whole thing is about. Phrased another way, there may be a way in which, if Trump hasn't put civil rights under attack, he's put the concept of civic inclusion under duress. If he hasn't supported discrimination in a direct sense, he's at least led one to wonder if discriminatory opinions are somehow ok. If he doesn't directly say he doesn't like social groups, he certainly doesn't put them more at ease. That, however, may be joined to the sense that the man sometimes simply doesn't know what he's doing, or, worse yet, that he's *trying* to undo democracy as serious business. It may be connected to what sometimes feels like a distinct lack of principle, or, if not that, oblivion towards reflectivity as the lodestar of a republic's foundations.[43]

Now, one need be careful about defining stability as an end in itself. American democracy *itself* emerged as products of regime overthrow, and civil disobedience is part of the democratic tradition.[44] Most European countries gained democratic constitutions as a product of revolt, and for my money, the Black Panthers and participants at the 1853 National Women's Rights Convention have a central role in the national narrative. Still, it's been wild. First Obamacare should be repealed and replaced. Then it should just be repealed. Then it should be left in place so that it might "implode."[45] Then there's nothing to allegations of connections between the Trump campaign and Russian interests. Then National Security Advisor Michael Flynn has to step down because he made misleading statements about the degree of contact he had with the Russian Ambassador. Then-Attorney General Jeff Sessions is a "great guy" – one of the few supporters from early in the campaign.

---

43 Thomas Christiano notes that it's tough to have democracy without "the citizen attempt[ing] to advance justice and the common good according to her lights." I.e., democracy involves deliberation over and above discussion. See Christiano, *The Constitution of Equality: Democratic Authority and Its Limits* (Oxford: Oxford University Press, 2008), 3.

44 See William Smith, *Civil Disobedience and Deliberative Democracy* (London: Routledge, 2013).

45 Madeline Conway, "Trump on Healthcare: 'Let Obamacare Implode,' then 'We'll Get it Done,'" *Politico*, July 28, 2017, http://www.politico.com/story/2017/07/28/obamacare-repeal-fails-trump-responds-241094.

Then Sessions is criticized because he recused himself from the investigation into connections between the Trump campaign and Russia because he *also* had contact with the Russian Ambassador.[46] Press Secretary Sean Spicer, famous for his high-octane insistence that Trump's inauguration was the best-attended inauguration in presidential history "period!" (it wasn't), left the White House because Trump wanted to place friend and supposed fellow-vocalist-for-the-everyman Anthony Scaramucci in the position of White House Communications Director. Scaramucci was then fired after ten days for having teed off with a row of profanities in discussion with a *New Yorker* reporter.[47] Chief of Staff Reince Priebus stepped down on July 31st – Priebus being a symbol of connection with the traditional Republican Party. Steve Bannon's nationalist wing of the party was supposedly ascendant – Bannon having been brought on to sharpen the Trump campaign, after which he transitioned to White House chief strategist. Then Charlottesville. And Bannon was gone – that while Trump hurled Bannon-like Molotov cocktails at civic concord. It makes one's head spin. After years of conspiracy theories about Obama's citizenship and indecipherable ideas like "Hillary Clinton founded ISIS," it feels like institutionalized politics have been put on a lurching ship. If anyone has read *The Republic*, it feels like the bit about the boat captain, only it's 3 AM, the cap's knocked back a few Macallans, and he's simply yelling, "go here;" "go there!"[48]

Again, fine. Never mind Nixon sanctioning break-ins or maintaining an enemies list. Belgium went almost two *years* without a government not long ago, and fistfights have broken out on the floor of Taiwan's parliament.[49] Recent years

---

46 Peter Baker, Michael S. Schmidt, Maggie Haberman, "Citing Recusal, Trump Says He Wouldn't Have Hired Sessions," *The New York Times*, July 19, 2017, https://www.nytimes.com/2017/07/19/us/politics/trump-interview-sessions-russia.html.
47 Glenn Thrush and Maggie Haberman, "Sean Spicer Resigns as White House Secretary," *The New York Times*, July 21, 2017, https://www.nytimes.com/2017/07/21/us/politics/sean-spicer-resigns-as-white-house-press-secretary.html; Alexandra Wilts, "White House Communications Director Anthony Scaramucci 'Forced Out by John Kelly,'" *the Independent*, July 31, 2017, https://www.independent.co.uk/news/world/americas/us-politics/anthony-scaramucci-donald-trump-white-house-communications-director-resigns-quits-a7869936.html.
48 Though the site has a relatively consistent anti-Trump orientation, the turnaround in the Trump White House is well-illustrated in Andrew Prokop, "The Chaos of the Trump Administration, in One Picture," *Vox*, August 18, 2017, https://www.vox.com/policy-and-politics/2017/8/18/16170400/bannon-fired-trump-administration.
49 Angelique Chrisafis, "Eurozone Crisis Forces Belgium to Finally Form a Government," *The Guardian*, December 1, 2011, https://www.theguardian.com/world/2011/dec/01/eurozone-crisis-forces-belgium-government.

of EU parliamentary debate have featured MEPs accusing each other of being "Nazis," and haranguing reporters Trump-style would be just another day for the heads of many other states.[50] Politics is messy; that's hardly news. Still, are we looking at orchestrated chaos? Is all the to and fro intentional? Or is Trump – and perhaps some of those around him – *trying* to hit notes that can clearly be heard, yet throwing in enough other noise such that some of those notes linger for those who *want* to hear them, yet for those who *don't*, it becomes possible to claim that they're not there?

I'd put it this way: you won't convince me to give up my American passport anytime soon. American institutions are strong, and Trump hasn't been able to maneuver without fetters. A vibrant political culture opposes him, and there will be a government after he leaves – a government perhaps more sympathetic to civil society and brotherhood in the democratic body. Again, Nixon often comes to mind – not because the Mueller investigation will prove Trump's a crook, but concerning the atmosphere of nastiness and a sense of government as about scoring "points." Still, it often appears Trump picks themes he *knows* will sound out of place in the second decade of the twenty-first century – that to *in fact* speak to groups that *have* become disenfranchised because their views *aren't* majority anymore. It's rough. If, as the American Declaration of Independence (1776) maintains, it's "self-evident" that "all men are created equal" and have an inalienable right to "life, liberty and the pursuit of happiness," one has to ask whether one is taking one's job seriously as leader of a polity *built* on such ideals when one engages in discourses one *knows* will contradict the sensibilities of groups who long had to struggle to achieve recognition as members of said polity – that above and beyond groups who see the inclusion of previously marginalized brothers and sisters as a victory for the society as a whole. Napalm politics *can* leave a lot of forests burned.

I take that to mean the following: one can talk about such issues on the terrain of national ideals. One might discuss the American Constitution, the American Revolution, or specific legislation from the national past. One might discuss the United States' role in the world or the meaning of the experiences of American life. One can talk about national narratives, and one can discuss which President is the aberration and which is the norm. One might *also* discuss *human* ideals, however; one might discuss ideals engaged by *wide* varieties of

---

50 See, e.g., The Telegraph, "Parliament Fights Around the World," March 15, 2013, http://www.telegraph.co.uk/news/worldnews/9931916/Parliament-fights-around-the-world.html.

communities and discuss the social atmospheres we might want to *create*. One might discuss the goals that *democratic* peoples place in front of themselves, and what the meaning of social betterment in fact is. Indeed, the U.S. has advocated for and assisted in the construction of universal socio-political standards; it helped to build the institutions through which such standards are advocated for as well as enforced.[51] Simply put, blowing dog whistles that perhaps-don't-quite-sanction-white-supremacism-yet-don't-help-undo-it – whistles wrapped in enough auxiliary noise to either strategically or *de facto* distract from the fact that such whistles are being blown – brings the American government to at least partially abandon the high ground it hasn't always, but theoretically *should* (and on more than a few occasions, *has*), maintained. Even if it's temporary, it makes America look worse than it should, to say nothing of worse than it *could*. The image of America becomes clouded: is it a "shining city on a hill" or an angry nation concerned with infighting? Of course, if one wants to grant Trump points for not even claiming to do *that* (make the U.S. look good, or occupy the moral high ground), one might give him something there. Perhaps he deserves honesty credit for not even *claiming* to be interested in higher ideals or declaring that principles don't matter, and then following through. The next day, though, he'll likely tell you that's *not* what he's doing (speaking "honestly;" that, he's being a "strategist" or "deal maker") – that while another prominent White House figure is shown their way out the door. And when you see such a happy reaction on the faces of figures with some dubitable views, and you look in the other direction and see someone looking at the ground while holding a megaphone behind their back, I, anyway, would be hard-pressed to say that honesty is the first thing that comes to mind. Now, I can't be the *only* one who hears that faintly pitched sound in the air, can I – a sound that makes certain people's ears prick up while others are less sure about what they heard? It feels like a tone that *is* meant to be heard and not – one causing a lot of dogs to start barking and people to grip their heads, yet which presents a certain logic if barking dogs and a lot of headaches are part of what one wants.

---

51 See, e.g., Samuel Walker, *The Rights Revolution: Rights and Community in Modern America* (Oxford: Oxford University Press, 1998), 89–114. See also Roger Normand and Sarah Zaidi, *Human Rights at the UN: The Politics of Universal Justice* (Bloomington: Indiana University Press, 2008).

Codas of Anger and Silence
Finding Resolution from the Yugoslav '90s (December 12, 2017)

Abstract: *For those of us who lived through the '90s, Yugoslavia was a dismaying shock. The justice process is winding down now; most important players have been processed by the UN's Criminal Tribunal for the Former Yugoslavia. Some of the last cases, however, brought drama – outbursts and a suicide. It's a macabre coda to the Totentanz of the Yugoslav wars – a dance which need be remembered, but which it's a relief to see come to an end.*

Potentially, the past few weeks at the International Criminal Tribunal for the Former Yugoslavia have been unparalleled. Firstly, one of the individuals who has to be considered one of the top handful of war criminals from the 1990s Yugoslav conflicts – Ratko Mladić – was finally sentenced. It was a more than six-year process, from his May 2011 arrest in a small village in the province of Vojvodina in Serbia's north country to his November 22nd sentencing in The Hague. The trial had never been uneventful – Mladić had never been shy about interrupting proceedings. The episode ended in a final outburst of anger and vileness, however, as, in the course of his sentencing, Mladić announced that the accusations and verdict against him were based on "lies," and that he would violate the mothers of the officers of the court. The eruption was to no avail. Global opinion had spoken, and while Mladić escaped from one charge of genocide, he was convicted of another, as well as several counts of crimes against humanity and violating the laws of war.[1] It was a dramatic coda to a period

"Flag of Yugoslavia. Close Up" @ yui / shutterstock.com 245369776

---

1 See Own Bowcott and Julian Borger, "Ratko Mladić Convicted of War Crimes and Genocide at UN Tribunal," *The Guardian*, November 22, 2017, https://www.theguardian.com/world/2017/nov/22/ratko-mladic-convicted-of-genocide-and-war-crimes-at-un-tribunal.

already marked by dramas of the kind that most of us don't want to see: dramas marked by violence, murder, and death.

The Bosnia Serbs weren't the only group to commit atrocities during the 1990s conflicts that shocked not only Europe but the world, however, and few national groups haven't had at least *some* portion of their military or political leadership up for trials before the Tribunal. The Croats, for example, both within Croatia itself as well as on the Bosnian side of the border, *also* engaged in some regrettable violence and dubious ethnic politics over the years of the wars, and Bosnian Croat general Slobodan Praljak was among a number of figures sentenced for crimes committed in the fighting in and around the city of Mostar – the destruction of the town's bridge, Stari Most, being one of the conflicts' iconic images. Praljak's reaction to his sentencing for war crimes was even more dramatic than Mladić's. Upon the announcement of the verdict, Praljak declared that he was "not a war criminal," and that he would have no part in the justice to come. The court's decision was illegitimate in his view, and he rejected the whole thing. Then, in what can only be described as a stunning move, he drank a bottle of poison in full view of the court. Proceedings were suspended as presiding judge Carmel Agius looked on flabbergasted, unsure of precisely what to do.[2]

Now, the Yugoslav Wars, which lasted from 1991 to 1995, or 1999, depending on how one counts (does one stop with the Dayton Peace Accords or with the end of the war in Kosovo?), were a shock. I'm not sure anyone expected the Cold War's end to involve mellifluous peace; the U.S. had of course committed hundreds of thousands of troops to fighting Saddam Hussein in the Gulf War in 1990, and civil conflict around the world was on as hot a boil as ever. The usual battle over resources and sovereignty were afoot in what one social theorist has called the global "periphery," and the world's leading military powers still packed significant punch.[3] Still, disarmament was in discussion and an atmosphere of optimism, perhaps best articulated by books like Francis Fukuyama's *The End of History and the Last Man* (1992), hung in the air. It might not be that communism's defeat was "good;" capitalism's inequalities had caused a great deal of misery over its two hundred some-odd year history. However, the reasons to

---

2 See Bowcott, "Bosnian Croat War Criminal Dies after Taking Poison in UN Courtroom," *The Guardian*, November 29, 2017, https://www.theguardian.com/law/2017/nov/29/un-war-crimes-defendant-claims-to-drink-poison-at-trial-in-hague-slobodan-praljak. Prajlak was pronounced dead within twenty-four hours.

3 See Immanuel Wallerstein, *World-systems Analysis: An Introduction* (Durham, NC: Duke University Press, 2004).

go after each other ideologically had at least been reduced, and it wasn't fully uncommon to allow oneself visions of an era of concord and peace.[4] For many, the Yugoslav conflicts represented a karate-chop to this idea. Though it had never been part of the Soviet Bloc, Yugoslavia, as the last of Europe's socialist states, dissolved into the kind of politico-ethnic and nationalistic frenzy not seen since the first half of the twentieth century in the context of the two world wars. It was hard not to feel that a moment with potential had been lost.

Bosnia got the worst of it. I.e., Slovenia managed to break off with remarkably little conflict. When the wealthiest of the Yugoslav republics declared independence, a smart set of military maneuvers and Serbian president Slobodan Milošević's desire to hold as many of the remaining Yugoslav states together as possible kept the battle for Slovenian independence down to a week or two. A few dozen people were killed and, though any life lost in war is a tragedy, it was but a drop in the bucket compared with what was to come next. The Serbo-Croat War, or Croatian War of Independence, as some call it, involved tens of *thousands* of deaths and, though one might have suspected that the term was older (perhaps related to the Second World War or the Armenian Genocide), the Croat portion of the Yugoslav conflicts birthed the vocabulary "ethnic cleansing" – a product of the killing and population displacement around the village of Voćin in 1991 (a Serb paramilitary unit murdered some dozens of innocent Croats, and populations from both ethnic groups fled or were pushed out in different directions).[5] Still, the *Bosnian* War – with which the Croatian War of Independence was intertwined – brought the mayhem and killing to their height. The most ethnically and religiously diverse of the Yugoslav states, Bosnia became the central battleground for the multiple claims to ethnicity and sovereignty that ripped Federal Yugoslavia apart. Bosnian Serbs and Croats wanted territory contiguous with the Serb and Croat states, if not incorporation into those states themselves. Bosnian Muslims felt ganged-up on as, while they were the country's largest ethnic group (about 45%), Serb and Croat minority populations were sizable as well (about 32 and 18–19%). The latter also had the backing of the heftier republics within the dissolving Yugoslavia as Slobodan Milošević and Franjo Tuđman threw their support behind their brother and sister populations. As one

---

4 See Mikkel Vedby Rasmussen, *The West, Civil Society and the Construction of Peace* (New York: Palgrave MacMillan, 2003), 140; Leonie Murray, *Clinton, Peacekeeping and Humanitarian Interventionism: Rise and Fall of a Policy* (London: Routledge, 2008), 1; Francis Fukuyama, *The End of History and the Last Man* (New York: Penguin, 1992).

5 See Drazan Petrovic, "Ethnic Cleansing – An Attempt at Methodology," *European Journal of International Law* 5, no. 1 (1994): 342–59.

observer put it, the whole thing resulted in a "clusterfuck": per the *Oxford English Dictionary*, a "botched undertaking" defined by a "disorganized" or "chaotic" state.[6] The Croats were fickle, at times agreeing with Serbia to slice up Bosnian territory but then, once the tide turned against the Serbs behind NATO airpower, rounding on the Serbs as *de facto* Bosnian allies and throwing their weight behind the effort to push back both Bosnian Serb paramilitaries as well as the Yugoslav army itself. The Serbs had traditionally been the most powerful of the Yugoslav states, with Milošević controlling the resources of the JNA (Yugoslav Army). His bankrolling of the *Bosnian* Serbs to do his dirty work in Bosnia-Herzegovina (with the Bosnian Serb army commanded by Mladić) resulted in his own indictment by the Yugoslav Tribunal (though he died before proceedings were brought to an end). The Bosnian Muslims, or Bosniaks, though not always innocent, were largely left to fend for themselves; left with few military options, their move was to play for recognition in the West. Again, few in the Yugoslav Wars can be seen as simply "clean." Praljak, and figures like Bosniak commander Naser Orić, were properly investigated and involved in highly dubious acts.[7] It's nonetheless fair to say that Milošević, Mladić, and Bosnian Serb *jefe* Radovan Karadžić, have come to symbolize the worst of the violence and evil involved in the whole 1990s Yugoslav affair. They've achieved a kind of totemistic status vis-à-vis crimes against humanity and disregard for the value of human life.[8]

---

6   Oxford English Dictionary, "Clusterfuck" (2018), http://www.oed.com/view/Entry/2 57244?redirectedFrom=clusterfuck#eid. See also Jens Lapidus, *Easy Money: A Novel*, trans. Astri von Arbin Ahlander (New York: Random House, 2012).
7   Orić was a Bosniak military commander who led raids on several Bosnian Serb positions, but also regional towns, in and around Srebrenica, one of which killed eleven civilians. He was convicted by the Yugoslav Tribunal of failing to prevent the deaths of a number of Bosnian Serbian detainees as well as the mistreatment of others. It should be noted that, after a two-year prison sentence, Orić had his conviction overturned. And, indeed, a Bosnian court also recently absolved him of war crimes. Still, Orić represents the grey zone in which many events took place during the Yugoslav wars. Civilians and non-combatants were harmed at his men's hands and, at the very least, there was a legal question mark behind the military actions and treatment of prisoners with which he was involved. See Rafaëlle Maison, *Coupable de résistance?: Naser Oric, défenseur de Srebrenica, devant la justice international* (Paris: Armand Colin, 2010); Deutsche Welle, "'Defender of Srebrenica,' Naser Oric, Acquitted of War Crimes," December 30, 2018, https://www.dw.com/en/defender-of-srebrenica-naser-oric-acquitted-of-war-crimes/a-46517517.
8   See Norman Cigar and Paul Williams, *Indictment at The Hague: The Milošević Regime and the Crimes of the Balkan War* (New York: New York University Press, 2002).

Now, measuring evil is hard. One can't offhand dismiss nationalism – many of us are involved with it – there may be moments when killing is justified, and the transition from one political system to another is never an easy affair. Western political parties with dubious attitudes have gained increasing power in recent years (I often wonder how supporters of Germany's Alternative for Germany or the Danish People's Party would behave had *they* been Bosnian Serbs in the 1990s), and the rights of peoples vis-à-vis one another can be a fraught issue indeed. Still, the symbolic position of Milošević, Mladić, and Karadžić isn't without reason. Were there elements within the Croat government that pushed hard for war, including forcing Serb populations out of Croat territory? Yes. The expulsion of Serbs from the Krajina, or the Eastern sector of Croatia, is a well-known event vis-à-vis the end of the war. However, Serbs were also pushed out of towns by Croats not only in the Krajina, but other areas as well – and not only at the end of the conflict, but as part of the war's early days as well.[9] Might Franjo Tuđman and his government have been more sensitive to – indeed, shown *any* interest in – the experiences of Serbs in relation to *Croat* nationalism, especially in light of Croatia's history in the Second World War? Clearly. Hundreds of thousands of Serbs were either displaced or killed in concentration camps in the so-called Independent State of Croatia, allied with the Axis in the first years of the 1940s – a point on which Serbs in Croatia and elsewhere in the dissolving Yugoslavia harped again and again.[10] During the Bosnian phase of the war, did *Muslim* militia leaders *also* commit atrocities as fighting in the country sank to the worst of its depths? They did. Again, if you were a Serb in Kravica around Christmas of 1993, you would have witnessed terrifying raids and *ad hoc* killing led by figures like the aforementioned Orić, who, post-imprisonment by the Yugoslav Tribunal, apparently found a second career as a fitness buff.[11] Still, one of the stunning dimensions of the Yugoslav Wars is how much of certain episodes – including speech and actions that fed directly into genocide, war

---

9   Around Vukovar, e.g., an early hotpoint in the war, the violence against and ethnic cleansing of Croats was intense, including the murder of Croatian civilians and prisoners of war. However, there were elements on both sides pushing at the other's populations, and refugees were forced out in both directions. See Norman Percy (producer), *The Death of Yugoslavia: Wars of Independence* (United Kingdom: BBC, 1995).
10 See Sabrina P. Ramet, ed., *The Independent State of Croatia* (New York: Routledge, 2007).
11 France24, "'Srebrenica Defender' Awaits His War Crimes Verdict," November 30, 2018, https://www.france24.com/en/20181130-srebrenica-defender-awaits-war-crimes-verdict.Yugoslav Tribunal

crimes, and crimes against humanity – was captured as a matter of record, and directly on film. In a range of excellent works – from the BBC's *The Death of Yugoslavia* (1995) to the two-hour-long multinational production *A Cry from the Grave* (1999) – one can simply *see* Milošević manipulating Yugoslavia's status *qua* sovereign state in conjunction with Serb national sentiment for his personal gain. One can *watch* Karadžić announcing that Bosniaks faced "extinction" before the Bosnian parliament lest greater concessions be made to Bosnian Serb demands. And, in film footage from the town of Srebrenica, near the Bosnian-Serbian border, one can watch Mladić declare – face flush to the camera – that it was time to take "revenge" on the "Turks;" that the area was to be returned to the "great Serb nation." Srebrenica is obviously a headline issue in all this. In roughly a week and a half in July 1995, somewhere in the area of 8000 Bosniak men and boys were simply murdered. Using the vocabulary that the Clinton Administration adopted vis-à-vis events in Rwanda roughly a year before, it was at the very least an "act" of genocide. It represented the worst variety of murderousness in an atmosphere already pervaded by the absolute stink of death. At least in one area, an entire people were gone after. They were pinpointed by way of identity, and a killing machine was set into motion. Especially in light of the Holocaust, that one would discuss such things in a *European* context in the late twentieth century bordered on the unfathomable. It was hard to imagine – no more, no less.

A number of issues emerge in relation to all this; the trials, the killing, the wars, the hyper-nationalism – the entire tragic *gestalt*. The first of these might be how such a thing could have been brought to happen generally, yes, but also, particularly in *Europe*? I.e., is it such a massive contradiction with the European tradition that populations went after each other so savagely, and is Europe *really* the paradigm of modern rationality and progressive ideologies that we sometimes make it out to be? I'll say but two things. Firstly, precisely what Europe "is" is deeply contested. One recent claim on the issue, e.g., posits that Europe has actually been a matter of *two* visions: a supposedly rationalistic North defining itself, occasionally imperialistically and sometimes priggishly, in opposition to a supposedly more romantic South, and that South then providing a more diverse picture of European life in which a more passionate, sometimes obscurantist, set of beliefs sometimes made their way to the fore. I.e., it's been posited that figures from Montesquieu to Hegel to Locke brought us the figure of "man as man" and forwarded notions of the logical, independent subject on which most democratic philosophies have been reliant. Here Europe becomes the picture of "enlightened" London, Paris, or Berlin, promoting ideas that would become central to international law and concepts of the "rights of man."[12] That's while *others* have posed a picture of Europe as more diverse, taking in traditions from not only its borderlands, but the Islamic world as well. There might be a broader range of philosophies at work with potentially different views of the subject that might have *also* had play in European life.[13] I'd be shy to say which vision "won," or which is the "true" Europe. Still, from *philosophe* notions of rational Enlightenment to the revolutions that convulsed Europe throughout the eighteenth and nineteenth centuries to ideas of science and progress, certain notions of politics, education, and the possibilities of the subject seem to mark the run of at least the *modern* European past. Certain concepts *may* have been dominant in European life, and they may be those we classically note. Historians Peter Burke and Hayden White, e.g., have argued that certain concepts of science, commitments to empirical truth, notions of the individual mind, and schematizations of historical progress were hallmarks of the European ideal. Nothing marks European culture like notions of "linear" development, Burke has claimed, while the idea of a "science of freedom," as another historian has put it, may mark the European legacy from the end of the seventeenth century until now.[14] It's not a ridiculous

---

12 See Roberto M. Dainotto, *Europe (In Theory)* (Durham, NC: Duke University Press, 2007), 49.
13 Ibid. This is an extremely complex point as it can reproduce ideas of a rationalist Europe versus a supposedly more obscurantist world outside the West – something I don't want to do. Indeed, insofar as the point might also specifically involve the issue of *Islam*, one has to take care; that somehow it bears a set of ideas distinct odds with Western ideas of rights is a deeply controversial idea. Still, one need be aware of particular claims that multiple global cultures may *in fact* hold different worldviews – including senses of sovereignty and subjectivity – and that the point is in part the claimed "rationalism" of Europe as being an occasion for the domination of colonization of people supposedly holding *alternative* worldviews. "Different," or "alternative," in this case, doesn't mean of "lesser." It may designate difference, or alternative, and recognizing historical tapestries as more complex than we might imagine. See, e.g., Hamid Mowlana, "Theoretical Perspectives on Islam and Communication" in *The Global Intercultural Communication Reader*, ed. Molefi Kete Asante, Yoshitaka Miike and Jing Yin (London: Routledge, 2008), 283–96. See also Reza Afshari, "On the Historiography of Human Rights: Reflections on Paul Gordon Lauren's *The Evolution of International Human Rights: Visions Seen*," *Human Rights Quarterly* 29, no. 1 (2007): 1–67.
14 Peter Gay, *The Enlightenment: An Interpretation, vol. II: The Science of Freedom* (New York: Knopf, 1969). See also Peter Burke, "Western Historical Thinking in a Global Perspective: 10 Theses" in *Western Historical Thinking: An Intercultural Debate*, ed. Jörn Rüsen (New York: Berghahn, 2002), 19; Hayden White, "The Westernization of World History" in *Western Historical Thought*, 111–8.

idea. The world's democratic political systems claim their origins in the work of figures like Montesquieu and Locke, and one simply can't miss the role of important European political upheavals in spreading ideas of emancipation and equality in law.[15]

Fair enough. That's the Europe we like, and the Louvre and Humboldt University are Europe, as are the French Revolution and, in some ways, the American.[16] Europe is Marie Curie and Samuel Pufendorf, Isaac Newton, and Albert Einstein. Still, the flip side of this has been that Europe also has a *long* history of viewing some people as more "ready" for rights than others and supposedly universal liberties *not* being liberties Europeans have accorded to all. I.e., because intellectual development and rationality were decided "things," one could use "science" to see who had attained them and who had not. If one had achieved a particular mode of knowledge or "variety" of thought, one was "developed," or in accordance with humanity's "teleology." If one *hadn't* achieved such things, someone would have to be sent to teach you, and your political freedom accordingly held back. Here, we get in the idea of rationality part of the justification of imperialism in the name of things like "civilization" and "progress," if not "natural law."[17] Of course, *that's* then compounded by the fact that Europeans haven't always had the highest degree of success applying universalistic concepts of humankind to *each other*. European states have often been surprisingly tribal on historical bases, and Europe's cultures have frequently competed for pride of place (debates of German *Kultur* versus French *civilisation* are exemplary of this [what one scholar has called the "civic" model of citizenship – citizenship as about legal rights as opposed to culture or ethnicity – has not always played the dominant role]).[18] Of course, then there's the fighting. That's been not only a matter of the twentieth century's two World Wars – vortices into which the rest of the

---

15 See, e.g., Lynn Hunt, *Inventing Human Rights: A History* (New York: W.W. Norton, 2007); Jonathan Israel, *Democratic Enlightenment: Philosophy, Revolution, and Human Rights* (Oxford: Oxford University Press, 2011). See also Arvind Sharma, *Are Human Rights Western?: A Contribution to the Dialogue of Civilizations* (Oxford: Oxford University Press, 2006).

16 I simply point out that, originally, the American Revolution was a revolution of Europeans against Europeans, and that the principles off of which the country was built were in essence European ideas. See Israel, *Democratic Enlightenment*.

17 See, e.g., Brett Bowden, *The Empire of Civilization: The Evolution of an Imperial Idea* (Chicago: University of Chicago Press, 2009). See also Bill Ashcroft, Gareth Griffiths, and Helen Tiffin, eds., *The Post-Colonial Studies Reader* (London: Routledge, 2006).

18 See Anthony D. Smith, *The Nation in History: Historiographical Debates about Ethnicity and Nationalism* (Cambridge: Polity, 2000).

world became sucked – but the Napoleonic Wars, the Franco-Prussian War, the first Balkan Wars (1912-3), the Crimean War, the Greco-Turkish War, and many, many others. Indeed, from Paris' *Arc de Triomphe* to the *Völkerschlachtdenkmal* in Leipzig to Nelson's Column in Trafalgar Square, Europe *memorializes* these conflicts, posing them as central to national identity.[19] Yes, Europe can be celebrated for its humanism and insistences on things reasoned. However, it has also been the seat of some of the world's worst violences, to say nothing of having fostered both moments and movements organized not only around ethnocentric nationalism, but racism and anti-Semitism in the most rote sense. Ask anyone who experienced the Pogroms, the Dreyfus Affair, or the rise of the Nazis if *they* read European history as the history of realizing "man as man."[20]

I'll round that out by saying this: in many ways, Europe's recent history has concerned *breaking* with such pasts. Ideologically, the communist world sought to do so. An essential claim of communism – "real, existing socialism" having been part of at least *Eastern* Europe's past from the end of the Second World War until, well, about the time of the Yugoslav Wars – was that histories of conflict and oppression were predictable in societies that competed over wealth. People in competition with each other either collectively or individually in relation to power and resources will get caught up in ideologies not only justifying competition, but seeking *victory* in said competition – wherein exploitation if not abuse becomes normalized as a matter of course.[21] Of course, communist Europe, which practiced its own varieties of oppression, is gone, and we're left with liberalism supreme. This means market-driven economics tied to political democracy which, though equally hard work may not be equally rewarded, *does* provide relative freedom of speech, freedom of movement, freedom of work and travel, and institutions supporting such ideals. That's a Europe we again know, and a Europe with virtue. That's at the same time that vocabularies of "Heimat statt Multikulti" (homeland over multiculturalism), a campaign slogan of Germany's *Alternative für Deutschland*, or political advertisements for groups such as the Danish People's

---

19 See, e.g., Siobhan Kattago, *Memory and Representation in Contemporary Europe: The Persistence of the Past* (Farnham: Ashgate, 2012).
20 See, e.g., Neil McMaster, *Racism in Europe: 1870-2000* (New York: Palgrave MacMillan, 2001). See also Alan Kramer, *Dynamic of Destruction: Culture and Mass Killing in the First World War* (Oxford: Oxford University Press, 2007); Michael S. Neiberg, *War and Society in Europe: 1898 to the Present* (London: Routledge, 2004).
21 These were essential points made by Marx vis-à-vis the relation between economics and social ideology. See Domenico Losurdo, *Class Struggle: A Political and Philosophical History* (New York: Palgrave MacMillan, 2016).

Party featuring phalanxes of Nordic faces over subscripts like "we have so much to protect" (never mind Victor Orban's "anti-Soros" campaigns) can make one wary.[22] While no place in Europe is undergoing the kinds of transformations that played into the Yugoslav conflicts, more than a few Europeans are concerned to hold nationalist extremes at bay. That's such that culturalist attitudes *don't* become laced with tinges of violence and we find reversions to darker moments of the European past. Rationalism and universalism have deep roots in Europe. Not a small part of recent European projects, however, have been dedicated to consciously promoting such legacies out of awareness that histories of ethnicism, xenophobia, marginalization, and degrees of both military and social violence have often made Europe's picture more complex.[23]

In any case, beyond that – beyond thinking about different sides of the European past – a second point is considering what kind of *crimes* in which figures like Milošević, Mladić, and Karadžić, though also Praljak, were engaged. Yes, Milošević, Mladić, and Karadžić have a kind of negative iconic status as modern-day war criminals and defilers of international law. Many know their names, and for that reason – that a consensus has built-up via which they're akin

---

22 See, e.g., Götz Bonsen, "Doris von Sayn-Wittgenstein: 'Deutschland ist so unbeliebt wie nie zuvor,'" *shz.de*, https://www.shz.de/17265076; Thomas Klose Jensen, "Eksperter: Dansk Folkeparti vinder på modkampagner," *DR*, https://www.dr.dk/nyheder/politik/eksperter-dansk-folkeparti-vinder-paa-modkampagner. Accompanying Denmark in the Scandinavian world is the Sweden Democrats with their slogan "Keep Sweden Swedish," and we are of course aware of events like the crowds applauding the fire at a migrant hostel in Bautzen, Germany. See David Crouch, "The Rise of the Anti-Immigrant Sweden Democrats: 'We Don't Feel at Home Anymore, and It's Their Fault," *The Guardian*, December 14, 2014, https://www.theguardian.com/world/2014/dec/14/sweden-democrats-flex-muscles-anti-immigrant-kristianstad; Samuel Osborne, "Crowds 'Cheer' as Fire Breaks Out at Home for Refugees in Germany," *The Independent*, February 21, 2016, http://www.independent.co.uk/news/world/europe/crowd-cheers-as-fire-breaks-out-at-home-for-refugees-in-germany-a6887416.html.

23 Obviously, the EU plays into this as well. Intended to promote "peace, security, and progress" via the recognition of essential rights across borders and founding itself in democratic governments, the body explicitly calls on the heritages of the "the Renaissance and the Enlightenment" as laying the foundation for its cultural and political *raison d'être*. See Council of the European Communities, "Treaty of the European Union" (1992, preamble), https://europa.eu/european-union/sites/europaeu/files/docs/body/treaty_on_european_union_en.pdf; European Commission, "New Narrative for Europe" (2015), http://ec.europa.eu/assets/eac/culture/policy/new-narrative/documents/declaration_en.pdf.

to latter-day Hitlers or Stalins. Again, though, what have figures like Milošević, Mladić, and Karadžić, (and perhaps Praljak) *done* – not just in general, but relatively *precise*, senses? How might one consider the crimes they committed, and what's the *nature* of the violence with which they were involved? What's the *heart* of violations like "crimes against humanity," and how do we understand the nature of that "heart?" I'll again note that it's remarkable to watch film of central figures discussing claims driving the Yugoslav Wars. It's remarkable hearing – *hearing* – interest in making one or the other region ethnically "pure," and it's wild to watch open threats against neighbor populations and bold-faced declarations of intents to destroy them or drive them out. Still, what does that concern? What's the essence of the violations that such things involved? Indeed, in view of the fact that we live in a world of "insidious leniencies" and "unavowable petty cruelties," as one philosopher put it – that invasive acts of degradation may be part of everyday life – how can we put words on the concepts at work in at least *some* of the cases concerning the former Yugoslavia and say "here's *how* those are rights violations and here's where they transgress not only how conflict is supposed to go (the laws of war), but the essential privileges and freedoms that *all* should have (human rights)?"[24] How can we go to the *deepest* level of what Milošević, Mladić, Karadžić, and, again, Praljak, did, and say something about *that* – the ground floor of human rights violations and the fundamental level of what such crimes concern?

I'd like to focus on genocide for a moment – that as, within the panoply of crimes committed by the figures named above (Praljak excepted), it's the most basic. Genocide is the most frightening, egregious, and the most laden with historical baggage. It's provocative: among what one might think of as human rights crimes, genocide is usually noted as "non-derogable." As phrased by the United Nation's International Covenant on Civil and Political Rights (1966), one might impose the "sentence of death…for the most serious crimes in accordance with the law."[25] Potentially – potentially – states might allow for certain modes of killing with a certain level of legality.[26] States also have rights to go to war – there is a right to "individual or collective self-defence" if one is attacked, and

---

24 Michel Foucault, *Discipline and Punish: The Birth of the Prison*, trans. Alan Sheridan (New York: Vintage, 1979), 308.
25 United Nations, "International Covenant on Civil and Political Rights" (1966, article 6), http://www.ohchr.org/en/professionalinterest/pages/ccpr.aspx. Hereafter ICCPR.
26 I would, however, point this out as generally not in human rights spirit. The ICCPR uses the vocabulary of "countries which have not abolished the death penalty," indicating that human rights would prefer if one did. See ibid., article 6.

there are provisos for international intervention in the context of humanitarian crisis.[27] Under *no* circumstance, however, is one supposed to destroy a "national, ethnical, racial, or religious group" in whole or in part.[28] Go after individuals *en masse* based on identity and you've committed an absolute crime. Sure; one might suspend particular rights in times of emergency; societies might limit certain freedoms and liberties under particular types of conditions.[29] Going after racial, ethnic, national, or religious groups, though? Get caught and have it proved, and one is on crimes-against-humanity level.[30]

Now, significant about discussing a document like the Civil and Political Covenant is that it involves the words of the UN's Convention on the Prevention and Punishment of the Crime of Genocide (1948) – what is in fact the *central* international instrument defining the crime of genocide, as well as the censure against it. Significant about *that* is then that the Genocide Convention's conceptualization of the idea – "genocide" – is up for debate. I.e., as fundamental as the idea is, some would say that the Genocide Convention's definition of genocide is too narrow. Worked-out by the jurist Raphael Lemkin in the 1940s, it is noticeable that the term does *not* include class or political affiliation. Translatable to "gene killing," or "tribe" or "racial" killing, the concept *was* thought primarily in relation to ethnic and cultural identity, and it was thought in relation to nations, with the nation as a kind of "ethnie," or geno-cultural community.[31] It's true that in the book in which Lemkin introduced genocide as a concept, *Axis Rule in Occupied Europe: Laws of Occupation, Analysis of Government, Proposals for Redress* (1944), he discussed political *techniques* for genocide. Lemkin noted how

---

27 United Nations "Charter of the United Nations" (1945, article 51), http://www.un.org/en/sections/un-charter/chapter-vii/index.html. See also Michael Byers, *War Law: Understanding International Law and Armed Conflict* (London: Atlantic, 2005).
28 United Nations, "Convention on the Prevention and Punishment of the Crime of Genocide" (1948, article 2), https://treaties.un.org/doc/Publication/UNTS/Volume%2078/volume-78-I-1021-English.pdf.
29 Usually, this involves certain levels of freedom of expression, freedom of movement, or the normal course through the justice system. However, such things are highly controversial, and should be introduced only under the strictest restrictions. See Victor V. Ramaraj, *Emergencies and the Limits of Legality* (Cambridge: Cambridge University Press, 2008).
30 See Michael Byers, *War Law: Understanding International Law and Armed Conflict* (London: Atlantic, 2005).
31 The "ethnie" is a term nationalism scholar Anthony D. Smith has used to describe conceptions of the national community as ethnic. See Smith, *The Ethnic Origins of Nations* (Oxford: Blackwell, 1991).

the levers of institutional and ideological power might be manipulated to make genocide *happen*.³² What it was, however, was the "destruction of [peoples];" it was the elimination or eradication of a "biological structure" and the social accouterments that accompanied it. It was the destruction of a line of descent and a cultural world that went with it. That makes things complicated. March thousands if not millions of people off to a death camp because of a political conviction (something many people could hold), and it's unclear what to call it. Many would say "genocide." Not the Genocide Convention, though – something that makes one think.³³

There are two points here. Firstly, that genocide is "officially" defined as about "people," or a space between culture, ethnicity, and biology, doesn't preclude that politics and ethnic identity might intersect. It doesn't mean that one can't *make* politics via the "culturalized self," or in relation to a sense of historical identity. One can belong to a nation in purely civic or legal terms, and perhaps even those terms alone. Still, among the issues in Yugoslavia was the *conversion* of cultural, ethnic, and religious identities *into* political groups demanding rights. The issue was partly groups *claiming* legacy, ancestral lands, and assertions that, true or not, various groups were not receiving their rightful inheritances or that, along cultural or ethnic lines, particular groups were being marginalized or oppressed (and, indeed, being ethnically Khmer or Russian didn't save one's backside in Pol Pot's Cambodia or Stalin's USSR).³⁴ Was Milošević a Serb nationalist in an

---

32 This involved the promotion of political parties furthering the interests of occupying powers in addition, of course, to the obvious point that it involved those out to eliminate specific ethnic or religious cultures (the Nazis were the obvious example; however, Lemkin also notes Norway's Nasjonal Samling and the Dutch National Party as the types of collaborationist parties that might help genocidal conditions). See Raphael Lemkin, *Axis Rule in Occupied Europe: Laws of Occupation, Analysis of Government, Proposals for Redress* (Clark: The Lawbook Exchange, 2005).

33 See, e.g., Beth van Schaak, "The Crime of Political Genocide: Repairing the Convention's Blind Spots," *The Yale Law Journal* 106, no. 7 (1997): 2259–2291; Martin Shaw, *What is Genocide?* (Cambridge: Polity, 2007); George J. Andreopoulos, ed., *Genocide: Conceptual and Historical Dimensions* (Philadelphia: University of Pennsylvania Press, 1994).

34 Nor did being German necessarily save one in Hitler's Germany. I.e., there are multiple modes of belonging to a national community, and even if "ethnicity" is the preferred mode – and it not-infrequently is – *maintaining* that ethnicity doesn't necessarily guarantee one a place at the national table. Still, there can be a lethalness to mixing national identity with ethnicity – one that becomes dangerous at the moment when ethnicity is politicized. See, e.g., Jeff Spinner, *The Boundaries of Race, Ethnicity, and Nationality in the Liberal State* (Baltimore: Johns Hopkins University Press, 1994); David McCrone

authentic sense? Hard to say. One gets the sense that he felt a system change coming and he sought to turn events to his advantage. Comparatively, Mladić and Karadžić come off as the true zealots – concerned with the fate of the ancestral "folk" (where someone like Praljak falls on this spectrum is hard to say).[35] Still, some suggest that definitions of genocide *should* include class and political ideology as killing on mass scales is killing on mass scales, and the primary issue is membership in a group. In any case, however one cuts it, the killing in the course of the Yugoslav Wars was deleterious. Racial, cultural, *or* political, it was oriented towards the "destruction" of "societ[ies]," as one scholar puts it, or radically marginalizing or eliminating communities in either a political or cultural sense.[36] If genocide *must* be thought of as "gene killing," maybe political killing isn't genocide in the strictest sense. Regardless of how one phrases it, however, at stake was the destruction of people where they lived, and in the name of contradicting *other* people's claim to what they saw as sovereign right.[37]

Now, what's significant about *that* – significant about saying that "yes, central actors from the Yugoslav Wars were involved in genocide and crimes against humanity" regardless of how one defines such things – is the issue of what the problem with genocide and crimes against humanity *is*. It's the *essence* of killing on such scales, and what it means to undermine basic laws of deportment and human address. It's the *heart* of what it means to fundamentally undermine others' existences, and to run rampant across societies, snuffing out lives. Of course, no one wants to be subject to murder. Few look for humiliation, demonization, or to be stereotyped. I can't see anyone looking for "extermination, enslavement, [or] deportation" – vocabularies at the heart of the crimes against humanity lexicon.[38] Still, invoking one commentator's terminology, the problem may exceed "bare life." The issue with genocide and crimes against humanity

---

and Frank Bechhofer, *Understanding National Identity* (Cambridge: Cambridge University Press, 2015); Smith, *The Nation in History*.

35   In essence, Praljak seems to have been an operative as opposed to an ideologue – i.e., his crimes were military in nature, though, of course, military conduct overlaps with humanitarian issues. I.e., he participated in a criminal operation. However, there doesn't seem to be the same level of evidence of ideological ethnic hate. Se e Selma Milovanovic, "Slobodan Praljak: War Criminal or Croatian Hero?" *Al-Jazeera*, November 30, 2017, https://www.aljazeera.com/news/2017/11/slobodan-praljak-war-criminal-croatian-hero-171130181546531.html.
36   Catherine Baker, *The Yugoslav Wars of the 1990s* (New York: Palgrave, 2015), 1.
37   Ibid.
38   M. Cherif Bassiouni, *Crimes against Humanity in International Criminal Law* (The Hague: Kluwer, 1999), 1.

may not be whether someone is allowed to *live*, but what life should be *about*.³⁹ The problem may be the *kind* of existence we should have, and the possibilities allowed us as human beings when our rights are *recognized*. The issue might not be only the destruction of bodies, but the destruction of souls and minds. The issue is not just killing and enslaving physical beings. It's killing and jailing people with *expressions* and *ideas*. A stake are people with goals they'd like to accomplish and desires about what they'd like their lives to be about. It's people with modes of reflection and things they wish to do and say.

Here, I set-up human rights as a goal. I invoke those dimensions of rights ideas that involve legal privileges, but also privileges that should have legal status because they represent not just life's sustenance, but its sustenance in a fuller, richer sense – life beyond the minimum, or life as it *should be*. I approach human rights as addressing things as they should be, but the "should" being something we should *have*. This is a specific approach to rights. It's a way in which human rights sometimes don't *read*. When human rights proclaim that "everyone has the right to a standard of living adequate for the health and well-being of himself and of his family, including food, clothing, housing and medical care," that's addressing baselines.⁴⁰ When rights argue for the "right to life," or prohibitions against slavery or torture, they're not asking for much.⁴¹ When rights argue against "arbitrary arrest, detention or exile," they seem to set ground floor goals; they're defining a line between either obliteration and abuse or not.⁴² We need such lines; one doesn't get far without eating or sitting indefinitely in jail. However, what about *good* living standards? What about opportunities for economic *improvement*? What about *creativity* in one's life and social *inclusion*? What about self-expression, and the possibility of contributing to the world; leaving one's thumbprint and legacy or inheritance? Minimum guarantees are necessary; there is little without life. Still, "baseline" experiences and "minimum" standards are likely not the level at which most of us would like to define the arc of our lives.

Thankfully, those aren't rights' limit. "Enough" isn't always enough where human rights are concerned. "Bare life" isn't the entirety of rights' philosophy,

---

39 Giorgio Agamben, *Homo Sacer: Sovereign Power and Bare Life*, trans. Daniel Heller-Roazen (Stanford: Stanford University Press, 1998).
40 United Nations, "The Universal Declaration of Human Rights" (1948, article 25), http://www.un.org/en/universal-declaration-human-rights/index.html. Hereafter UDHR.
41 Ibid., article 3, 4.
42 Ibid., article 5, 9.

nor is the rote stopping of murder and torture. Looking at rights documents, e.g., one should have not only the basics of welfare but the right to work *and* free choice of employment; there should be a chance for labor as a mode of self-expression. If one reads rights texts, one should have not only "acceptable" standards of living, but the right to an education and the possibility to participate in a community's cultural life.[43] In the context of human rights, one has the right to share in society's technological advances and gain exposure to the benefits of science. One has the right to social services, yet also to rest and leisure.[44] One has the right to exist, but also free thought, democratic participation, and to discuss what one believes. We're not just born, but "born free and equal in dignity and rights." One has *liberty* and intellectual worth over and above rote properties of the body. One has evaluative and judgmental capacities in addition to a physical state. The body may provide the human being with certain needs. *The* human being, however, is found in the mind and the exercise of one's reflective capacities – in part the basis for instituting free speech, educational, cultural, and civil rights.

My point is as follows: *that's* what's violated when one extinguishes a group or uses the tools of violence to marginalize, silence, or destroy. *That's* what's killed when people's existences are damaged, and, whether seen through the lenses of ethnicity, class, or politics, their humanity is attacked or devolved. *That's* what's undermined when one pulls the rug out from under others in ways that are existential or puts their being at risk. The French call it *esprit* and the Germans call it *Geist* – "spiritedness," it's also been termed, or θυμός in ancient Greek: the ineffable spark of humanity and hard-to-define yet all-important basis of who we are. It's *jouissance* – a particular *je ne sais quoi*, or intangible part of human life and existence in the world.[45] It's, yes, breathing lungs and a heartbeat; it's taking in oxygen and a rote ability to move. It's also the ability to move *somewhere*, however, or maintain a soul, desire, and imagination one would like to achieve. *That's* what genocide is about: that humans might not just seek *life*, but *full, satisfactory* lives. Exterminating people means going after not only existence but *deeper* levels of experience – levels on which humanity becomes *human*, or, using Hegel's vocabulary, we can *in fact* see "man as man." Should we be shocked if human rights violations happen in Europe? Not necessarily. As involved as the

---

43 Ibid., article 27.
44 Ibid., article 25.
45 See Costas Douzinas and Conor Gearty, eds., *The Meanings of Rights: The Philosophy and Social Theory of Human Rights* (Cambridge: Cambridge University Press, 2014).

continent has been with notions of progressive humanity, it's also been involved with a lot of jingoism and abuse. There's been a good deal of xenophobic and imperialistic mentalities as part of the European past. Still, inheriting an intellectual line coming from figures like Montesquieu, Locke, and Hegel, "free development of [the human] personality" is what *human rights* are about.[46] Europe did help to leave behind a legacy of ideas suggesting that, in Paris, in the Balkans, or Rwanda, one should have a chance to lead a *thoughtful* existence and consider one's opinions about the world. One should, yes, have "security," as the French Declaration of the Rights of Man and Citizen (1789) put it. However, one should also have "liberty," "brotherhood," and a shot at "happiness," or self-realization in one's life.[47] Convicting those who have participated in genocidal acts and war crimes is a matter of fighting extinction and basic murder. It is also, however, about realizing that one has trampled on human potential and the ability of people to think and say as they will.[48]

To that extent, how does one make a summary statement about Ratko Mladić standing on the hills overlooking Sarajevo and insisting that his snipers shoot down on the town in ways intended to create maximum terror? How can one consider Slobodan Praljak turning a blind eye to, if not encouraging, camps imprisoning non-Croats in support of "Herceg-Bosna" – the Croat mini-state declared in parts of Bosnian-Herzegovinian territory for the bulk of the '91-'95 war? How do we paint a picture of Milošević strong-arming the Montenegrins such that he could prosecute his war under *Yugoslav* authority – that as opposed to in the name of his ambitions for the Serbian state? What *of* Naser Orić terrorizing Serb populations; a move that played its own role in the events that played out around Srebrenica?[49] How do we react, a quarter of a century on, to Karadžić insisting that no one was involved with war crimes while he knew full well of the mayhem caused as Bosnian Serb forces marauded through Bosniak villages?[50]

---

46 UDHR, article 22.
47 Yale Law School, "Declaration of the Rights of Man" (1789), http://avalon.law.yale.edu/18th_century/rightsof.asp.
48 Of course, Montesquieu, Locke, and Hegel are hardly the only figures to contribute to the history of rights – they're used here as emblematic of a particular commitment to the notion of reason and historical progress in European history. However, there are of course an enormous range of other thinkers which might be brought into that fold. See footnote 21.
49 See footnote 7.
50 As the Srebrenica massacre was in full swing, Karadžić declared on camera, in English, that "our army is very, very responsible; people, civilians, as well as UN personnel, are

How do we react to such *Totentanzen* – "dances of death" we relive as judgments are delivered and codas are put on stories via the opinions of international courts and the judgments of a global community?

One point concerns anger – the sheer aggression, if not rage, involved in, if not putting one's neighbors to death, then at least pushing them out of communities in which they had often lived for hundreds of years. It's the coldness involved in going after another's self-expression – worlds people built – and making policy around discrimination against identities. It is a matter of base ugliness; an unwillingness for compassion and an abrogation of sympathy. It's a continual hollowing out of human emotion and forcing the realization of people's worst fears. It's ironic; given the intractability of some of the claims made around territory and identity over the course of the wars, certain of the peace plans advocated vis-à-vis especially the wars' Bosnian phase amounted to ethnic partition; they essentially reflected what many of the worst actors in the Yugoslav Wars *sought*.[51] Populations *were* moved, and not everyone returned to the towns from which they came. Especially Bosnia was divided into ethnic enclaves with Republika Srpska and the Croat-Bosniak Federation *still* unhappy with each other.[52] Yugoslavia's violence felt raw and confrontational; its prosecution felt related to the id. It felt like – and was – an assertion of one's being at the expense of another's, and involved negation in the most meaningful sense. The anger expressed by figures like Mladić and Praljak in the course of their sentencing concerned the realization that they knew they now had to pay a price. They knew a bill had come, and their freedom was about to be denied. Still, in a *gestalt* sense, their expressions of outrage and acrimony felt not only emblematic of the harshness, coarseness, and jagged nature of the entire Yugoslav affair.

---

completely safe and secure" – a point that was clearly a performance. See Percy, *The Death of Yugoslavia: The Gates of Hell*.

51 Perhaps the most obvious example of this was the Owen-Stoltenberg Plan, proposed in 1993, devolving Bosnia-Herzegovina into three ethnic states. All peace plans proposed in the course of the '91-'95 wars, however, involved some level of ethnic partition or division. See Jutta Paczula, "The Long, Difficult Road to Dayton: Peace Efforts on Bosnia-Herzegovina," *International Journal* 60, no. 1 (2004/5): 255–72. See also, e.g., Maja Zuvela, "Bosnian Serbs Celebrate Divisive National Holiday, Defying Top Court," *Reuters*, January 9, 2017, https://www.reuters.com/article/us-bosnia-serbs-holiday/bosnian-serbs-celebrate-divisive-national-holiday-defying-top-court-idUSKBN14T1T9.

52 See, e.g., Katarina Ristić, *Imaginary Trials: War Crime Trials and Memory in Former Yugoslavia* (Leipzig: Leipzig University Press, 2014); Jo Shaw and Igor Štiks, eds., *Citizenship after Yugoslavia* (London: Routledge, 2013).

They felt like the last course, ugly scream of an era; a mottled *Zeitgeist* shoving its hand through the surface of a grave. It brought back the dissonant tones of tragedy – a dissonance time might have allowed us to forget, yet Mladić's ranting and Praljak's suicide brought screaming back.

    Still, after justice comes silence. In not only the Yugoslav court, but any court, after the sentence is delivered, the convicted need be led from the courtroom and reflection might begin. Whatever ranting and raving will be done will now be done in seclusion; as convicted, one's ability to scream out loud, or at least have one's screaming heard, will be reduced. It's just that international legal systems eschew capital punishment. Yes, death sentences bring silence. They're not needed, though, to stop the music of the band; they're not needed to muffle throes of anger. Silence descended as Mladić was removed from the courtroom and his case was closed; quiet came as lawyers packed away their files, and judges stepped down from the bench. Praljak stilled his own voice, defiantly but completely, in a sentence of his choosing. I don't know about its justice – only that there was stillness after the rage of a war criminal who closed his own affairs. Others will be tried by the Yugoslav court; the docket isn't clear. Still, the outbursts and then silencing of Mladić and Praljak, feel like a particular music's last bars. Codas continue a piece of music, revisiting central themes. They also end works, however, wherein, thankfully, the writing of a new piece can begin.

Art, Being, and Human Rights
A Hamburg Exhibition
(February 2, 2018)

Abstract: *Wolfgang Tillmans held a provocative exhibition in Hamburg come the end of 2017. It evoked thoughts about the dynamics of art history and how publics relate to art of high concept. It also, however, gave way to reflections on human rights – is there a place where human rights and art making the existential statement intersect?*

The Kunstverein in Hamburg held an interesting exhibition a couple of months ago – one I managed to see just before it came to an end. It was work from the photographer Wolfgang Tillmans – though he's more than just a photographer – and what amounted to a room-size installation of work done in multiple media from the 1980s up to the present (in the exhibition material, the earliest work is noted as from '84 [or '87; it's a framed laser copy of a photograph taken in '84], and the latest pieces date from last year [2017]). The Kunstverein, one of Germany's, if not Europe's, oldest art associations, sits in a building towards Hamburg's city center, not far from the train station, and a brisk-but-not-challenging walk from Hamburg's Alster, standing as part of an "art mile" that includes a number of top-class institutions: the Bucerius Kunst Forum, the Deichtorhallen (sitting opposite the Kunstverein), the Museum für Kunst und Gewerbe (Museum for Art and Industry), and the Hamburger Kunsthalle, or the main art museum for Hamburg city – the one most culture mavens and visitors to the city would go to first. The Kunstverein, or "Art Association," is the bohemian among these. It includes space for working artists, has a no-bones-about-it entryway, and makes the least effort to pretty itself up (indeed, it often features that smell working art studios can have of fresh paint; something I enjoy). The main gallery is but an open space loft-style, or perhaps in the style of a transformed warehouse. I haven't visited the Kunstverein often enough to know if they change the space

Photo of exhibition by author.

for each exhibition. The walls and pillars nonetheless look solidly grounded, wherein my feeling is that, in the Kunstverein, the space is largely the way it is. If you've met working artists, the whole thing feels as though it has something to do with that.

The exhibition had the fabulous title "There Were 30 Years between 1943 and 1973. 30 Years from 1973 Was the Year 2003," and it constituted a modern extravaganza featuring the high concept which has perhaps been art's calling card since the start of the twentieth century. It's hard to say; straight lines may have been falling apart by the time Van Gogh jacked up the psychedelics in the 1880s, and it appears that before what most historians see as the *real* start of the twentieth century (the years around the First World War), Marcel Duchamp had already nailed an upside-down bicycle wheel to a stool and started toying with the idea that one might put such a thing somewhere on display.[1] Regardless of when they started, however, art's last hundred years have involved a *lot* of moves towards what writer Tom Wolfe has called the "painted word" – art *in fact* based on concept as well as the idea that, even when one engages in realism (take someone like Duane Hansen), that realism need be "hyper," or turbo-charged, somehow (one might also look at a figure like Ron Mueck).[2] Such moves have created disorientation. Art historian David Carrier has used the concept "museum skepticism," and it's an interesting idea. While it's not precisely the way in which he meant the term, vastly greater publics have had access to art over the last one hundred years, including "fine" versions of it. That's at the same time that many of us are unsure of what to do with today's and recent yesterday's art – in part because it's not always easy to tell what it is.[3]

Now, what's disorienting, or perhaps a bit "confusing," about Tillmans' "There Were 30 Years" is precisely that: figuring out what one is looking at. Certainly,

---

1 On historical time-framing, see Eric Hobsbawm, *The Age of Extreme: The Short Twentieth Century 1914-1991* (London: Abacus, 1995). Reportedly, the first iteration of Duchamp's famous Dadaist bicycle wheel came in 1913. See also Caroline Cros, *Marcel Duchamp*, trans. Vivian Rehberg (London: Reaktion, 2006).
2 See Tom Wolfe, *The Painted Word* (New York: Bantam, 1976).
3 See David Carrier, *Museum Skepticism: A History of the Display of Art in Public Galleries* (Durham, NC: Duke University Press, 2006); Jeffrey Wilson, review of *Museum Skepticism: A History of the Display of Art in Public Galleries* by David Carrier, *The Journal of Aesthetics and Art Criticism*, 65, no. 3 (2007): 338–9. Carrier's actual point is a conceptual one: do museums contain "art," or but physical artifacts whose "art" only exists in historical context? Carrier is nonetheless concerned with public relations with artistic artifacts – my jumping-off point for the appropriation of his term.

one doesn't (or didn't [the exhibition is finished now]) look at a *single* thing. Most of Tillmans' work has a hybrid character – either a combination of unexpected visual cues or an eclectic blend of materials – and, taken together, it can be difficult to know precisely where to focus. Still, a ring of photos formed the basis of the exhibition – a range of subjects shot in provocative technique and involving everything from figures in portraiture to geometric configurations to works with a faded-away newspaper feel – and there were works of social commentary, such as the piece providing the title for the show ("There Were 30 Years between 1943 and 1973. 30 Years from 1973 Was the Year 2003"), as well as works which reflected on both German and global history via realistic but fictional images of postal stamps, oft-referring to international organizations or moments in the post-Second World War past. There were video projections with distinctly photo-like qualities cast into corners with color-enhanced, topographical themes, and there were nature scenes depicting canopies of trees as well as scenes where it was hard to tell if one was looking at the forest or inside someone's house. At the center of it all was an array of display tables of the kind that one might use to display insects or rare books (tables with aluminum legs holding clear, glass cases). Those were filled with arrangements of stones, shells, and other objects usually accompanied by pieces of paper explaining the distances between historical events (always symmetrically; "x amount of time stands between these events; however, x amount of time also stands between the last of those events and something more contemporary"). This gave jarring results as the dates created lines of association one might not expect (e.g., 1969 was twenty-four years from 1945, and twenty-four years back from now is 1993 [wherein one is asked to think if the Second World War and the world of the First Iraq War are somehow connected, with the Vietnam War as the bridge]). Four points bookended the exhibition. Two pointed to the outside world. On either side of the room, one ascended a short set of stairs to look out picture windows at passing traffic (on the west side) or at the train tracks and the delivery alley to the museum (on the east). On the two other sides (north and south) were images of the ocean: one right-side-up, the other upside-down, both noticeably large. One image was photographed (the right-side-up one), with the other consisting of a looped video of waves cresting in and out from the shore (the upside-down one – with its "upside-downness" helping to mark its presence). The whole thing was accompanied by a repeating audio track piped through speakers peppered throughout the exhibition. The music was a kind of atonal chanting. It might have been Gregorian modal singing, only it sounded like the Gregorians had visited the Trappists and the Trappists had put out a few too many beers.

Now, in all fairness, the whole thing was only characterizable as "disorienting" to a certain extent. Yes, Tillmans gives his viewer a lot to take in. The man is clearly not afraid of pastiche as he weaves a fine tapestry and there are a lot of individual threads. All of it *was* supremely executed, however, and it's possible to see forms in many of his photographs. It's also not as though the more abstract shapes weren't discernable, and the connection of the time spans Tillmans noted with the arrangement of the stones and other objects in the display cases was hardly impossible to figure out. If I had to make an appraisal, I'd say it was like listening to Wagner, or the rock band Yes. One might not like it. However, if one had the eye or the ear for it, a wider symphony emerged constructed of some quite compelling parts. The Kunstverein referred to "There Were 30 Years" as a "cineastic whole." Looking into the matter, "cineastic" appears to be a word in German, but not English. The idea is nonetheless a vast visual and aural panorama creating a deep, holistic experience – like watching Stanley Kubrick's *2001* in the theater, or Wagner's Ring Cycle at Bayreuth.

Now, of course, there *is* always the question of what to do with the idea of art that demands a particular "eye or ear." Are we involved in a kind of elitism when we talk about such things (one must have the "eye or the ear for it!") and what *do* we do if art *isn't* comprehensible to the average Joe or Jill? Again, more than a few art historians have noted that, as with many things, art has moved out of the domain of the exclusive as the world has democratized. "The birth of the museum is a significant symbol of the French Revolution," art historian Jennifer Barrett has noted, as, what one gets with the emergence of the "Atlantic Revolutions" and then again the nationalist revolutions of the nineteenth century is a trend towards more public access to *all* of society's institutions, including those concerned with education, representation, modes of aesthetic reflection, and the contemplative powers involved therein.[4] The mindsets of modernity can be criticized for many things: overweening imperialism, running over people in a demand for progress, industrial-driven conformity, and joining us to the hip with technologies that may have harmed as much as helped (it's great to drive, but all that CO_2 *has* caused some problems).[5] Still, people's involvement in cultural

---

4   Jennifer Barrett, *Museums and the Public Sphere* (Malden: Wiley Blackwell, 2011), 57. On the vocabulary of "Atlantic Revolutions" – the democratic revolts of the late eighteenth century (France and America are the leading examples) – see R.R. Palmer, *The Age of Democratic Revolution: A Political History of Europe and America 1760-1800* (Princeton: Princeton University Press, 2014).

5   See Andrew Feenberg, *Heidegger and Marcuse: The Catastrophe and Redemption of History* (London: Routledge, 2005).

institutions *has* increased, and in our times (say, the second half of the twentieth century up to now), such things have *really* taken off.⁶ That's not only as a matter of public funding or the arts as part of educational systems, but thinking the arts as a matter of *right* and a particular social mentality involved therein. It's not the most-recognized set of concepts from the world of human rights. It doesn't get talked about in the same way as, say, the right to life or the right to legal equality. The theoretically preeminent statement on what our rights are supposed to *be*, however – the Universal Declaration of Human Rights of the UN from 1948 – notes that "everyone has the right [to] freely…participate in the cultural life of the community, to enjoy the arts and to share in scientific advancement and its benefits."⁷ Nothing should keep one away from one's society's intellectual production, painting, sculpture, music, and theater included. From a minority group? You should have access to the arts. From a historically oppressed gender? You should be able to see something at the theater. Hold a particular political persuasion? You should be able to go to a museum. And, perhaps most convincingly, if your family can't afford to put art on its walls, cities, municipalities, states, and nations should give you access to the art that's nailed to *their* walls and not charge you too much to see it. Of course, just because the UN (or even a national law) says you should have access to the arts and scientific production doesn't mean that every town or county is investing millions in museums; public funding for the arts remains a debate for good reason. Still, around the world, the attitudes represented in the Universal Declaration mean that *many* more people might choose to go to a museum or exhibition on the weekend than was the case, say, *before* World War II. That's while the notion of access raises the question of how access might *happen*, or precisely what the ability to "get in touch with art" *means*. In other words, we can talk about education, public funding, or uses of public space. We can put paintbrushes in kids' hands and fund national and community theater. Still, there might also be a question as to whether those who *create* art have a duty to speak in ways that *allow* people contact with it, or provide an intellectual way *in*. As part of the access issue, is there an obligation on the part of those who create art to speak in accessible vocabularies and to at least

---

6 A nice sense of this, including specific discussions of democracy, culture, and the arts, may be found in Hobsbawm's four-volume appraisal of modern history: Hobsbawm, *The Age of Extremes*; Hobsbawm, *The Age of Revolution 1789-1848* (New York: Mentor, 1962); Hobsbawm, *The Age of Capital 1848-1875* (New York: Meridian, 1979); Hobsbawm, *The Age of Empire 1874-1914* (New York: Vintage, 1989); Hobsbawm, *The Age of Exremes*.
7 United Nations, "The Universal Declaration of Human Rights," (1948, article 27), http://www.un.org/en/universal-declaration-human-rights/index.html. Hereafter UDHR.

sometimes descend from the mountain of high concept into hills we imagine *many* might climb? Are fathomable modes of speech part of the idea that "art should be for all," and is the idea that one should at least *sometimes* make something people can understand part of the duty of the artistic thinker?[8]

For the vague criticism I'm levying at art for sometimes being overly academic, I'm about to offer a bit of an academic answer myself. I.e., as many concerns as I have about art as "the painted word," I'm on my way to offering a "painted word" answer of my own. However, I'd like to turn to the work of phenomenologists and hermeneuticists for a response – phenomenology and hermeneutics being philosophical movements that triangulated issues of perception, knowledge, and senses of existence, or what one might think of as the bread and butter, or "ground floor," of human being (the ways in which we are and know). Now, firstly, key figures from the philosophical movements I'm pointing to argued that we're not going to enter knowledge situations the same way. They argue that we approach the "knowing" of something the way we do, nothing more, nothing less. Put yet another way, one always knows *what* one knows, and that is always relative to *you*; you never know what you don't. Things – both concepts and hard "stuff" – are always "there" for me, wrote Edmund Husserl, father of this kind of thinking; that because what I see and know is always exactly that (what I see and know [what's there, of any kind, is simply what it is]).[9] I'll rephrase: we always find ourselves where we are, and, given that there's a lot of us in many places, the diversity of human relations with the world means a low likelihood of approaching things in the same way.

This means a few things. Firstly, perspective is inevitable. Because you stand in a place and see things as you do, you have one (a perspective), and it defines you. It's your cognitive space that you're bound in; it's just tough to be somewhere else. Secondly, though, because we exist through time and in the presence of *other* subjectivities, what we see or hear isn't always a matter of *choice*. If you're a basketball player, someone can pass you the ball whether you want it or not. If the basketball is part of your field of vision, that's how it is (and if your neighbor *is* blasting Wagner or Yes, you'll have to deal with that). However, we *reflect* on what we see or hear – we *process* what enters our field of vision – and we may want to move in relation to *that*. We may *investigate* something we see

---

8   In addition to Barrett, see Lambert Zuidervaart, *Art in Public: Politics, Economics, and a Democratic Culture* (Cambridge: Cambridge University Press, 2011).

9   Edmund Husserl, *Ideas Pertaining to a Pure Phenomenology and to a Phenomenological Philosophy*, trans. F. Kersten (Dordrecht: Kluwer, 1983), 51.

or know, or establish *new* knowledge relationships with it. We may want to walk *towards* something that one puts in front of us, or inquire into the meaning of their statement. Indeed, it may be difficult to *not* do such a thing as knowledge, even a simple sense of the presence of something, may be impossible absent reflection. Put another way, as we *don't* approach things the same way, what one person says or communicates to another may well come off quite differently for the person to whom it's said than to the person who does the saying. Getting to know something involves traveling the distance between where one is conceptually and *another* conceptual place, or a place where one will look at something from a different angle. And, as anyone knows who has ever traveled somewhere, getting somewhere takes work. It takes elbow grease – it demands *some* kind of effort. Indeed, all of us feel this when we read something, or enter into conversation – that the motor has to go on, and the labor of reflection has to begin. Now, some things might feel difficult to read and other things simpler. We might feel we more readily understand a friend's discourse as opposed to someone new's or a stranger's. One is nonetheless always involved in overcoming the distance between the thing one is looking at or trying to understand and where one stands oneself. Interpretation (another word for this) is just something we do; it's always present for us, it always takes time, and it's never labor-free.[10]

In this context, "simplification" is tricky business. At the very least, it's a move whose results are hard to calculate. It's hard to say how one will react to a "paring down" of something, or even if "paring down" is how "paring down" will be received. Art history bears this out. Sometimes, simplicity has brought near-virulent reaction. Artists like Cy Twombly or Franz Kline, who have at least sometimes gone explicitly for senses of not doing anything complicated at *all* – but squiggles on a page or relatively simple brushed lines – have had to suffer from *massive* outcries of "what's that about?"; "Why are you wasting my time?" People have had something not complicated at all thrown at them and they've thought, "what the heck is that?" One of music's most controversial pieces, John Cage's 4'33", is perhaps the music world's easiest to understand. The thing is four and a half minutes of silence played on any instrument with sheet music that's essentially empty. We love Andy Warhol today; no museum showing

---

10 This is a highly classical view of perception and development, related much to German concept of *Bildung*, or a kind of transformation of understanding via intellectual labor. See W.H. Bruford, *The German Tradition of Self-Cultivation: 'Bildung' from Humboldt to Thomas Mann* (Cambridge: Cambridge University Press, 1995). See also Joseph D. Parry, ed., *Art and Phenomenology* (London: Routledge, 2011).

his stuff won't be packed. Initially, though, many weren't sure what to do with his Campbell's Soup cans or his stacks of reproduced Brillo boxes – things you can buy in the grocery store around the corner.[11] Not a small number of artists use found objects – elements surrounding us every day, be they bits of metal, scraps of wood, bubble gum wrappers, or what have you. However, man, the number of times you can go to a museum and hear, "hey, I can find stuff too!" is astounding, or at least extensive. Does that mean that Yo-Yo Ma shouldn't show up on Sesame Street or Leonard Bernstein shouldn't have conducted his Young People's concerts? No. It's nice when an artist provides stripped-down examples of their work and puts their *own* words on their creations, slowing the tempo down. Still, if reproductions of objects we see in everyday life or but lines on a page are "hard" to comprehend, we might be careful in dictating what's "accessible" and what's "not" because, *really*, we might be discussing what we *like*, or what catches our fancy. We might be discussing what makes us feel good or what we *feel* makes sense. And, in *that* context, we might also be discussing notions of "acceptability," or ideas having to do with a great many things other than the work itself. We may be on the terrain of taste and the ways that gets produced.[12]

Here, art becomes a free speech issue. I.e., it involves not only the right to speak complexly, but also to speak *diversely*, or in multiplicious ways. We might not only be involved with the ability of someone to say what they *want* – that a sovereign being might choose for him- or herself – but with the idea that what some have termed the "culture industry," or the *selling* of things as artistic expression, can be so broad and hard to see beyond that, lest societies make it policy to hold up *alternatives*, everything can get pulled into the pool of sanctioned taste. This cuts two ways. Firstly, there is a question of allowing pop art (or perhaps popular "culture") to become art "itself." Without *some* challenging of the standards of "high" culture, not only might the Beatles be just a minor sensation from some English town, but John Coltrane's *Giant Steps* or Miles Davis' *In a Silent Way* might be missed as masterpieces too. Taste dictated "from above" can restrict, and supposed purveyors of aesthetic truth might not always be correct.

---

11 Robert Hughes, "The Rise of Andy Warhol," *The New York Review of Books*, February 18, 1982, https://www.nybooks.com/articles/1982/02/18/the-rise-of-andy-warhol/.

12 I'd just indicate that the seminal critic Clement Greenberg made this point in his essay "Can Taste Be Objective?" "There the masters are, and they are there by virtue of what has to be a consensus of taste." Indeed, Greenberg took things a step further, indicating that "nothing" but taste makes the greats great. See Greenberg, "Can Taste Be Objective?" in *Homemade Esthetics: Observations on Art and Taste* (Oxford: Oxford University Press, 1991), 31–9.

On the other hand, was Bruno Mars' *24K Magic* really the "album of the year" in 2017? Among *all* the music produced that year, was it "the best," or just the most *popular*, somehow? A healthy society will allow you to say what you want; you should be able to play Beethoven or Run DMC.[13] The *healthiest* society, however, might not only *allow* for different kinds of expression, but *support* them and put them into public view. It might not only say "yes, we have to *deal* with that," but "let's let that thing *breathe* a bit such that we might find out if there's *value* in it." *Reader's Digest* and *Spark Notes* should very much be available. They're useful and help people out. If you have access to *Reader's Digest*, however, you should also be able to get the book. That's what the Kunstverein tries to do. It looks for experimentation. It's interested to provoke. The museum has a public function; it's concerned to let everyone in. In providing access, however, it doesn't guarantee that you needn't bring your thinking cap. The Kunstverein makes the choice to provide experiences with the potential to challenge the norm at the same time as democratically saying, "welcome; this is yours too."[14]

Still, over and above meditations on speech and access, and over and above considerations of complexity and interpretation, "There Were 30 Years" set off another train of thoughts concerning human rights. It provoked *another* set of meditations on freedom, privilege, sovereignty, and our relations with the social body. It instigated another set of reflections concerning human possibility and our essential social relations. For this observer, anyway, the Tillmans exhibition also addressed the *nature* of the being who has rights – the *nature* of the creature who is the *subject* of social communication, law, politics, and cultural life. "There Were 30 Years" discussed that to which the concept of rights *speaks*, and how we might relate to the multiple experiences that thing involves. Tillmans' installation was evocative of concepts concerning that "member of the human family," as the Universal Declaration puts it, who *involves* themselves in social experience,

---

13 See Cass R. Sunstein, *Democracy and the Problem of Free Speech* (New York: Free Press, 1995); Paul Kearns, *Freedom of Artistic Expression: Essays on Culture and Legal Censure* (Portland: Hart, 2013).

14 The Kunstverein doesn't publish a mission statement. A look at the museum's exhibition history, however, reveals a history of engaging noted, paradigm-challenging artists, as well as takes note of the institution's public function; that, *qua*, association, it's there for Hamburg and, as located in a major metropolitan center, for Europe and the world as well. See Kunstverein in Hamburg, "Geschichte" (2017), http://kunstverein.de/kunstverein/geschichte/index.php. On the "culture industry" concept, see Theodor Adorno and Max Horkheimer, "The Culture Industry: Enlightenment as Mass Deception" in *Dialectic of Enlightenment: Philosophical Fragments*, ed., Gunzelin Schmid Noerr (Stanford: Stanford University Press, 2002), 94–136.

and who may – née, *does* – deserve access to institutions and the ideas involved therein.

I'd put it this way. Firstly, human experience is holistic. I again turn to the phenomenologists and hermeneuticists. One finds oneself in a "world," Husserl notes – a world that's there in a "literal" and "figurative" sense.[15] We have a space around us that relates to the *fullness* of our being – what we can see and what we but "sense," what's factual and what's impression, what's historical and what is "now." We have intuitive ideas and concrete perceptions and we have senses of things both distinct and not. We imagine things as possible, yet have a sense of limitations as well. We live in zones of black and white – yet with no small amount of grey. We have every manner of experience moving around us and filling large swatches of our day. Tillmans captures this in the range of his work. In "There Were 30 Years," we got images of the human being that were both clear and indistinct, crystalline and cloudy. We gained surreal images of our lifeworld as well as images with photographic literality. We had references to historical time, yet the idea that history concerns today. We got the sense that humanity relates not only to concepts, but to sounds, pictures, things in motion yet also things standing still. An aesthetician named Mikel Dufrenne once wrote that "expression establishes a singular world…[expression] proceeds from an internal cohesion which is only amenable to the logic of feeling."[16] Yes, we see certain things at certain moments with our attention going here and there. However, we move in a full experiential space at all times, bearing with us the complete range of our being at any point. We take the full range of our existence with us like a halo, or an orange sun behind the clouds. It's a full experiential world we have: sticky and dry, sweet and sour, and arid as well as moist.[17]

---

15 Husserl, *Ideas*, 51.
16 Mikel Dufrenne, *The Phenomenology of Aesthetic Experience*, trans. Edward S. Casey (Evanston: Northwestern University Press, 1973), 180.
17 This is a touch complex in as, technically, phenomenology emphasizes the "directedness" or "intentionality" of consciousness – that one provides certain things with a particular concentration, wherein, in fact there's a certain way in which one *isn't* dealing with everything all at once. However, the trick with this – and phenomenology tends to occupy this simultaneously common-sense-yet-also-not-easy-to-understand territory – is that one looks at what one looks at. I.e., those things one has in consciousness, no matter how vague that consciousness might be or its particular character, are conscious and present to one. Sure, one might look at a coffee cup and see *nothing* else. How often does one do that though? Is one not seeing many things at one time? And even though one's consciousness might be so directed, might one not also be seeing one's coffee cup, its surroundings, and that evening's grocery list (i.e., be of several minds

That's at the same time that Tillman's exhibition reminds us that that being is grounded *somewhere*. The perceiving human sees the earth from the earth, and the world is seen from within itself. Though our experience is full – it's always the totality of what it is – it is nonetheless bound. Experience plays out within limits and is had within spaces where human beings *are*. Experience is had on *terra firma*; not in abstracted ether or the mist of ideas. As I see it, Tillmans represented this with the oceans and the windows pointing to the train tracks and the streets. He represented this via the bookends he placed around the installation and through placing *its* variety of expression (and our experiences) within limits. A world is akin to a continent with shores. One always has a horizon – a space in which vision and sensibilities unfold. Visions and sensibilities *will* be multiple – blurry, yet distinct, a world of reason yet also gut feeling. Still, our visions and sensibilities will always be located *in* this world – the place we inevitably are. They will be where human beings are *bound*, and to which everything we do pertains. Our world can have moments of quiet contemplation in the manner of the space *inside* the exhibition hall; we can have controlled territory for discreet thought and places filled with stillness. We can also have moments of movement and bustle, like the traffic in the street; there are moments where we simply can't escape the noise. Still, such possibilities play-out within the boundaries of the world *itself*. They happen in a space that is concrete, and not to be surpassed. One can run from one shore to the other. However, one will always *hit* a shore. Being is broad but finite; large yet limited. It's had on a continent – a reality that "There Were 30 Years" captures well.

Now, what interests me about this is that it's here we find the subject of rights. In some ways, this *is* the subject of rights. This is who should *have* rights – and, indeed, rights in any way; not just to education or intellectual production, but to legal representation, participation in government and access to food, clothing, housing, and medical care. It's he or she who has the right to privacy, yet also the right to speak out. It's who should be addressed by national constitutions but, I submit, also the declarations addressing *everyone's* existences and the freedoms and privileges we *all* should share. Rights concern flesh and blood

---

at once)? And might not the politics of the day, or one's relations with one's friends, also be playing in the background? *That* demands an entire setting to which we relate; a universe in which we find ourselves, however vague certain senses of it may be. I.e., as phenomenology also puts it, we drag a "lifeworld" around with us everywhere we go – the totality of that world which surrounds one. Good introductions to these points may be found in Dermot Moran, "Editor's Introduction" in *The Phenomenology Reader*, ed. Dermot Moran (London: Routledge, 2002), 1–26.

individuals, here, on this earth. Rights concern people who are "born" among us, with the same limitations as everyone else.[18] People have rights by virtue of their humanity; because they're part of the human species – the creatures we are in space and time.[19] We are caught in worlds where movement and stillness play out; where experience is both loud and quiet. We live in spaces indoors and outdoors, both facile to read and hard. *That goes for all of us*, however, because we can be but nowhere else. The earth exposes us to limits; we can't but orient ourselves towards it. It also, however, *provides* everything for us as it's the shelter of humankind. Whether by accident or intention, Tillmans somehow captured that.

Now, do such things have to be phrased in terms of "human rights?" Is a *political* vision of the individual either the best or a necessary way to discuss an *artistic* installation? Is a theory of political society a relevant mode of analysis when talking aesthetics or histories of art? In looking at something like "There Were 30 Years," are we discussing the policies of nations, social justice, or the "aspirations" of a "common people," as human rights are wont to address? Are we discussing a social or juridical theory in any determined sense?

It depends on what one takes law and politics to concern; what one takes freedom, privileges, and the considerations of our relations with each other to be about. It depends on how one delineates the object of social theory, and what one thinks juridical discussion entails. Rights are a way of discussing politics, yes. They are a way of discussing ethics and law. Rights concern visions of world order, modes of conflict resolution, as well as problems of sovereignty and force. Rights are about behavior, social contracts, and theories of what the human being deserves. Such things, however, concern *experience*. Such things are based on the idea that one has "reason and conscience," and a place where those play out.[20] Such things concern the idea that we're an issue because we indubitably *are* – otherwise, there's no discussion to have. Rights are "political," yes. However, rights are also *human* rights in that they concern *life*; they concern *us*, the fact of our being, and that we will need to legislate that. We can have different outlines of the rights we *want* – one might be a liberal, authoritarian, a free thinker, or

---

18 UDHR, article 1.
19 See, e.g., Micheline R. Ishay, *The History of Human Rights: From Ancient Times to the Globalization Era* (Berkeley: University of California Press, 2004), 3.
20 UDHR, article 1. Some relevant points on these issues as they relate to philosophy and human rights is available in Johannes Morsink, *Inherent Human Rights: Philosophical Roots of the Universal Declaration* (Philadelphia: University of Pennsylvania Press, 2009).

conformist. One might have an open sense of self-expression, or think it should play out in certain boundaries. Our existence will have to be *dealt with*, however, and that in relation to individuals whom we *also* might realize as concrete. Those are individuals that *are* there, also having experiences of definitude and uniqueness that we may need bear with us, like everything else.

It's hard to know where to leave off. Regarding art, philosopher Martin Heidegger once said that "world withdrawal and world-decay can never be undone."[21] The context for a work of art will never be recovered as time dislodges works from their original setting. However, *the work had a setting. The entirety of the work depends on what that setting was.* Art is related to a totality of historical affairs and is fully related to the historical situation it finds itself in. Regarding rights, we might turn to the vocabulary of John Humphrey, one of the lawyers central to setting words on modern rights and institutionalizing them among us. Composing rights, Humphrey posited, concerns thinking the relation between the "individual and society." It has to do with tackling the *gestalt* range of problems that have "puzzled mankind since Old Testament times and before."[22] It concerns an *in toto* assessment of humanity, and a survey of our atmosphere. Had they met, Heidegger and Humphrey wouldn't likely have gotten along. Heidegger was an arch-conservative, skeptical of liberal individualism and the trappings of the modern world. Humphrey was the *arch*-liberal, politically progressive and with forward-looking social goals. In discussing issues like art, however, Humphrey might have found Heidegger spot-on. Art comes at us holistically because it speaks to from where humanity comes; it emerges from our "realm," or where we must be and *are*. Yet Heidegger might have seen Humphrey as also correct. Approaching rights the right way – completely – is a broad endeavor. It takes on the range of experiences that, somehow, we ask the *artist* to elucidate. It takes on the canvas between sun and moon – or between the seas, and in the spectrum between activity and silence.

For me, that means this: in our day and age, we can be thankful that notions like human rights survive – that we have an "ideology after 'the end of ideologies,'" as it's been put, or that, that in an age of ironies and an era in which lines rarely seem straight, we have a modicum of ideals and enough naiveté for optimistic beliefs.[23]

---

21 Martin Heidegger, "The Origin of the Work of Art" in *Poetry, Language, Though*, trans. Albert Hofstadter (New York: Harper and Row, 1971), 40.
22 In Roger Normand and Sarah Zaidi, *Human Rights at the UN: The Politics of Universal Justice* (Bloomington: Indiana University Press, 2008), 147.
23 Conor Gearty and Costas Douzinas, "Introduction" in *The Meaning of Rights: The Philosophy and Social Theory of Human Rights*, ed. Costas Douzinas and Conor Gearty (Cambridge: Cambridge University Press, 2014), 1.

That's while we can also be glad that art – some art – pursues the comprehensive statement; that grandiose and perhaps a bit disorienting though it may be, some are willing to point out our existential bounds and indicate the geographical-yet-ontological space that maps out where we be. There's no demand that art do that. Heidegger might be right – it might be a totality to which art responds; it might be that art is always a product of its world – and all of it, all the time. That doesn't mean that's what everyone will want to *discuss*, however, or that if an artist *doesn't* want to discuss such things, that they necessarily should. Being should be addressed in many ways, through a variety of media, on many scales, and in ranges of modalities. Books, music, science, simple talk about a million things – we need it all. We need multiple modes of insight into our surroundings, and music played with a thousand notes. Still, for those of us looking for a cartography of human existence – a map of our playing field – it's nice that someone tries; it's nice that *some* art traverses the floor of our world, and puts up markers at its bounds. And for those *not* looking for such cartographies, it's nice that they've been made anyway. That's for the moment that, for whatever reason, one becomes interested to seek them out – that one might *look* for a roadmap of our limitations and possibilities, and might reflect on what our rights and privileges concern: the flat-out reality of being, and our confrontation with a here and now. Of course, that's a here and now that outlines all we both do and have: life, death, struggle, emancipation, victory, bondage, and freedom – as well as any other experience a rights, nay human, subject in fact might have.

Justice and the Confrontation
Human Rights and Social Politics
(February 12, 2018)

Abstract: *The Larry Nasser case has been made headlines in the U.S. as well as throughout the world. It concerns issues of gender, social power, and reactions to abuse. It also involves manners of the prosecution of justice, however, and the meaning of practices like victim impact statements. I am clearly for the empowerment of victims – especially vis-à-vis decisive issues such as gender equality. Can there be something dangerous about the manner in which Nasser was confronted at his trial, though? Yes. While also attempting to make clear why actions like Nasser's represent the deepest of rights violations, I try to show that we have something to think about in terms of confrontations with the convicted in terms of the potential spectaclization of such moments.*

It's been an intense year around gender and social politics in the United States. As with so many things, the Trump phenomenon has provided a special backdrop to the whole thing. Firstly, there were the weird stances that Trump, historically supportive of abortion rights, suddenly took under his campaign in an attempt to appeal to arch-conservatives: that, as he put it, there should be some sort of "punishment" for women deciding to terminate a pregnancy. Now, opposing a practice because of a cultural conviction I can buy. Instituting *punishment* for what, even if you support it, is generally recognized as a gut-wrenching choice? We're on *Handmaid's Tale* territory there, and no one will convince me otherwise.[1] Of course, then there was the infamous "grab 'em by the pussy" *Access Hollywood* tape that emerged a few weeks before the election. Such a thing would have torpedoed the candidacy of almost any other public

"Statue of justice" @sebra/ shutterstock.com 283151966

---

1 Obviously, this is opinionating. Punishment for abortion in the twenty-first century – in a liberal state – is nonetheless a massively heavy-handed move. For a

figure. For Trump, however, it was taken as but "locker room talk;" "boys being boys." Of course, such lowbrow sexism led directly to the main post-election protest march – the January 2017 "Women's March" that played out not only in Washington D.C., but in cities around the world. The march didn't focus exclusively on women's issues. Seen from my eyes, though, the point was that the dismissive attitude Trump often displays towards women's issues might be emblematic of a larger, unthinking attitude that he and some of his supporters sometimes take towards the disempowered and historically disenfranchised generally. I.e., the attempt wasn't only to fight misogyny specifically. It was to fight misogyny as representative of a level of dismissiveness towards social difference at-large.

In any case, the question of women in American and, to some extent, global, social life became amped-up come the Weinstein affair. In October 2017, well-known Hollywood mogul Harvey Weinstein was identified as having had behaved like a letch while wielding his star-making power – sexually harassing models and actresses in casting couch-like scenarios, and engaging in behaviors characterizable as simultaneously tragic and cliché. Of course, this launched #MeToo, via which not only ranges of Hollywood personalities, but tens of thousands of women from across American life (and, indeed, other parts of the world), revealed stories of moments from when they had been pushed around, abused, harassed, or otherwise treated in ways they shouldn't. It led women to try to underline how diverse yet similar some of their experiences with gender mistreatment could be.[2] Results were dramatic. Actors were fired from TV shows. Talk show hosts left their desks. Senators lost their seats, and women's issues dominated headlines in ways they hadn't in many years.[3] Then came the Nassar affair. It had been building for a while. However, it burst into public view at the end of 2017 when it became clear that Larry Nassar, a former U.S. gymnastics team physician, had sexually abused athletes in the course of treating

---

recent, since-the-election commentary on this issue, see Richard Wolffe, "Donald Trump's Only Fixed Position on Abortion is His Disdain for Women," *The Guardian*, July 1, 2018, https://www.theguardian.com/commentisfree/2018/jul/01/donald-trump-abortion-supreme-court.

2   For a good overview of #MeToo, see Sophie Gilbert, "The Movement of #MeToo," *The Atlantic*, October 16, 2017, https://www.theatlantic.com/entertainment/archive/2017/10/the-movement-of-metoo/542979/.

3   See The New York Times Editorial Staff, *#MeToo: Women Speak Out Against Sexual Assault* (New York: New York Times Educational Publishing, 2019)

them – athletes often quite young. The abuse had sometimes taken place in his doctor's office, even with the parents nearby (revolting), and the whole thing involved combinations of trust-building and gaslighting that make one's stomach churn.[4] The issue became a media sensation as some the victims were high-profile – some of America's best-known gymnasts – and Nassar was convicted to a set of prison terms adding up to well over a hundred years. The affair again underlined that, whether a matter of public discourse, private behavior, or on-the-job conduct, America and the world had much to think about in terms of gender, power, and social capital. To be sure: "power and social capital" seem like vague, academic terms. Nassar nonetheless took advantage of such things and hurt a lot of people in the process.

Now, a feature of the Nassar trial was a phenomenon that has become increasingly common in American justice – affording victims the opportunity to make direct statements to those who perpetrated crimes against them. "Victim's impact statements," they're commonly called, and they're extensions of a victims' rights movement that's picked up steam since the '70s. The movement comes from a couple of different sources. One is a conservative, law-and-order ideology where the philosophy is that citizens who have their heads screwed on straight don't commit crimes and people are responsible for their behavior, full stop. I.e., if people do things they shouldn't, it's with the perpetrator, not the society, that fault lies. Victims should be understood *as* victims, and there should be liberal limits as to how restitution is thought.[5] That doesn't always mean fire-and-brimstone expressions of revenge. Survivors of the 2015 Dylan Roof Charleston shootings, e.g., forgave Roof before he was sentenced to death.[6] No one *need* have forgiven anyone, though, wherein the point becomes emotional catharsis as much as any

---

4 A good commentary on this can be found in Caroline Kitchener, "Larry Nassar and the Impulse to Doubt Female Pain", The Atlantic, January 23, 2018, https://www.theatlantic.com/health/archive/2018/01/larry-nassar-and-the-impulse-to-doubt-female-pain/551198/.
5 My phrasing here might be a bit pejorative. There is a particular harshness in culturally conservative positions on justice (indeed, particularly *American* culturally conservative approaches to justice). Nonetheless, they exist within the spectrum of ideas on justice, particularly within a criminal context. The range of ongoing discussion of that issue is well-captured in Jonathan Jacobs and Jonathan Jackson, eds., *The Routledge Handbook of Criminal Justice Ethics* (London: Routledge, 2017).
6 See Mark Berman, "'I Forgive You.' Relatives of Charleston Church Shooting Victims Address Dylan Roof," *The Washington Post*, June 19, 2015, https://www.washingtonpost.com/news/post-nation/wp/2015/06/19/i-forgive-you-relatives-of-charleston-church-victims-address-dylann-roof/?utm_term=.268fda18061d.

attempt to realize anything specifically legal or concerned with examining social causations for the act.

Other streams behind victims' rights, however, come from decidedly different sources. The women's rights and civil rights movements have *also* advocated for broadened notions of victims' privileges based on ideas that (*a*) certain kinds of crime involve a certain kind of oppression in which simple sentencing isn't enough, and (*b*) articulatory space, or the space to fully say one's piece, is important for the individual to recover their wholeness *qua* person. In other words, but handing down sentences for misogynistic or racist behavior doesn't do enough to raise awareness of the issues a crime might involve. It also doesn't it provide the restoration of voice necessary for either the victim or their social group to *overcome* the experiences of having been abused or otherwise putdown. "Depending on their social location, people see different forms of abuse," cultural studies scholar Joshua Price has written.[7] One person's misogyny might be someone else's locker room talk. Perhaps, though, when it's been determined that it *wasn't* just locker room talk that took place, the person who was the victim of abuse deserves the chance to say how *they* experienced the situation and *their* sense of the so-called "talk" in question. Of course, that's to the extent that we're interested to allow "locker room talk" at all.[8]

It's a tough row to hoe. Is allowing victims "the right to be reasonably heard at any public proceeding in…district court involving release, plea, sentencing, or any parole proceeding," as the U.S.' 2004 Crime Victims' Rights Act puts it, the best carriage of justice?[9] Is the confrontation of the convicted by the victim how fairness and law are supposed to play out? Do we want to put emphasis on catharsis in the justice system and, if yes, to what degree and how? The Nassar case involved some intense instantiations of victims' rights. Now, I'll get this out of the way immediately: there's no justification for Nassar's actions. Fair sentencing is fair sentencing, and "brute" but begins to describe what the man is and was. Every woman involved deserves to know that maximum attention will be paid to their experiences and that the society will fully address the meaning

---

7 Joshua M. Price, *Structural Violence: Hidden Brutality in the Lives of Women* (Albany: SUNY, 2012), 2.
8 Obviously, free speech is welcome. There may be a difference between free speech and *mean* speech, however, wherein, as Catherine Mackinnon points out, societies have decisions to make about what words are acceptable and what words discriminate. See Mackinnon, *Only Words* (Cambridge, MA: Harvard University Press, 1993).
9 *Justice for All Act of 2004*, House Resolution 5107, 108th Congress, 2nd Session (January 20, 2004), § 3771.

of the issues involved. Still, *one hundred and fifty-six* victims spoke at the Nassar trial, with more than a few testimonies covered extensively by the media. The trial judge noted that it was her "privilege" to sentence Nassar to one hundred and seventy-five years in prison – a number akin to *two* life sentences. The judge also found it important to note that she had signed Nassar's "death warrant" – a grim and ominous proclamation. The whole thing happened in full view of anyone who wanted to watch (one only needed turn on cable TV to see it), and though involving catharsis (comprehensible), the process included shaming – the *public* shaming – of a person who, though reprehensible, remained, and, we imagine, *continues* to remain, in fact, that: a person like the rest of us, at root.[10]

Now, my immediate reaction was to think of this via human rights. What's the basic problem with sexual abuse? It detracts from the dignity that everyone should have. It invades the victim's privacy and personhood – domains that should somehow be protected by law. It's true: not every legal system practices "maximum" realizations of human rights – that as either as matters of principle or law. In the neighborhood of sixty countries maintain the death penalty, e.g., something not *forbidden* under human rights, but certainly not in human rights' *spirit* – the right to life being among basic rights' foundational principles.[11] Still, lest nations are interested to say that they abrogate, or deny, rights concepts (few are), they often at least *attempt* to gesture in the direction of broad swathes of rights standards and the liberties and privileges that all are supposed to have. Here, we are talking about not only "freedom" – the ability to do as one likes – but the idea of the inherence of the human being and his or her intrinsic worth. At issue is the ineffable spark of humanity, or the *esprit* that defines what the human

---

10 One might make the argument that someone who engages in acts like Nassar's *isn't* human – in the same manner that some might want to claim that Hitler, or history's other great mass-murderers, might be less than so. That is a fabulously dangerous position, however, as it opens up the space for arguing that some humans *de facto* aren't that, potentially leading to mindsets that figures such as Hitler (or perhaps Nassar) used to justify their positions.

11 See William A. Schabas, *The Abolition of the Death Penalty in International Law*, 3rd ed. (Cambridge: Cambridge University Press, 2002). This is, of course, controversial to the extent that international intervention by force of arms to *prevent* human rights violations might involve denying some the right to life – wherein, there is a question as to how fundamental the right to life actually is in human rights (is it absolute, or isn't it?). Still, as many acknowledge, take away life, and there are few human rights to discuss; life is the premise to asking rights questions. See also Ian Park, *The Right to Life in Armed Conflict* (Oxford: Oxford University Press, 2018); B.G. Ramcharan, ed., *The Right to Life in International Law* (Dordrecht: Martinus Nijhoff, 1985).

being might be. We are concerned about that part of us which *is* human and which might experience the humanity of others as well as the humanity of ourselves. Simply put, play with that hard-to-define-yet-nonetheless-determinate spark that defines us and you're not only playing with the humanity of a specific individual, but the essence of humanity at-large. That, though, circles back to the individual. Because one *is* human, one should always be treated via humane standards. Standards don't apply to thin air. They apply to *people* who should be accorded dignity and, generally, dignity in equal amounts.

This forms the basis for ranges of rights legislation in both national and international contexts. That's especially in the domain of civil rights. I call this the "civil rights" domain because civil rights intersect with identity and one's ability to speak and be recognized. For sure, people need to be kept alive. Food, housing, and shelter (gathered under the heading of socio-economic rights) are fundamental human needs.[12] No bread or water, and, wow, is there no discussion about particularly much to have. However, one doesn't provide such things simply for themselves. The point isn't just keeping people *alive*. The point is to facilitate *thought*. The point is allowing *articulation*. The point is to help participation in *democracy* and aiding someone in voicing their *opinion* – explaining and reflecting on their worldview. One simply can't engage civil liberties and one's possibilities for self-expression unless one has a reasonable relationship with one's being; one need be allowed one's sense of self and to feel secure that one can reflect on one's thoughts without undue interference. When you invade someone in a way that for many crosses into territory that's perhaps the most intimate, one disturbs that relationship. One upsets the connection one has with one's self– that via attempting, anyway, to dictate the terms of one's self-relationship *for* someone; interfering in their general sensibilities as they maintain them for *themselves*. One gets deeply into another's existential space and starts to move the furniture around – that in ways for which no one asked. There are a million things one could say about such acts. At the very least, however, they're disorienting. They cut the legs out from under one's mental space and

---

12 See UDHR, article 25. This is not unproblematic. As many note, so-called socio-economic rights (e.g., food, housing, and shelter) are often not well-protected. That's as they demand resources reallocation – something hard to demand under conditions of private ownership. Still, I but appeal to the idea embodied in the UDHR that, optimally, anyway, better societies wouldn't let people starve or freeze. See Mary Robinson, "Advancing Economic, Social and Cultural Rights: The Way Forward," *Human Rights Quarterly* 26, no. 4 (2004): 866–72.

can be felt as fundamentally destabilizing. And in cases bearing trauma, one isn't talking about a momentary loss of orientation. One is talking about a set of actions whose effects linger like a plague, or a pestilence that it's tough to get to go away.[13]

In this context, proactive protection for at-risk groups becomes important. Protection of those who have been historically vulnerable becomes a priority. Such things have played out in a number of contexts. Legislation like the American Civil Rights Act of 1964 or the Covenant on the Elimination of All Forms of Racial Discrimination (1965) from the UN combat discrimination along the lines of ethnicity and race. They contend that any "doctrine of superiority based on racial differentiation" is false and that we need to keep our eye open for any social practice that not only professes racism, but engages in *any* kind of cultural marginalization.[14] Minors have been the subject of special protection as people in their formative stages of development should be able to develop in peace, and young minds should be able to develop without hardship or oppression.[15] Indigenous peoples and migrant workers have also seen covenants worked out in their name, as such groups have *also* experienced demotion to second-class status and bars to participating in societies in the manner of dominant groups around them.[16] Now, we're obviously here discussing the terrain of minority rights. We're discussing the rights of people who often exist in smaller numbers than other groups in the societies in which they find themselves. That's not the only way to discuss "minority," however. "Minority" can concern power status, or the historical roles people have occupied. It can concern being pushed to the bottom of the totem pole by forces we either accept knowingly, or whose

---

13 See Linda LeMoncheck, "Taunted and Tormented or Savvy and Seductive?" in *Sexual Harassment: A Debate* (Lanham: Rowman & Littlefield, 1997), 1–96. See also Diana T. Meyers, *Subjection and Subjectivity: Psychoanalytic Feminism and Moral Philosophy* (London: Routledge, 1994).
14 United Nations, "International Convention on the Elimination of All Forms of Racial Discrimination" (1965, preamble), https://www.ohchr.org/EN/ProfessionalInterest/Pages/CERD.aspx.
15 See Antonella Invernizzi and Jane Williams, eds., *The Human Rights of Children: From Visions to Implementation* (London: Routledge, 2011).
16 See United Nations, "Convention on the Rights of the Child" (1989), https://www.ohchr.org/EN/ProfessionalInterest/Pages/CRC.aspx; United Nations, "International Convention on the Protection of the Rights of All Migrant Workers and Members of Their Families" (1990), https://www.ohchr.org/EN/ProfessionalInterest/Pages/CMW.aspx.

momentum we accede to without reflection or thought.[17] Vis-à-vis gender, is sexual assault a one-way street? Are women sexual abuse's *only* victims? No. When it comes to sexual assault, however, women are by far its primary sufferers, and we might *still* be fighting with structures that, as Simone de Beauvoir put it, often relegate women to the status of the "Other."[18]

Now, a document like the Convention on the Elimination of All Forms of Discrimination against Women (1979) doesn't reference sexual assault, rape, harassment, or any other form of sexual violence in an explicit sense. The Convention's focus is on non-discrimination and assuring women's access to social and civic space. The document thinks in terms of institutional marginalization and the legal denial of rights.[19] Again, though, what is sexual assault or harassment if not a form of exactly such things? Is sexual harassment of any kind not an "exclusion or restriction made on the basis of sex?"[20] Is not *not* reacting to "social and cultural patterns of conduct" that put women in vulnerable positions not a mode of pushing individuals to the side or suggesting they *needn't* be treated like everyone else?[21] Is not sexual harassment or violence a matter of "impairing or nullifying" women's social recognition and seeing someone as *not* having the same privileges as others?[22] Is not treating women as objects a mode of "stereotyping" we're supposed to have done away with?[23] It's a national shame that the United States has not ratified the Women's Convention (which it hasn't). It's also shocking that America's own Equal Rights Amendment has continually fallen flat.[24] Part of the reason this has happened, however, at least it's been claimed, is that the principle is already in American law: you're not supposed to

---

17 See Helen Mayer Hacker, "Women as a Minority Group," *Social Forces* 30, no. 1 (1951): 60–9. See also Simone de Beauvoir, *The Second Sex*, trans. H.M. Parshley (New York: Vintage, 1989).
18 See Maria Bevacqua, *Rape on the Public Agenda: Feminism and the Politics of Sexual Assault* (Boston: Northeastern University Press, 2000).
19 See Anne Hellum and Henriette Sindig Aasen, eds., *Women's Human Rights: CEDAW in International, Regional and National Law* (Cambridge: Cambridge University Press, 2013).
20 United Nations, "Convention on the Elimination of All Forms of Discrimination against Women" (1979, introduction), http://www.ohchr.org/EN/ProfessionalInterest/Pages/CEDAW.aspx.
21 Ibid., article 4.
22 Ibid., article 1.
23 Ibid., article 4.
24 Gilbert Y. Steiner, *Constitutional Inequality: The Political Fortunes of the Equal Rights Amendment* (Washington, DC: The Brookings Institution, 1985).

discriminate; people *can't* be treated differently because of who they are. I.e., ratified women's conventions or not, you're technically not supposed to put people in situations where either their person or their agency as a civic actor can be denied.[25]

To that extent, it's the case that we should never brook such behavior, and we must get rid of sexual violence root and branch. Whether concerning a President or a pauper, norms that facilitate harassment aren't good enough, and when accusations of such things are *brought*, they should be approached with the highest level of gravity. Indeed, not only when a case is brought and a verdict reached, but *before*, victims deserve a recovery process reinforcing their recognition as social subjects and buttressing their sense of personhood. Victims deserve to heal, and they should be offered a sense of their belonging in life's public and private contexts. Some healing might come at the convicted's expense in the instances where conviction happens, and there are arguments that convictions don't happen frequently enough.[26] Perhaps there are ways to confront perpetrators – demonstrated perpetrators – in which *that* person's personhood isn't detracted from or their being isn't *also* degraded. Perhaps there are ways to construct oneself as a full being in front of someone that has undone one's being without undoing *their* being, and not expanding circles of hurt and ill will. Perhaps there are ways to make it clear that one won't be held down and that neither others nor oneself should ignore or forget who one is: a human being with the same status as everyone else.

I'm thus comfortable with victim's impact statements. I get it – fully – and I have full affinity with victims' rights. It's important that people don't feel powerless for long, and that "restorative justice," as it's been called, in fact, restores.[27] A crime should not have lasting effects, and the idea with crime

---

25 For American law vis-à-vis the concept Austin Sarat, ed., *Civil Rights in American Law, History, and Politics* (Cambridge: Cambridge University Press, 2014); Alan B. Morrison, *Fundamental of American Law* (Oxford: Oxford University Press, 1996); Coromae Richey Mann, *Unequal Justice: A Question of Color* (Bloomington: Indiana University Press, 1993).

26 See Andrew Van Damm, "Less Than 1% of Rapes Lead to Felony Convictions. At Least 89% of Victims Face Emotional and Physical Consequences," *The Washington Post*, October 6, 2018, https://www.washingtonpost.com/business/2018/10/06/less-than-percent-rapes-lead-felony-convictions-least-percent-victims-face-emotional-physical-consequences/?utm_term=.c51b319c5c52.

27 See Ruth Ann Strickland, *Restorative Justice* (New York: Peter Lang, 2004), 38.

is that it *is* wrong and doesn't represent how things should be.[28] Still, the convicted's personhood *is* an issue. There *is* a question as to whether there's a moment at which punishment turns into "spectacle," as it's been put, as opposed to the execution of fairness or just contract.[29] "Eye for an eye" may be a form of justice – and victim impact statements aren't that. Punishment involves pain. Even the most liberal penal systems, oriented towards rehabilitation, involve boxing the individual in. They involve conditioning people and instructing them on right and wrong – standards they have to *accept* as opposed to participating in the creation of those standards themselves. Individuals *will be* dictated to and, even if subtly, expected to obey.[30] Indeed, it's been pointed out that's what well-functioning societies may do – inculcate varieties of obedience and discipline in *all* of a polity's members, whether those individuals are labeled "criminal" or not. I.e., if not dehumanization, then at least deconstructing and reconstructing the human being, may naturally be part of the punishment process.[31]

Still, one can't go *too* far down that road. You can't just run *roughshod* over another person's essence and some ground floor level of their human status. Using one commentator's vocabulary, we have to use our "highest moral precepts

---

28 Christopher R. Williams and Bruce A. Arrigo make the nice point that the definition of crime has change over the years: it's alternatively been a considered a defect of the soul, a matter of sin, a breach of social contract, a kind of hedonism as well as an idea with no firm foundations as the concept is socially constructed. What seems to *me* the point is that, regardless of the particular way one defines it, the general social assumption is that it's not supposed to be there. Otherwise, there's no need for redress. See Williams and Arrigo, "Introduction: Philosophy, Crime, and Theoretical Criminology" in *Philosophy, Crime, and Criminology*, ed. Christopher R. Williams and Bruce A. Arrigo (Urbana: University of Illinois Press, 2004), 1–39.
29 See Michel Foucault, *Discipline and Punish: The Birth of the Prison*, trans. A.M. Sheridan (New York: Vintage, 1979).
30 Hyman Gross makes the interesting point that many – though not all of us – feel "abhorrence" at the idea of punishment: we know that we're going to do something to another human being that, generally, we don't want to. However, that underlines that fact – we're going to *do* something to another human being, and it's likely to be less than pleasant. See Gross, *Crime and Punishment: A Concise Moral Critique* (Oxford: Oxford University Press, 2012), 1.
31 Indeed, it's been pointed out that's what well-functioning members of society may in fact do – assent to varieties of obedience and self-discipline. See, again, Foucault, *Discipline and Punish*. See also Rob Canton, *Why Punish?: An Introduction to the Philosophy of Punishment* (London: Palgrave, 2017), 177–99.

and political ideals."[32] We can't *just* invade another person's personhood, regardless of what they've done. Again: countries have latitude to make their own laws and it's clear that standards of justice are not the same. Some nations might have put a figure like Nassar to death while others might have stoned him, sterilized him, or removed a limb. Still others might have ignored his crimes and simply let him go free.[33] Nonetheless, we have to be clear: no one is supposed to be subject to "degrading treatment or punishment."[34] No part of punishment is supposed to be "cruel."[35] "Inherent dignity" is *not* to be denied to *anyone*, whether it's someone you like or not.[36] You can't stick your thumb in a wound and swirl it around. This is part of the reason why, until the 1970s, victim impact statements weren't much present in law. It's also why, though they're now common in the U.S., they're handled circumspectly in many parts of the world.[37]

A few points are salient here. Firstly, there might be a difference between waterboarding someone and allowing individuals whose dignity, to say nothing of legal rights, have been violated to *confront* an individual proved guilty. I.e., in human rights regimes, the concept of "degrading treatment and punishment" and notions of "cruel" punishment are related to torture. In international law, they're related to the panoply of rights ideas that emerged post-1945 in reaction to the Second World War – specifically Nazism. Totalitarian regimes, as one commentator has noted, became not just totalitarian, but perpetrated "horrors."[38]

---

32 Samuel Moyn, *The Last Utopia: Human Rights in History* (Cambridge, MA: Harvard Belknap, 2010), 1.
33 See Matthew Pate and Lauri A. Gould, *Corporate Punishment around the World* (Denver: Praeger, 2012).
34 United Nations, "International Covenant on Civil and Political Rights" (1966, article 6), http://www.ohchr.org/en/professionalinterest/pages/ccpr.aspx.
35 Ibid., article 7.
36 Ibid., preamble.
37 See Jonathan Doak, "The Victim and the Criminal Process: An Analysis of Recent Trends in Regional and International Tribunals," *Legal Studies* 23, no. 1 (2003): 1–32; Kevin R. Gray, "Evidence before the ICC" in *The Permanent International Criminal Court: Legal and Policy Issues*, Dominic McGoldrick, Peter J. Rowe and Eric Donnelly, eds. (Portland: Hart, 2004), 303. Doak actually makes the argument that accept of victim's impact statements is expanding. In a limited way, he's right. However, as Gray notes, they *are* still primarily an American phenomenon, and are considered to involve extensive complications.
38 J. Herman Burgers and Hans Daniels, *The United Nations Convention against Torture: A Handbook on the Convention against Torture and Other Cruel, Inhuman or Degrading Treatment or Punishment* (Dordrecht: Martinus Nijhoff, 1988), 5.

Totalitarian regimes were involved in camps. They were involved in medical experiments. They sent out death squads. They were involved in violent segregation and stigmatization. They practiced forced relocation and posed intense threats to the bodies of individuals and their everyday lives. People were made to experience systematic dehumanization and pain from which they might not recover. *Nationally* – in American law – the notion of "cruel and unusual punishment" dates to the 1790s and the eighth amendment to the U.S. Constitution: the idea being that law shouldn't be applied arbitrarily (as totalitarian regimes tend to do), and there be consistency to judicial practice's fundamental workings. Now, Larry Nassar might be shamed. The trial judge might have grandstanded and piled on. It was intense to see someone just launched into, as awful as the things were he had done. Still, Nassar *will* be (and was) taken away, wherein he won't have to confront the women he abused *after* his trial and, legally, he's not to be abused in confinement.[39] Nassar's life won't be pleasurable, and his career stops. He won't enjoy life as he did outside prison, and his freedom is denied. He'll nonetheless get three meals a day and presumably die of old age. Fingernails won't be pulled out and the only re-education he'll be sent for – assuming some kind of therapy or rehabilitation will be part of his imprisonment – will be to fix his misogynistic and pedophilic tendencies. Nassar won't be persecuted for his background or gender, and his physical body will be limited, but not hurt. He'll be punished within the law for something he actually *did*.

Indeed, in terms of the statements of Nassar's victims and the general way they came off, the media plays none-too-small a role. There's a *context* to our view of how the Nassar trial played out, and the vociferousness of the proceedings may have been magnified due to their extensive press coverage and the intersection of that coverage with popular attitudes towards justice. "Aly Raisman 'Almost Passed Out' During Larry Nassar Testimony," Fox News proclaimed; a fog of evil hung over the proceedings because of a stink that followed *him* – the evil-doer (a variety of the conservative, "you commit the crime and *you* bear responsibility for that" argument; "if you've done something, we can go after you however we want"). "Larry Nassar, I Hate You," headlined *The New York Times*, picking up the words of Emma Ann Miller, one of Nassar's victims.[40] Anger, enmity, and

---

39 Yes, prison abuse happens, and child molesters, especially, have a reputation of becoming its victims. Technically, though, prisoners are not supposed to be subjected to violence by other prisoners. See Kristine Levan, *Prison Violence: Causes, Consequences, and Solutions* (New York: Routledge, 2012).
40 See Sarah Stein Kerr and Neeti Updahye, "Victims of Abuse Speak: 'Larry Nasser, I Hate You,'" *The New York Times*, January 22, 2018, https://www.google.dk/search?q=%22

the viscerality of experiences were what need be underlined. A father to three of Nassar's victims went after Nassar in the courtroom; Randall Margraves made profane comments during sentencing proceedings. The judge expressed sympathy, offering to facilitate Margraves in expressing his anguish. He would also have a chance to confront Nassar and express what was on his mind. At the confrontation, however, Margraves asked for "five minutes in a locked room" with this "demon" (the "demon" being Nassar [he wanted to meet him alone]). The judge said no. Margraves then ran across the courtroom, trying to punch the convicted. He was restrained. However, Fox News again: "Dad Who Charged Larry Nassar Receiving Hundreds of Donations." Victims were booked on CBS' *This Morning* and NBC's *Megyn Kelly Today*. Joy Behar, from the popular afternoon chat show, *The View*, delighted in the idea of Nassar running into someone "alone," in his prison cell. We all knew what would happen then; he'd be beaten up if not raped himself. No media outlet wasn't covering the event, and the point was anger and hate. Again, were the articulations of Nassar's *victims* important? Clearly. What happened, after all, happened to *them*. Was the content of the case newsworthy? Undoubtedly – not only in itself, but also due to the cultural moment in which we find ourselves. Few news outlets were trying to *under*sell the statements of victims and their families, however, and it was anger and revenge that took the headlines. I don't know. In deeply divided times in American if not global society, it seemed that every news outlet could tap into outrage and various calls for retribution without treading into overly fraught waters. On this issue, anyway, Americans could unify in their hate.[41]

Larry+Nassar%2C+I+Hate+You%22&rlz=1C1GCEA_enDK782DK782&oq=%22L&aqs=chrome.2.69i57j69i65j69i59j35i39l2j0.2759j0j4&sourceid=chrome&ie=UTF-8. It's but one article. There were, however, hundreds.

41 See Morgan M. Evans, "Aly Raisman 'Almost Passed Out' During Larry Nassar Testimony," *Fox News*, January 25, 2018, http://www.foxnews.com/entertainment/2018/01/25/aly-raisman-almost-passed-out-during-larry-nassar-testimony.html; Amy Lieu, "Dad Who Charged at Larry Nassar Receiving Hundreds of Donations," *Fox News*, February 3, 2018, http://www.foxnews.com/us/2018/02/03/dad-who-charged-at-larry-nassar-receiving-hundreds-donations.html; Mythili Sampathkumar, "Larry Nassar: Judge Says 'No Way' Will She Punish Abuse Victims' Father For Trying to Attack Disgraced Doctor," *The Independent*, February 2, 2018, https://www.independent.co.uk/news/world/americas/larry-nassar-trial-video-attack-judge-punish-father-sex-abuse-victim-a8192346.html; Sarah Stein Kerr and Neeti Updahye, "Victims of Abuse Speak: 'Larry Nassar, I Hate You,'" *The New York Times*, January 23, 2018, https://www.nytimes.com/video/us/100000005695934/more-of-nassars-victims-come-forward.html.

And indeed, it can't be under-underlined that there *were* extraordinary dimensions to the Nassar case. *Hundreds* of women were involved in the suit. Nassar admitted to around a dozen incidents, wherein abuse on an extensive scale was an admitted matter of fact. Nassar's abuse was systemic, and the situation involved some rarified institutions – not everyone works for the American Olympic team, and Nassar was connected to the medical school of a university with real prestige.[42] Nassar's violations of medical ethics disgust, and the fact that Nassar *didn't* admit to more than a dozen cases of abuse brought its own drama too. Even in defeat, he wasn't precisely contrite.[43] Resonating with #MeToo, there was value in saying, "this is what abuse looks like when it goes unchecked." Workplace, professional, and even simple social circle lasciviousness can turn into something else, and one should be clear what "something else" can be.

There are yet further salient points, however. There are further issues we might consider about the carriage of justice, and how it played out. I.e., a particular focus might need to be put on the *amount* of abuse and the way that intersected with media coverage. We have to ask ourselves questions regarding numbers and what abuse does – how invasive it can be. Still, I'd put it this way: is one sexual assault less important or dramatic – less of a call to action – than two hundred? Do we want it to be the *quantity* of abuse that catches our attention and grabs headlines? Or, do we want it to be the *fact* of abuse that matters in whatever amount it takes place? Do we want it to be the *recognition* of violation, tragedy, and assault that is our priority, or should it be only because the *amount* of violations crosses a particular threshold that we decide to pay attention to a case?

The answer has to be the former. Again, dozens – hundreds – of individuals were hurt by Nassar. Many were affected by his lechery, and he conducted his violations from positions where he could affect a lot of people. Nassar abused positions of power, and situations in which individuals were physically prone. The individuality

---

42 The school has decided to share culpability too. See Mitch Smith and Anemona Hartocollis, "Michigan State's $500 Million for Nassar Victims Dwarfs Other Settlements," *The New York Times*, May 18, 2018, https://www.nytimes.com/2018/05/16/us/larry-nassar-michigan-state-settlement.html.

43 Jeffrey Toobin of *The New Yorker* argued that Nassar in fact *remade* the case for cameras in the court – that *because* he didn't admit to as many crimes as he had committed that the viscerality of his effect on the many young women he harmed need be highlighted. See Toobin, "How Larry Nassar's Trial Made the Case for Cameras in the Courtroom," *The New Yorker*, February 12, 2018, https://www.newyorker.com/news/daily-comment/how-larry-nassars-trial-made-the-case-for-cameras-in-the-court.

of those experiences, however, constitutes their importance. Individuality is the *grounds* on which subjectivity is violated. It's in the individual where we find the subjectivity that can *speak* of its abuse, and the subjectivity that might *recover*. It's in individuality that we find the locality of the rights that might be stripped away and the locale of the voice that might be silenced. Whether a particular experience is comparable with another is only interesting on an analytical basis. Yes, when indignities are committed against so many people, it's endemic. It's an abuse that must be handled via law. However, Aly Raisman, Emma Ann Miller and all others involved deserve to have their experiences heard as *theirs* – in the context of the fact that it happened to *them*, and not because they figured into abuse of a particular *amount*. I.e., we hope that Nassar would have been as vigorously prosecuted had his abuse involved just a few individuals as opposed to the over one hundred that it did.[44]

Moreover, we should perhaps expect media coverage; it's perhaps something which may be needed. Cultural discussions *should be* had around issues like the Nassar case, and women should feel empowered to use their voice in public. The outlets we have to drive discussion are the outlets we have to drive discussion, and we have to deploy those the best we can. Still: do we always do ourselves the biggest favor with the *way* we drive discussions? Are we asking questions that might *really* solve – or *help* to solve – issues like the Nassar case in the *broadest* sense? Are we asking the questions that need to be asked? Or are we involved with an almost religious-like focus on the notion of evil without discussing complexes of social, political, and legal factors to which damaging behavior might relate? Are there things which *contribute* to individuals taking turns such as Nassar's, and do not *all* of us bear part of the bill when respect for basic rights goes fundamentally off track? Do we solve the "problem that has no name," as Betty Friedan put it, by turning cases like Nassar's into dramas?[45] Or, are we missing a chance

---

44 Ray Surette brings up the point of "predator criminals as media icons." I.e., it is the most spectacular crimes that tend to get attention – often instigate legislation – and one way that crimes can often feel "spectacular" is if they involve many victims. This spectaclization of crime, however, easily washes over the fact that crimes are crimes, spectacular or not. See Surette, "Predator Criminals as Media Icons" in *Media, Process, and the Social Construction of Crime: Studies in Newsmaking Criminology*, ed. Gregg Barak (New York: Garland, 1994), 131–58.
45 See Betty Friedan, *The Feminine Mystique* (New York: W.W. Norton, 1963). This is a slight modification of Friedan's idea – that women in the mid-twentieth century suffered a hard-to-name discontentment. However, that discontentment was attached to women's social role and everyday, unsaid oppression. These are issues with which #MeToo would say is right at the heart of the problem.

to have a more analytical discussion of women's rights because we're caught up in the idea a specific person – Nassar – is the "devil"?[46] It's noticeable, e.g., that, even in the face of all that's been going on vis-à-vis gender, there is relatively little discussion about reforwarding America's Equal Rights Amendment – the attempt to grant women a recognition on par with the focus on race provided in the Civil Rights Act.[47] Yes, there is talk about the gender wage gap and paid child leave; as much as we need, though? And why in the holy high heck has the U.S. *not* ratified the Convention on Discrimination against Women, a basic gesture in the direction of women's rights on the international stage? Why is sexually exploitative social imagery of and about women in any number of media not on the agenda when talk shows launch into their *spiel*, and what of the digs at women based on physical appearance coming from places like the occupant of the White House? Nassar did unforgivable things. They should never be justified. Is there *no* social fabric surrounding what he did, however – one larger than U.S. Olympics, the medical profession, Michigan State or, most specifically, *him*? Is *Nassar* really the problem, or do we have to look at more extensive factors at play? Only the most committed social libertarian would say "no."[48]

In any case, primary may be the concept of personhood. Primary may be the universality of the human essence that underpins notions of rights – the rights of victims, the rights of the accused, the rights of the convicted, the rights of those who have lived free of crime, the rights of those experienced crime, and the rights of those who *might* become victims of crime in the future. Primary is the self-proprietariness of body and soul and assuring that individuals don't become alienated from themselves; primary is that our existence is connected to sovereignty and control over oneself. Rights bring obligations – accepting their normativity and allowing rights for others. Rights aren't easy to realize and they

---

46 It wasn't "devil." However, as noted, "demon" was the term used by the father who attacked Nassar in the courtroom, and who gained not a small amount of sympathy from the American public.

47 See, e.g., Garrett Epps, "The Equal Rights Amendment Strikes Again," *The Atlantic*, January 20, 2019, https://www.theatlantic.com/ideas/archive/2019/01/will-congress-ever-ratify-equal-rights-amendment/580849/.

48 Of course, some would say that some of the attention the Larry Nassar case got involved just though: shining a light on a general situation regarding gender relations and misbehavior on a larger social scale. Again, though, that was amidst a large wash of focus on Nassar himself – not unjust, but again, also perhaps not the whole issue. See Caroline Kitchener, "Larry Nasser and the Impulse to Doubt Female Pain," *The Atlantic*, January 23, 2018, https://www.theatlantic.com/health/archive/2018/01/larry-nassar-and-the-impulse-to-doubt-female-pain/551198/.

need be *practiced*; rights' effects can't always be felt because rights stand on paper. Rights demand a culture – a commitment to their value. They demand education and dissemination of their existence throughout the social body. Rights aren't only for the virtuous, though. They don't fully disappear because one did something wrong. One maintains rights because one is "part of the human species."[49] One has rights *inherently* – via membership in a global community. One maintains rights because once they're dented or dinged for anyone, they're dented and dinged for us *all*. Attacking one human being means attacking all of us. That's because all who are human *are* human – whether we're the best example of our humanity or not.

The question is thus whether one seeks to deconstruct another's personhood or not. The question is whether one goes after another by will. Do we try to disassemble the humanity another human being has, or are we trying to recover *ourselves* and find ways to live our lives? Are we looking to recover, or are we looking to take others' down? Those convicted of crimes have rights and privileges removed. That's how paying for crime goes; one *won't* have the life one had. The idea of conviction is conviction – it's that things *won't* continue as they did before. Still, does one want to degrade a person's sense of self more than will be done via punishment alone? Has either one or the society around one *stopped* viewing the person as a person – a being with core meaning and value they maintain; that because the moment we stop according people such things is the moment we start down a slippery slope? It's an obtuse example. However, war crimes trials relating to the former Yugoslavia have involved some nasty characters. They involved political and military puppet masters responsible for tens, if not hundreds, of thousands of deaths. The deaths in question were discriminatory: religion, language, nationality, and ethnicity all played into their grounds. Indeed, gender was an issue too as rape was a grim reality in more than a few of Yugoslavia's conflict zones. Slobodan Milošević, Ratko Mladić, Radovan Karadžić, and others in their circles committed war crimes and crimes against humanity. They mangled fellow human beings and snuffed out thousands and thousands of lives. They treated people as objects; pieces to be moved around geographical chessboards in violent games of ethnic politics.[50]

Still, a few things of note. Firstly, the death penalty wasn't used in the Yugoslav trials. It's a sidebar. However, capital punishment wasn't part of the Yugoslav court's

---

49 Micheline R. Ishay, *The History of Human Rights: From Ancient Times to the Globalization Era* (Berkeley: University of California Press, 2004), 3.
50 See Catherine Baker, *The Yugoslav Wars of the 1990s* (London: Palgrave, 2015).

statute under the aegis of UN justice. Why that remark? Because what is perhaps the maximum crime was *not* subject to maximum punishment – the obliteration of the person who committed the crime as such. One *could* have done more. One *could have* adjusted jurisprudence to allow for the obliteration of people who had obliterated others. One could have said, "you did this, and the same will be done to you." However, the perpetrators were kept *alive*. The law suggested that they should be allowed existence. They should have *some* mode of speech, modicum of movement, and some form of basic care. Those convicted at the Yugoslav tribunals weren't denuded of any and all experience. The *legal* reaction wasn't "kill them!" It was to make sure that justice was served, and that it was served on roughly humanitarian terms.[51]

The proceedings also went forward absent victim impact statements. I.e., the Yugoslav trials involved sanctioning no oaths or declarations of personal affect – that either for restorative purposes or to assuage individual anger or the desire to speak. Survivors of massacres and concentration camps testified as *witnesses*. Those affected attested to *evidence*, attempting to relate to facts and the outlines of *what happened*. They attempted to paint a picture of the *situation*, and describe precisely what was *done*. Testimony could be heart-wrenching and near-indescribable. It involved indelible scenes – scenes many thought we were done with come the "new world order" of the 1990s (the worst ravages of war).[52] Still, there was no pointing anyone out as a "monster," and no space was carved out to tell someone they were "hated."[53] The viscerality of the circumstances was

---

51 Eric Stover makes the point that it's easy to claim that "therapeutic value" was an important part of the Yugoslav trials – and it may well have been. However, he also notes that one doesn't in fact know the extent to which that's the case and in what way, wherein, in the first instance, the importance of the trial was justice and prosecuting human rights violations in themselves. See Stover, *The Witnesses: War Crimes and the Promise of Justice in The Hague* (Philadelphia: University of Pennsylvania Press, 2005), 131.

52 This is of course the vocabulary used by George Bush, Sr., to address the post-Cold War world. That involved many things – some things potentially dubious (e.g., would it be a world dominated by the American agenda?). However, for many, the post-Cold War world also represented opportunities to expand human rights in the absence of the ideologically driven battle between communism and capitalism. Indeed, Bush himself referenced the expansion of human rights in his description of the "new world order." See, e.g., Mortimer Sellers, ed., *The New World Order: Sovereignty, Human Rights and the Self-Determination of Peoples* (Oxford: Berg, 1996).

53 This is not to say that testimonies weren't poignant. However, the tone was relatively staid, matter-of-fact, and reflective. A good sense of the atmosphere may be found in International Criminal Tribunal for the former Yugoslavia, "Through

made visceral due to the *crime*, with the salient point being that *that* should be dealt with above all else. Emotion involved describing an event and the idea that we might internalize the wrongs involved as each of us felt like we should. We might consider the meaning of the crime in its broad contexts and have information about it to take account of in our thoughts. The point was getting murderers off the street, however – not going after another individual's *person*. The issue wasn't *degrading* someone, or hollowing-out their being. The point was the *opposite*: assuring that universal humanity was accorded to *everyone*, and that dignity *itself* was sustained. It was to uphold a universal essence and saying, bar none, that deserves respect. That meant doing that. Certainly, that was if you were the victim of a crime. However, it was also if you had perpetrated one as well.

I'll end with this. I'd never take away a victim's right to speak. The twentieth century is unimaginable without Elie Wiesel, Malala Yousafzai, or Liu Xiaobo. Imagine no women's rights movement, civil rights movement, or movements on behalf of justice for the poor. Imagine a world absent anger, outrage, or activism against wrongs long done, and streets empty of protest or activists for rights-based change. Imagine us *not* being clear on Nassar's crimes, how they affected women or our communities – that in both specific and general senses. Nassar had to be stopped, his violations discussed, and knowledge of them gained. We had to be precise about what took place, including the clear and unmistakable testimony of victims. A cultural momentum also shouldn't be lost. Women speaking their piece about a range of issues, from the worst abuse to more subtle forms of harassment, has been significant – on par with any instance of rights activism. As victims' rights movements proceed, however, they might consider their objectives. Are they looking to *solve* social problems, or but restore individual subjects? Are they looking to but *bring* issues to attention, or to give issues the *deepest* address? Are they looking to restore by building the foundations of a person up, or putting another in a position where their foundations become torn down? Do we *punish*, or do we *spectaclize*; is it *examples* we're looking for, or the stopping of a crime? I can accept a punished Larry Nassar. I don't need him to go free – either now, or in his old age. A life sentence is fine with me as is the end of his career. What I *really* want, however, is for what *made* Larry Nassar to go away. I'd be pleased if there were *fewer* cases where we needed to decide if anger should be released as part of the healing process, and appropriate outlets to express hate wasn't a pressing problem. As courts do their business, is basic *dignity* their point?

Their Eyes – Witness Justice," August 13, 2014, https://www.youtube.com/watch?v=giY5opbx4xs.

Or do they look to protect the humanity of some, while leaving room for others' humanity to be attacked? Nassar didn't exhibit such consideration himself. He ignored others' humanity, and, for my sake, he can join Yugoslavia's murderers on a desert island. Still, I wonder if turbo-charging emotions is the best way to address what he did. I wonder if watching someone convicted be gone after personally in a justice setting isn't akin to pinning a scarlet letter on someone's breast. Indeed, even if we accept that there's no justice without spectaclization – which there might not be – then we have to ask if spectaclization is the *point*, or if we should minimize such things in the name of larger principles; namely, assuring that the humanity justice defends doesn't become eroded *itself*. In my view, we to need make according dignity to *everyone* justice's principle – even when we accord dignity begrudgingly, or in relation to a figure like Nassar that we think and perhaps *is* the worst of the worst. The point is to register a wrong. It isn't, and really can't be, to strip down another human being's fundaments because even the worst of wrongs is among the things they've done.

Trespassing the Untrespassable
Poland and Its Holocaust Speech Law
(March 21, 2018)

Abstract: *Poland has done something quite controversial: passed a law that suggests that any mode of blaming the nation for the Holocaust is illegal. Fair enough – Poland isn't responsible for the tragedy. However, is that kind of legislation necessary? And does it have much to do with the Holocaust? Or is it rather about the nationalist politics sweeping Europe as well as Poland specifically? Moreover, how does the concept of a "Holocaust speech law" relate to human rights? Not well, I'd say.*

Note: As of summer, 2018, Poland's country's parliament backtracked on the most severe part of the legislation discussed in this piece, removing the possibility of jail time for asserting the country as culpable for the Nazi genocide. Lesser penalties, however, remain in place.[1]

It's been a complex time in Polish history. A country perhaps prone to a particular intensity about its identity – it has historically suffered badly in being caught between the European behemoths of Russia and Germany – what once appeared as a leader in the post-Communist world's turn to liberalism now appears a leader in anything but. I know; there's a lot of debate as to what the Solidarity movement was actually about, and perhaps things generally regarding the end of the old Eastern Bloc were more complex than the simple march to liberal

"Flag of Poland or Polish banner on rough pattern texture background" @Miro Novak / shutterstock.com 268625996

---

1   Rick Noack, "Poland's Controversial 'Holocaust Law' Set to Be Reversed after Global Outcry," *The Washington Post*, June 27, 2018, https://www.washingtonpost.com/news/worldviews/wp/2018/06/27/polands-holocaust-law-caused-an-outcry-now-in-a-surprise-its-being-largely-reversed/?utm_term=.54867c5cd11c.

democracy sometimes portrayed in the "be like us" West.² Still, a hope for liberal consensus very much hung in the air in the '90s, and it felt like a new moment might open up not only for the world, but for Europe specifically. Fascism had been defeated, the Communist period endured, and it might finally be possible to realize modicums of personal liberty and varieties of economic progress that non-liberal ideologies had denied. That the two largest vote-getters in the Polish Third Republic's first parliamentary election in 1991 came from the center and center-left didn't seem a coincidence. It appeared to reflect the rough progress of the slow "wagon train" that authors like Francis Fukuyama claimed was chugging towards destination "liberal project."³ Democracy and free markets had won, and that was it.

Now, Poland isn't the only country now swinging violently towards the right. It's a Europe-wide, and indeed global, phenomenon. However, that doesn't make it any less the case in Poland. People more in the know than I can make deeper genealogical arguments about where Polish nationo-populism comes from, and how long it's been going on. A turning point, though, seems to have been the election of the Kaczyńskis – brothers Lech and Jarosław. Riding a wave of corruption scandals, economic problems, and government spending cuts to power in 2005, the Kaczyńskis and their new Law and Justice party represented a new formation in Polish politics gathering a range of forces from the right. Now, Law and Justice had competition – the center-right Civic Platform, which had run the previous government, wrested power away from the Kaczyńskis between 2007 and 2015, wherein Law and Justice's first run in government was short. However, pushing intense EU skepticism, preaching economic populism (the defense of welfare, lowering the retirement age, etc.), coupling Polish patriotism with a defense of conservative Catholicism and an intensely anti-immigrant stance, and playing on notions that the little man and woman had somehow been done in by elites and runaway globalism, PiS (the Polish acronym for Law

---

2   See Dariusz Aleksandrowicz, Stefani Sonntag and Jan Wielgohs, eds., *The Polish Solidarity Movement in Retrospect: A Story of Failure or Success?* (Berlin: Gesellschaft für sozialwissenschaftliche Forschung und Publizistik, 2009); Günther Heydemann and Karel Vodička, eds., *From Eastern Bloc to European Union: Comparative Processes of Transformation since 1990* (New York: Berghahn, 2017).

3   Francis Fukuyama, *The End of History and the Last Man* (New York: Penguin, 1992), 333, 338.

and Justice) took back power in a dramatic way come 2015. With the elections of that year, the party emerged holding not only the presidency, but having a parliamentary majority on its own (a rarity in European politics) – and this time, it was determined not to let go. Firstly, the party floated conspiracy theories around the one brother's, Lech's, death. Killed in 2010 in a plane crash on his way to commemorate the 1940 Katyn Massacre (a seminal event in Polish history), both his brother and Law and Justice at-large pushed the assertion that Russia was somehow involved in bringing the plane down and that EU officials assisted in a cover-up. The prime target has been Donald Tusk, fellow Pole, former Prime Minister, and co-founder of the archrival Civic Platform – and now President of the European Council. Indeed, things got so extreme that on March 9th of last year, Tusk was re-elected as Council President with all twenty-eight Council votes *except* that of his own country; then-Prime Minister and PiS member Beata Szydło argued that Poland's "priorities" weren't being taken seriously – the priority apparently being that it be more seriously pushed that the EU *was* involved in a cover-up and that Polish nationalists were the victims of cabalistic campaigns.[4] Then, not long before *that*, the legislature moved to invest the government with the right to hire and fire all heads of state media. President Andrzej Duda signed that bill into law as one of the first acts of 2016, making it easier to narrow the voices the voting public heard.[5] Of course, as part of the government beating the traditionalist drum, it attempted to foment support for a petition accumulating around 450,000 signatures that asked for a full ban on abortion – a move the PiS might have won had not significant street protests taken place.[6] The *pièce de résistance*, however, perhaps concerns the judiciary, where, in a pair of bills, what had been more dispersed control over the ability to appoint judges to the country's highest courts became centered on

---

4 See Don Murray, "Jaroslaw Kaczynski's Conspiracy Theory Drives Poland's Sulky EU Policy," *CBCNews*, March 28, 2017, http://www.cbc.ca/news/world/poland-jaroslaw-kaczynski-european-1.4042243. See also Ivan Krastev, "The Plane Crash Conspiracy that Explains Poland," *Foreign Policy*, December 21, 2015, http://foreignpolicy.com/2015/12/21/when-law-and-justice-wears-a-tinfoil-hat-poland-russia-smolensk-kaczynski/.
5 BBC, "Polish Media Laws: Government Takes Control of State Media," January 7, 2016, http://www.bbc.com/news/world-europe-35257105.
6 See BBC, "Poland's Tussle Over Abortion," October 6, 2016, http://www.bbc.com/news/world-europe-37449903.

the parliament and, to a lesser extent, the presidency – again, both now run by a single party. The PiS said it was rooting out old communists in the legal system. The head of the country's judiciary oversight committee said "baloney" – and, in protest, he resigned.[7]

Now to all the controversy and attempts to martial "the people" comes an extra addition: a law stating that "whoever claims, publicly and contrary to the facts, that the Polish Nation or the Republic of Poland is responsible or co-responsible for Nazi crimes committed by the Third Reich… shall be liable to a fine or imprisonment for up to 3 years."[8] I.e., as part of its ongoing campaign to either restore or appeal to national pride, it's now become illegal to blame Poland, even partially, for the late 1930s and early 1940s murder of 6,000,000 Jews and 5,000,000 Roma, Sinti, communists, Jehovah's Witnesses, and plethora of others. There are exceptions. Scientific research (presumably historical research), is exempted. Discover that Poles somehow *were* responsible for the Holocaust – and prove it – and you're technically ok. Artistic expression is also protected. Want to say something challenging established orthodoxy under the label of "aesthetic thoughts?" That's also alright (except, of course, that newly government-controlled media could denounce you). Generally, though, suggesting that Poland is in any way to blame for the Shoah or Nazi genocide – that it had a meaningful hand in events at all – is supposed to be taboo. Poles were *victims* of the Holocaust. They weren't Nazi clients, and they weren't henchmen of Hitler's anti-Semitic regime.

Now, this is complex. Firstly, there's no way to read the Holocaust law *qua* phenomenon except in the context of Poland's political climate, and in relation to the PiS agenda. It's hard to say – do nationalist politicians really *believe* in the need to defend national culture and promote the people's virtue, or do they see political opportunity in a sedimented idea paving the way to easy political points and advantageous maneuvering space in the halls of power (that nations are natural somehow, and that there's natural virtue in the "folk")? It's a tough call. Distinctions between opportunism and belief can be hard to tease out, and what's idealism and what's pragmatism is a tough question in anyone's life.[9] In

---

7 Deutsche Welle, "Poland: Head of Judiciary Watchdog," January 12, 2018, http://www.dw.com/en/poland-head-of-judiciary-watchdog-resigns-in-protest/a-42127723.

8 Times of Israel, "Full Text of Poland's Controversial Holocaust Legislation," *Times of Israel*, February 1, 2018, https://www.timesofisrael.com/full-text-of-polands-controversial-holocaust-legislation/.

9 It addresses the issue at a more intellectualized level than I'm addressing it here. However, Howard H. Schweber takes this issue on in *Democracy and Authenticity: Toward a Theory of Public Justification* (Cambridge: Cambridge University Press, 2012).

any case, like many rightist parties, the PiS has sensed something, and they're concerned to advance it as an idea. This is that people *in fact* feel left behind, many feel condescended to, some are uncomfortable with change and the unfamiliar, and there's something unfair about being governed from faraway places like Brussels or Strasbourg (Warsaw might be ok). In the space of modernity, few things are easier to turn to than the rights of the homeland and the notion that there's righteousness in one's cultural belonging. The PiS isn't alone in this; it's the mantra of near every right-populist party and, indeed, the Civic Platform *also* had its moments declaring "Poles, arise!" That's the point, though. No one is supposed to misunderstand the nation. Want to talk about abuse? How about those people the Nazis ran over in 1939 and then the Soviets in 1944-5? What about *them*? We're sorry about others. However, the point is how *we're* considered – that as "we" is the point of the nation-state.

And, indeed, there *have* been some blunders in this area. The most visible was Barak Obama's utterance of the phrase "Polish death camp" in a White House ceremony in 2012 where he posthumously awarded Polish Second World War resistance fighter Jan Karski with the Presidential Medal of Freedom (the highest civilian decoration the United States offers). Narrating some of Karski's exploits, Obama stated that he (Karski) had been smuggled into a "Polish death camp" to see in first person where Jews were being murdered; that he had been snuck in to see the villainy against which he was fighting. It's true: there were Poles, as was the case with all Nazi-occupied nationalities, who collaborated with the Germans. The most famous example is likely the "Navy Blue Police" (*Granatowa policja*), who found themselves roped into some dubious law and order operations and were involved with some round-ups of Jews.[10] Really, though, the number of collaborators was low in Poland (it's been noted that about a quarter of Poles were willing to fight the occupation whereas the number of collaborators was much, much less), and it's clear – indeed, more than– that responsibility for the entire system of concentration and death camps throughout Europe must be laid at Nazi Germany's feet.[11] Obama misspoke – he was trying to indicate the physical location of the camps he had in mind – and he was quick to apologize.

---

10 See Klaus-Peter Friedrich, "Collaboration in a 'Land Without a Quisling': Patterns of Collaboration with the Nazi German Occupation Regime in Poland during World War II," *Slavic Review* 64, no. 4 (2005): 711–46.
11 On Polish collaboration numbers, see ibid., 744. There *are* estimates that as many as a million Poles collaborated. However, there are also estimates that the number is as low as 7000.

"Nazi death camps" is the correct appellation. To say that they were the creations of the Polish government or its people would be as ridiculous as saying "French death camps" or that the Waffen SS was "Norwegian" because a handful of Scandinavians served in it.[12]

Still, are there no *indirect* senses in which Europe as a *whole*, of which Poland is a *part*, may have had *some* hand in a larger picture of the Holocaust? Is there *no* way in which anti-Semitism in even far off places like America didn't contribute to a global atmosphere in which Jews and other "undesirables" might have been allowed to die, and it became easy to look away from large groups of "others" and the "different" as they were pushed around and, in roughly 11 million individual cases, killed? Indeed, were there not even Jews, Roma, Sinti, and communists *themselves* who might be seen as culpable, collaborating at particular moments or perhaps capitulating in situations in which we, with the gift of hindsight (and not being caught up in events ourselves), wish they had held out? Yes. There *were* Danes, Swedes, and Norwegians in the SS, and there were Nazi supporters in all of those countries. Social democratic welfare systems isn't the *only* history of Scandinavian states, and it's similarly estimated that 3% of *Dutch* men were members of their version of the Nazi party at the start of the 1940s (yuck). The Vichy French regime forced Jews to *register* as such (so much for the grand tradition of *liberté*) and in 1939, the U.S. turned away the ocean liner St. Louis on which hundreds of Jews sought asylum, guaranteeing that many would end up in concentration camps (which they did). And yes, in 1941, Poles, regardless of whether they were ordered to do so by the Germans or not, forced hundreds of Jews into a barn in the town of Jedwabne and burned it. Everyone in it died, and it is an ugly tragedy that sits heavily on the souls of Poles with liberal beliefs. Whether in numbers from the dozens to the thousands, local citizens and police in every occupied land helped the Nazis in ways either central or oblique: pointing a finger to where someone was hiding, taking monetary or material reward or reprise for a list of names, pretending one didn't see something one knew one had, or putting on a uniform, even of but the local constabulary, and doing the Germans' bidding. Business deals were cut, and officials were paid off to save various people's hides. Now, does that prevent Poland's World War II history – including, perhaps even primarily, for ethnic Poles – from being tragic? No. Does it mean that *Poles* didn't end up in death camps, that they didn't

---

12 BBC, "Obama Angers Poles with 'Death Camps' Remark," May 30 2012, http://www.bbc.com/news/world-europe-18264036. See also Nikolaus Wachsmann, *KL: A History of Nazi Concentration Camps* (New York: Farrar, Strauss and Giroux, 2015).

provide a near-incomprehensible amount of slave labor for German industries, or that the country wasn't point one in Hitler's crazy plan for *Lebensraum*? Clearly not. Mostly Hitler, but also Stalin, simply ravaged the country; it was bombed flat and pillaged for all it was worth. As rough as Poland had it during the Second World War, however – and it was as rough as it comes – I don't think anyone gets a free pass on the Holocaust. The history of Jew-hating throughout the West and Europe – to say nothing of skepticism of anyone outside dominant national groups – runs too deep for anyone to escape introspection, if not a modicum of guilt.[13]

Of course, then there's the question of why, beyond advancing national pride, the PiS would feel compelled to push the Holocaust issue *now*? Yes, Law and Justice may be looking to score political points. They may seek to ensure that Polish suffering isn't forgotten in an effort to bolster sentiment that the nation is good; to let Poles know that they know that Poland matters too (and that it's [the PiS] they above everyone else who will broadcast that). With *that* issue, though – the *Holocaust*? Don't people *know* that about Poland; that it was a *German* issue, and that the idea of Poland as "responsible" for the Holocaust is somehow off? As much as there might be knuckleheads out there, or people not in the know – plenty of Americans wouldn't be able to name Thomas Jefferson as the Declaration of Independence's author, e.g., or as the country's third President – it's hard to imagine few having more than the most elementary education seeing Poland as anything but deeply oppressed during World War II, or the subject of aggression. I can't think of many who'd remember any high school history that would think blame for the Holocaust lay anywhere *except* with Nazi Germany, and that Poles played much except the virtuous role. That Denmark smuggled its Jews to Sweden, that the French underground sabotaged a lot of train tracks and factories, and that the Polish Home Army coordinated a massive fight against the Germans in 1944 in the form of the Warsaw Uprising, are iconic parts of resistance-to-the-Nazis legend. They're pretty well-broadcast through education

---

13 See Léon Poliakov, *The History of Anti-Semitism, Vol. IV: Suicidal Europe, 1870-1933*, trans. George Klin (Philadelphia: University of Pennsylvania Press, 1977). See also Philip Morgan, *Hitler's Collaborators: Choosing between Bad and Worse in Nazi-Occupied Western Europe* (Oxford: Oxford University Press, 2018); Peter Davies, *Dangerous Liaisons: Collaboration and World War II* (London: Routledge, 2004). Also of interest in the collaboration debate may be Isaiah Trunk, *Judenrat: The Jewish Councils in Eastern Europe Under Nazi Occupation* (Lincoln: University of Nebraska Press, 1972), at least partially addressing the issue of collaboration by Jews themselves.

systems around the world, as well as via popular media and any number of monuments that address the past.¹⁴

As I see it, the issue is again contemporary politics. However, this time, let me place it in broader context. I'd put it this way: the powers that be in the EU are none-too-happy about authoritarian swings within European ranks, and Polish (along with Hungarian) politics have been more than a small part of the focus. For the first time in the EU's history, the twenty-eight-state bloc invoked article 7 of the Union's treaty in relation to the issue of the country's judiciary (again, the "let's give PiS the power to essentially install judges"). That means if Poland doesn't *re*-decentralize authority in relation to judiciary appointments and dismissals, it risks losing EU-bloc voting rights. That's right. An organization Poland wanted badly to *join* come the '90s is telling the country that it's now in violation of the organization's basic rules. At the time of writing, Poland was preparing its response to the EU's charges. Put simply, Poland is attempting to make a distraction. "We're nationalists, not authoritarians," they're saying. "You want to see authoritarians? Look at the Nazis or communists. Poles aren't that."

Then there's the intense levels of debate around immigration, national right, multiculturalism, identity, and tradition within Europe *in toto*. There is *massive* tension in European politics and society between more cosmopolitanly-minded citizens – liberals who have multicultural visions of European life, and who aren't worked-up about national borders – and more parochially-minded citizens who see the nation-state's *raison d'être* as involving the defense of cultural tradition and see "the nation" as a basically monoethnic group.¹⁵ Now, numbers can be hard to invoke because the EU maintains the rule that asylum seekers have to apply for asylum in the *first* EU country they reach – meaning that coastal southern states have been inordinately pounded by large waves of asylum applicants, and, hence, new residents, allowing more northerly states to say the problem isn't theirs.¹⁶ However, when Jean-Claude Junker called for EU members to lend a hand to relieve the migration burden from challenged nations

---

14 Just for example, a standard, overview history textbook like J.A.S. Grenville's *A History of the World: From the 20ᵗʰ to the 21ˢᵗ Century* (London: Routledge, 2005), 269–271, notes all three events in the space of three pages.
15 See Pippa Norris and Ronald Inglehart, *Cultural Backlash: Trump, Brexit, and Authoritarian Populism* (Cambridge: Cambridge University Press, 2019); Mabel Berezin, *Illiberal Politics in Neoliberal Times: Culture, Security and Populism in the New Europe* (Cambridge: Cambridge University Press, 2009).
16 See, e.g., Justin Huggler, "EU Court Rejects 'Open-Door' Policy and Upholds Rights of Member States to Deport Refugees," *The Telegraph*, July 26, 2017,

vis-à-vis the millions that have come to Europe over the past few years, Poland said "no." Specifically, Poland, a country of over 35 million, was asked to take a touch over 6000 souls. Again, the answer was "nope; not us."[17]

The reason? Again, culture. Now, I'm not sure what individual Poles think about immigrants. Having had some connection with the country's academic circles, my sense is that attitudes in *that* context in Poland are as liberal as anywhere else; go to a university or the progressive parts of the larger cities, and you could be in San Francisco or left-wing Paris. Urban centers are urbane, and Poland's are clearly that. That's not where PiS gets its support from, though, and it's clear they're able to get by with- if not gain appeal from- some *virulently* anti-immigrant attitudes. Perhaps the party's central figure, Jarosław Kaczyński, once proclaimed that migrants might bring "epidemics," and that they carry "various parasites and protozoa" – a set of word associations out of the "worst-of-xenophobia" playbook.[18] After the 2017 terrorist attacks in Manchester, UK, Ryszard Czarnecki, a PiS representative to the European Parliament, argued that "we, Poland, are learning from the mistakes of others…and we will not open our doors to Islamic migrants;" *religion* might now be identified as a reason for keeping people away (thank God Czarnecki wasn't in Palestine in 1946 when Jewish terrorists blew up the King David Hotel).[19] And indeed, there was no reason to accept immigrants of *any kind*, Kaczyński claimed, because they haven't been "invited."[20] On a November 11, 2017, Polish Independence Day march, tens of thousands from fascist and neo-fascist groups, proclaiming explicitly racist

---

   https://www.telegraph.co.uk/news/2017/07/26/eu-court-rejects-open-door-policy-upholds-right-member-states/.
17 See Chris Harris, "Fact Check: How Many Refugees Has Each EU Country Taken In?" *EuroNews*, September 16, 2017, http://www.euronews.com/2017/09/26/fact-check-how-many-refugees-has-each-eu-country-taken-in. Of course, this concerns the post-2015 migration crisis, related partly to the Syrian civil war, in which millions fled towards European shores.
18 See Remi Adekoya, "Why Poland's Law and Justice Party Remains So Popular," *Foreign Affairs*, November 3, 2017, https://www.foreignaffairs.com/articles/central-europe/2017-11-03/why-polands-law-and-justice-party-remains-so-popular.
19 Radio Poland, "Refusing Islamic Migrants is the Only Way of Ensuring Security: Polish MEP," June 5, 2017, http://thenews.pl/1/10/Artykul/310243,Refusing-Islamic-migrants-is-only-way-of-ensuring-security-Polish-MEP.
20 Agnieszka Barteczko and Pawel Sobczak, "Poland Has Moral Right to Say 'No' to Refugees, Says Ruling Party Leader," *Business Insider*, July 2, 2017, http://www.businessinsider.com/r-poland-did-not-invite-refugees-has-right-to-say-no-kaczynski-2017-7?r=US&IR=T&IR=T.

views, descended onto Warsaw's streets. "Pure blood, clear mind" and "Europe will be white or uninhabited," some of their signage read; they were supposedly fighting waves of migration and "atheism."[21] Law and Justice on one hand expressed regret. Foreign minister Witold Waszczykowski asserted that such views were "reprehensible." Still, knowing that the PiS' right-wing merges into groups holding *precisely* such views, PiS mayor of Stalowa Wola in Poland's southeast helped to fund a trip for right-wing activists to Warsaw for the Independence Day march. Lucjusz Nadberezny said he was looking to support "patriotism." Expressions of racism were theoretically incidental.[22]

Again, what the Holocaust law does is put a different frame around all this. It tells us that Poles are exercising a constitutional if not human right to "defend the nation." It tells us that some Poles see Poland as *for* the Poles and that they are concerned about the idea of the right to a national homeland. Some Poles are skeptical of having to help others when there's so much to take care of "at home." And, in fact, *Poles* might be victims. They're misunderstood. They're seen in the wrong light. Sure, one might be a nationalist. Again, though, we need to take a hard look at *real* xenophobia and the kind that brought *it* (the Polish nation) egregious death. Poles can only be blamed for not going with Europe's plutocratic mainstream and resisting the condescension of the EU or citified elites. Sure – don't like Poland. There's no law that it like you either, however, and even though no one really is, don't say that the country is populated by fascists or oppressors. As long as it's not oppressing or doing explicit violence to anyone, the nation has the right to make its own politics, and for the people to be what it naturally "is."

Now, as that vocabulary seeps in – "rights," or "the right" – one does have to wonder: are there *not* certain human rights issues here? *Is* Poland compelled to play along with the international community, and help with migrants when it can? *Need* the nation respond to international standards and play by rules that others set? And, indeed, doesn't making a law that insulates a national group from blame for the Holocaust transgress senses of fundamental justice and cross baselines of ideals that should never be contravened? Does it not pervert free speech principles, and tramp on a territory that should be left pristine: the ability of victims of perhaps history's worst crime to simply remain that, with all of us

---

21 Lidia Kelly and Justyna Pawlak, "Poland's Far Right: Opportunity and Threat for Ruling PiS," *Reuters*, January 3, 2018, https://www.reuters.com/article/us-poland-politics-farright/polands-far-right-opportunity-and-threat-for-ruling-pis-idUSKBN1ES0BK.
22 Ibid.

confessing to whatever role we may have played, be that role large or small? I.e., though we can understand political contexts in terms of *analyzing* the Holocaust speech law, does the thing accomplish much positive as a form of addressing a memory that asks for a higher ethics, and promotes justice as our watchword – that instead of taking extraordinary efforts to avoid a blame that few accord?

About migrants and international law, or at least international norms: as a non-jurist, I can't 100% offer specifics. I can't lead one through all the legalities of migration law or, in the most technical sense, who's obligated to do what. In general, international rights treaties say that national sovereignty is a right – and, indeed, the *inter*national system is built off such ideals. "All peoples have the right of self-determination. By virtue of that right they freely determine their political status and freely pursue their economic, social and cultural development," asserts the International Covenant on Civil and Political Rights (1966), articulating a basic principle of international law.[23] "Peoples" are supposed to be able to express their will, and determine how national life should be. Still, rights documents *also* suggest that "everyone is entitled to a social and international order in which the[ir] rights can be fully realized."[24] Regardless of your national origin or where you come from, you're supposed to have a shot at *human* rights. Yes, nations can look away and act priggish. Human rights pacts don't note precisely how *many* refugees someone's supposed to take or not. Not taking on international obligations or trading in humanitarian norms, though – never mind throwing around vocabularies that inflame situations? That's not in human rights' spirit. It's definitely a path *away* from what human rights are intended to do.[25]

Now to the speech issue. No, limiting hurtful speech isn't a rights violation. Human rights are liberal. The preeminent human rights declaration, e.g. – the UN's Universal Declaration of Human Rights – argues that "everyone has the right to freedom of opinion and expression; this right includes freedom to hold opinions without interference and to seek, receive and impart information and

---

23 United Nations, "International Covenant on Civil and Political Rights" (1966, article 1), https://www.ohchr.org/en/professionalinterest/pages/ccpr.aspx. Hereafter ICCPR.
24 United Nations, "Universal Declaration of Human Rights" (1948, article 28), http://www.un.org/en/universal-declaration-human-rights/index.html. Hereafter UDHR.
25 As noted by former UN Secretary General Kofi Annan, human rights should "cross any border, climb any wall, defy any force." I.e., you – we (and everywhere) – have them, and we should have them. They're not to complain about. See Annan, "Message by the United Nations Secretary-General," in *Reflections on the Universal Declaration of Human Rights: A Fiftieth Anniversary Anthology*, ed. Barend van der Heijden and Bahia Tahzib-Lie (The Hague: Martinus Nijhoff, 1998), 18.

ideas through any media and regardless of frontiers."[26] Rights conventions don't set limitations on speech in any *immediate* sense. However, human rights also demand inclusion and non-discrimination – the idea that no one should be marginalized or feel their access to justice diminished. "Advocacy of national, racial or religious hatred that constitutes incitement to discrimination, hostility or violence," human rights documents proclaim, "shall be prohibited by law."[27] That's the basis for hate speech laws – the notion that words aren't "only words," as one voice puts it, but words can push people into mental ghettos as much as economic and social marginalization can push them into physical ones.[28]

Poland's Holocaust speech law relates to that idea – that words can hurt. It derives from the idea that Poles are being pushed into a "mental ghetto." However, it does so in a strange way. As framed by the law, the words that can hurt are against *Poland*; not minorities, the memory of Jews, or groups that continue to suffer from prejudice or persecution. It's a relatively well-developed nation that is persecuted according to the Holocaust law – and not those from that nation who *died* in the Holocaust (and that is millions), but those in a political discussion *today*. "We have to send a clear signal to the world that we won't allow for Poland to continue being insulted," deputy justice minister Patryk Jaki offered; comments like Obama's don't fly.[29] Despite its EU membership and high living standards (among the top quarter of global nations), *Poland* is a minority somehow, and the international community is discriminating against *it*. Moreover, that's by saying it caused the Holocaust.

Again, it's a disorienting if not mind-boggling idea; how much does that *happen*? How much money does the insulting-Poland-about-the-*Holocaust* business make? Will anyone get *anywhere* in halfway intelligent political discussion by suggesting that *Poland* killed Jews and Roma, or that the crematoria at Auschwitz were *their* idea? Will anyone get anywhere by saying that *Poles* thought up Majdanek, or that Polish scientists were interested in Zyklon B? No. Indeed, if one pokes around, one can *sometimes* read or hear the term "Polish Holocaust" or "Polish Death Camp" – including from Zofia Nałkowska, a historically important Polish author.[30] There can *clearly* be stereotypes about

---

26 UDHR, article 19.
27 ICCPR, article 20.
28 Catherine MacKinnon, *Only Words* (Cambridge, MA: Harvard University Press, 1996).
29 Ginger Hervey, "Polish Senate Approves Holocaust Law," *Politico*, February 1, 2018, https://www.politico.eu/article/polish-senate-approves-holocaust-law/.
30 This comes in her "Medallions" – short stories about the World War II experience. However, *à la* Obama, the reference was to the *geographical* location of concentration

Poland, and they're not always nice (anyone who's been the butt of a Polish joke can testify to that [and for my money, those should stop]). Insofar as I can see, however, anti-Polish prejudice is hardly the world's leading discrimination issue, and, as concerns the *Holocaust*, the charges used to push through the statute have done more to bring up the idea of potential Polish guilt than any discourse playing out in the center lanes of world politics. For sure: historians of the Second World War *have* investigated culpability in the Holocaust, and Poland experts have asked what Poles contributed specifically. Reflective Poles have considered such issues vis-à-vis their own country, and intellectual circles will discuss them. Events like Jedwabne are subject to debate and liberal Poles can be concerned that the nation is conscious of such things.[31] Still, in a couple of decades of moving back and forth between two continents, dealing with thousands of university students in their twenties, hundreds of colleagues of all ages, and more than a few members of the general public, I can't think of a single example of anyone *blaming* Poland for the Holocaust. I can't think of anyone suggesting that Poles were terrible collaborators, or that there was a plan hatched in Warsaw to murder Jews (never mind Poles themselves). Awareness that significant portions of the Holocaust happened *in* Poland? That exists. Knowledge that Poles were among the Holocaust's victims, and that they were used for vicious slave labor? I've heard that. Wondering if Poland played *any* role in the events of the Holocaust – in the same manner as the Dutch, French, Croats, or Belgians? One can hear that. Again, though, the idea that Nazi Germany was the prime mover in the Holocaust is an idea so obvious that for many, it needn't even be discussed. Perhaps there is some oddball who is convinced that Canada was the driving force behind British imperialism, or that the whole thing was engineered by Australians. It's such a weird concept, though, that I can't possibly imagine the Canadian or Australian governments needing to pass legislation to suggest that such ideas are wrong.[32]

---

camps, not who was responsible for them. Thus, this is another non-contribution to the problem identified by the Polish government. My thanks to Agnieszka Pantuchowicz for the reference. See Zofia Nałkowska, *Medallions*, trans. Diana Kuprel (Evanston: Northwestern University Press, 2000).
31 E.g., Tadeusz Piotrowski, *Poland's Holocaust: Ethnic Strife, Collaboration with Occupying Forces and Genocide in the Second Republic, 1918-1947* (Jefferson: McFarland, 1998).
32 This is potentially a problematic statement in a number of ways. Firstly, is imperialism equivalent to the Holocaust? Perhaps not. Still, by those who experienced colonization, it was hardly always a benign experience. Secondly, to the extent that we would at all

And, again, the *Holocaust*? *That's* the issue on which a nation needs to make its stand? It's vis-à-vis an event that, for many, symbolizes the worst human rights violation – the nadir of politics and society – that the PiS and its allies feel the need to proclaim "it wasn't us?" And, indeed, in *2018* – seventy years *after* the fact? Among all conceptual and historical territories, might we not think of the Holocaust as the area where sleeping dogs should just be allowed to lie, allowing people's understandings and memories of events to be what they are – that as the event *was* so severe and so deeply connected to violations of dignity and senses of the self that it should never become a matter of popular politics or the need to make contrarian statements? Isn't the *Holocaust* an issue where, people should be educated about it and have correct factual information, yes, yet one can back off a bit vis-a-vis politics in the name of keeping the focus on *the event*, and not on what those whose survived may or may not, in the most particular sense, have done? Would it be appropriate for the United States to pass a proclamation absconding itself of blame for *Poland's* destruction, e.g., or Hitler's invasion of the USSR? Would it be couth for the American government to say "not our fault Poles and Russians!" even if there might be a few who would blame some allies for not jumping more directly into the war?[33]

Ranking tragedy stinks. Is the Holocaust *worse* than, say, any of the twentieth century's *other* great tragedies – e.g., the Armenian genocide, the Cambodian killing fields, the millions killed in Stalin's forced farm collectivizations of the 1930s, the victims of death squads under Latin American dictatorships in the mid-twentieth century or events from the 1990s, like Srebrenica or the mass-killings in Rwanda? There are arguments to this effect. The Holocaust involved

---

discuss Canada or Australia here, as they were raised as specific examples, the country has been involved with its own violences in relation to native peoples. The move in that context over recent history, however, has largely been to apologize for wrongdoing. Now, of course, the point in the Polish case is to *abscond* Poland of responsibility – something it of course didn't have. Again, though, was anyone in any meaningful sense *blaming* Poland? It's a question of attitude. Is one looking to have a larger discussion of general, *human* responsibility for oppression and tragedy, or is one looking to have tedious discussion of who's to blame for what when one isn't really being blamed in the first place? See Melina Delkic, "Justin Trudeau Apologizes to Canada's Native Peoples, Something the U.S. Hasn't Done Publicly," *Newsweek*, September 22, 2017, http://www.newsweek.com/justin-trudeau-indigenous-peoples-canada-shame-669696; Dierk Walter, *Colonial Violence: European Empires and the Use of Force* (Oxford: Oxford University Press, 2016).

33 See Jan Karski, *The Great Powers and Poland: From Versailles to Yalta* (Rowman & Littlefield, 2014).

vast levels of organization. It included extensive cover-ups. It involved not only killing, but a long-term, slow-drip dehumanization and the ability of surprisingly large parts of a relatively well-educated society to turn a blind eye to something they knew was taking place. It was mechanized and industrialized. It took place in the heart of a continent often advancing itself as the paradigm of enlightened rationalism – the seat of science, civilizing ideas, and concepts of education and progress. Europe had seen anti-Semitism, jingoism, and xenophobia before the '30s and '40s. Somehow, however, over a roughly twelve-year period, the "heavens darkened," as it's been put, and a special kind of evil descended over the continent that we hope we never repeat.[34]

Is that *worse*, though, than people slaughtering each other to the tune of 900,000 in ninety days, as happened in Rwanda? From reeducation camps to murdering in the name of eradicating "privileged" populations, has not communism also brought a particular variety of evil? Do we not need to shine more of a light on holocaust in the *First* World War, given that the Turkish government largely refuses to acknowledge that the Armenian genocide exists? Perhaps we need to hear the sound of "many and one" in our tragedies: the idea that each one is unique, yet that they all share the catastrophe of human destruction and violations against the inherent worth of the human soul.[35]

In any case, what we know for sure is that the Holocaust is no *less* important than other tragedies. It invaded dignity and basic humanity no *less* than other events. It ended life on a colossal scale, violating everything we should stand for. It involved torture, marginalization, stigmatization, slander, the denial of civil liberties, and unequal application of the law *as much as* any moment humanity has seen. It's an overstatement to say that rights declarations – international, human rights declarations – were a result of the Holocaust. They had been on people's minds before that, and more interests were involved in getting people to discuss rights principles than Holocaust prevention. The Holocaust had effect on rights causes, however, as "never again!" became part of the rallying cry for more effective international law.[36] And that's because the Holocaust involved no-holds-barred discrimination and the attempt to eradicate a people.

---

34 Arno J. Mayer, *Why Did the Heavens Not Darken?: The "Final Solution" in History* (London: Verso, 2012).
35 See Ben Dorfman, "The Sound of Many and One: Bergen-Belsen" in *13 Acts of Academic Journalism and Historical Commentary on Human Rights* (Frankfurt am Main: Peter Lang, 2017), 203–20.
36 See Micheline R. Ishay, *The History of Human Rights: From Ancient Times to the Globalization Era* (Berkeley: University of California Press), 2004.

It created shock, depression, and revulsion when its full extent was understood, and it generates extensive despair when we consider it now.

Now, Holocaust memory isn't untrespassable. While one can imagine it being the object of hate speech laws (in Germany, e.g., Holocaust denial is a crime), it need also be an object of open thought and speech; research into the event's empirical truths demands the ability to criticize– say, vis-à-vis issues such as the *Judenrat*.[37] We also need be clear that focus on Holocaust memory *can* overshadow other important events; it's become such a focus of memorialization that one can be concerned that, as concerns tragedy, people think knowledge of the Holocaust is sufficient, and that's it. If humanitarians aren't aware of the plight of Cambodians in the '70s or tragedies unfolding in Yemen now, they need crack open a newspaper or a history book. If they're not aware what happened to Aboriginal populations in Australia or native populations in the U.S., they should try to watch a documentary film or two. Still, the lessons of the Holocaust are as close to the untrespassable as it gets, and its significance can never be *under*played. The Holocaust is a moral touchstone for which humanity maintains responsibility, regardless of whether certain parts of humanity bear a greater part of that responsibility than others. Again, it would be shameful if the Americans said, "we're not responsible for the Holocaust – go ask the Europeans; it had to do with their mindsets." It would be reprehensible if the French passed a law that said that genocide in the First World War wasn't *their* fault – "it wasn't us; go ask the Turks!" Indeed, say, in ten years, what if the German *Bundestag* passed a resolution saying that blame for the Holocaust belongs with an *earlier* generation of Germans and that those coming from, say, the '68 generation on, *aren't* responsible – and that should be a matter of law? It'd be true. However, it'd be awful. While I hate to play this card, there's a part of me that simply thinks it shames *Poles* who were murdered and forced to build the Nazi war machine at gunpoint that their nation would do this – say we don't own *your* deaths (the millions of them), even though you're ours. It's a disjunct from those who have passed, and a distancing of oneself from experiences that we all have to mourn.[38]

---

37 See again Trunk, *Judenrat*.
38 Indeed, with the increasing popularity of the far-right *Alternative für Deutschland*, it's worth noting that the sacrosanct nature of the Holocaust in German discourse has come under threat. Figures such as Thuringian party leader Björn Höcke have argued that it's time for Germany to stop moving so heavily under the weight of the event as enough time has now passed. Höcke even went so far as to call Peter Eisenman's well-known Holocaust memorial in Berlin not far off the Brandenburg Gate a "monument of shame" – that in the sense of keeping Germany in a historical guilt spiral.

What do we have, then, as regards Poland's Holocaust speech law? What does this odd mode of national self-assertion mean, and while it's *not* a mode of "trespassing the untrespassable," what is the significance of stepping on territory which is as close to that as we get, not only for victims of the Holocaust, but for senses of humanity and basic rights projects?

This is the worst kind of politics. No one is asserting Polish culpability. We're all aware that, despite what might be occasional acts of historical hurtfulness towards some of the Holocaust's central identity groups, "Poland" isn't to blame for events. No one thinks it was Poland's idea to build Auschwitz, and no one thinks *Poles* were members of Hitler's government. Poland didn't hold the Wannsee Conference – we know that – and no one thinks Felicjan Składkowski wrote *Mein Kampf*. Poland was *victimized* by the Holocaust. Poles *died* in death camps, and *Poland* was flattened by the Wehrmacht. *Poles* were characterized as among the Slavs that Hitler hated, and the country was raped during the War – no more, no less. My sense is that to the extent that collaboration happened, it was in the same manner it happened in other places – via some anti-Semitism, yes, but also simple fear and lack of surety about what to do. That's not what the Holocaust speech law is about, however. The Holocaust speech law is an attempt to reframe *other* things. It's an attempt to reframe debates about multiculturalism, migration, and international ideals versus the role of the nation-state. It's an attempt to reframe conflict with the EU, and the PiS' interest in power. It's an attempt to tell the national community that *inter*nationalism doesn't matter and to legitimize senses that thinking beyond borders is too complex. It's a strike against globalization and an attempt to refute ideas that anything matters other than what happens to the (and one's) "people." It's a bromide against political correctness and snobbish eggheads in the cities. I'd love to say that the law helps something. It's just hard to see *what*, though, other than the PiS itself. It feels like an instance of taking advantage of banality and a world on edge and hoping no one notices while one does.

This has been followed by controversy around the writings of Wolfgang Gedeon, who has appeared to show certain sympathy for resistance to Holocaust guilt, as well as invoked the strange phrases the "Jewishization of Christian religion" and "Zionization of Western politics." See Philip Oltermann, "AfD Politician Says Germany Should Stop Atoning for Nazi Crimes," *The Guardian*, January 18, 2017, https://www.theguardian.com/world/2017/jan/18/afd-politician-says-germany-should-stop-atoning-for-nazi-crimes; Rüdiger Soldt, "AfD Politiker Darf in der Parti Bleiben," *Frankfurter Allgemeine*, January 10, 2018, http://www.faz.net/aktuell/politik/inland/afd-duldet-antisemitischen-abgeordneten-wolfgang-gedeon-15384866.html.

As regards *human rights*, or notions that Poland, or perhaps the Law and Justice party specifically, have crossed moral baselines with its law, or is operating on a kind of extra-moral terrain, I'd suggest that's correct. Again, that's *not* because the Holocaust is a more holy tragedy than anything else. It's *not* because the Holocaust *necessarily* sits on a pedestal above all other rights calamities. It's not because there's something sacrosanct about the Holocaust when that thing is missing from everything else. It *is*, though, because the Holocaust is *as* holy as anything. It's because the abuse, degradation, and murder of six million Jews and millions of others, including Poles, *is* as bad as it gets. It's because those who perished are people like us, and they're like us regardless of where we live (i.e., they were human beings). It's because any of us who have ever felt marginalized or simply misunderstood are experiencing what was blown up on an infinitely exponential scale. Law and Justice can abscond itself of responsibility for any number of world tragedies, either in Europe or anywhere else. The party can declare that it wasn't responsible for famine in Darfur, or that it's not responsible for the rise of Islamic State. It can say that it didn't have anything to do with the Bataan Death March, or that Poles weren't responsible for the Nakba in Palestine. It can say that the Poles didn't kill Kennedy or that they didn't bring the common cold to the Americas. At the end of the day, however, that's not the point. Political point-scoring and patriotism based on conspiracy theory are and, here, such points have been scored and theories been put into discourse in the cheapest and most disrespectful way.

Shirtless on a Horse
The Revenge of the Vozhd
(March 29, 2018)

Abstract: *A quarter century after the Cold War, the course of Russian democracy has been complex. That's especially with eighteen years of Vladimir Putin, who has eaten solidly into whatever gains were made by liberalism during the '90s. Many things are difficult as concerns Putin's creeping authoritarianism. Not the least of those is how his approach mixes with human rights expectations. That's not particularly well.*

Until I was eighteen – well, perhaps until I was fifteen or sixteen (a lot of Americans warmed to Mikhail Gorbachev) – the country was the bogeyman. Russia. *Russia*. My God! Of course, it wasn't "Russia" then. It was the Soviet Union, which from 1940 on consisted of fifteen republics that are today independent countries (though a few Ukrainians might want to argue with me about that as concerns Crimea and the east of the country). There were plenty of ups and downs and ins and outs as concerns Soviet history as well as our senses of it. Indeed, it was my parents' generation, and their parents too, that *really* lived through the Cold War. I remember Brezhnev, though – he led the Soviet Union

"Location Russia. Green pin on the map." @Aaqib Husnain/ shutterstock.com 1210950115

when I was a schoolboy – and I remember the pair of colorless technocrats that came after his death: Yuri Andropov and Konstantin Chernenko, each of whom ruled the country for a year or two until *they* died too. I'd heard from my folks that they and their liberal friends became more Soviet-friendly with the rise of the energetic Nikita Khrushchev and the cultural thaw that came under his rule.[1] Until Gorbachev, though, for *my* generation, it was tough to tell what about the Soviet Union one might like; it seemed an awfully soulless place where

---

1   See Polly Jones, ed., *The Dilemmas of De-Stalinization: Negotiating Social and Cultural Change in the Khrushchev Era* (London: Routledge, 2006).

moves to counter-culture were simply quashed. Gorbachev brought *Glasnost* and *Perestroika*, however, and spontaneously jumped out of limousines in midtown Manhattan to mingle with New York crowds. Disarmament and reform were on the table, and for those of us who *wanted* to like socialism, it finally seemed like something was on offer. Of course, that was Gorbachev's undoing. Hardliners didn't like his reforms, and they sponsored a summer 1991 coup against him in which they bundled him off to a Black Sea resort. It was left to Boris Yeltsin and a popular movement to defend *some* level of people's input into the Soviet system – wherein, when Gorbachev *did* return, it was his end. Save Belarus, everyone in Eastern Europe had thrown the communists out, and on Christmas Day, 1991, the Soviet Union itself closed shop. The republics went their own ways, and, while socialist China and outposts like Cuba and North Korea still existed, the Cold War *de facto* shut down.

That brought interesting times. This was the "end of history" period written about by authors like Francis Fukuyama where there was for some the idea that a worldwide liberal revolution was underway and that, after all the turmoil with fascism and communism earlier in the twentieth century, it was now clear that modicums of political freedom and market economics were global society's path forward. History was a "wagon train," Fukuyama suggested, and it had pulled into station "liberal project."[2] And, indeed, such an arrival didn't seem *im*possible in Russia. Yes, the economy's privatization led to the rise of the oligarchs and the influence of a range of shady, mobster-like characters often involved in dubious dealings with members of government. No one would place 1990s Russia particularly high on anti-corruption rankings.[3] Still, if one looks at the results of elections in the period, there seemed to be *some* level of difference of opinion, a fair amount of debate, and a not-outside-the-norm democratic spread. The first presidential election for Russia was held in '91 with communism on its last legs, and Yeltsin scored 58.6% of the vote. That's a high number, but not impossibly so. The communist candidate pulled in 17.2%, and a liberal and independent each scored north of 7. It was a lot of Yeltsin, but not all Yeltsin all the time. Results weren't dissimilar in 1996 when the first round gave victory to Yeltsin again, but five candidates gained at least 5%. Indeed, when Vladimir Putin came to power in 2000, *his* vote share was 53.4%; good, but the Communist Party candidate gained

---

2   Francis Fukuyama, *The End of History and the Last Man* (New York: Penguin, 1992), 333.
3   See, e.g., David E. Hoffman, *The Oligarchs: Wealth and Power in the New Russia* (New York: PublicAffairs, 2002).

29.5% and the candidate for a liberal party called *Yabloko* gained the smallest hair under 6%.[4] Fast-forward to 2004, though, and things started to look different. Since that election, the lowest number Putin, or his appointed wingman, Dmitry Medvedev (who sat in the Presidency from 2008–2012), have scored is 63.6% (2012) – and, generally, Putin has gotten numbers north of 70. It's been one massive landslide after another. Of course, as most of us know, in the election this March, Putin got about 56 million votes from the roughly 75 million who showed up at the polls: 76.69%. That's not just a landslide but a waterfall dislodging half the mud in the hills above the town and causing a washout in the villages below. It leaves two options; maybe three: either Russians really love Putin – he's one of the most popular politicians on earth – or the man's found a way to convince Russians there's no other choice. Or, as can sometimes be the case in politics, the truth lies in between.

Now, more has been written explaining Putin and post-Soviet Russia than I can touch on here – and for the fullest account, I encourage readers to take up the references in my footnotes. Suffice it to say that things didn't go well with privatization. How could the *Communists*, who faded into near-irrelevance everywhere else in the old Eastern Bloc, still manage to score significant points in *Russia*? The transformation of an almost completely state-owned economy into a capitalist system in such a massive country created *incredible* wealth disparity

---

4   By way of example, in the German 2017 German elections, two parties scored over 20%, and five over 7%. In the 2017 British elections, two parties scored over 40% with a third scoring over 7%. In the first round of the 2017 French Presidential elections, three candidates scored over 20%, a fourth just under, and a fourth over 6%. The point is that there was a diversity of results in the Russian Presidential elections through 2000 that wasn't unlike counterparts in other European countries. See The Returning Federal Officer, "Bundestag Elections 2017," https://www.bundeswahlleiter.de/en/bundestagswahlen/2017/ergebnisse/bund-99.html#; House of Commons Library, "General Election 2017: Full Results and Analysis," September 22, 2017, http://researchbriefings.parliament.uk/ResearchBriefing/Summary/CBP-7979#fullreport; Le Conseil Constitutionnel, "Déclaration du 26 avril 2017 relative aux résultats du premier tour de scrutin de l'élection du Président de la République," April 26, 2017, http://www.conseil-constitutionnel.fr/conseil-constitutionnel/francais/les-decisions/acces-par-date/decisions-depuis-1959/2017/2017-169-pdr/decision-n-2017-169-pdr-du-26-avril-2017.148939.html; Centre for the Study of Public Policy, University of Strathclyde, "Results of Presidential Elections 1996 – 2004," August 12, 2015, http://www.russiavotes.org/president/presidency_96-04.php; The EU-Russia Centre Review, "The Electoral System of the Russian Federation" (2011, 34), https://www.files.ethz.ch/isn/143427/Review17.pdf.

and the concentration of ungodly amounts of capital into extremely few hands (if Lenin had been alive he would have had a heart attack; twice). The state had to have cash – *someone* had to buy industries the government couldn't afford to keep – and there were a handful of men who had the resources, or could at least get access to them in the West. They either got the cash or, as was more often the case, arranged to buy concerns at a fraction of their worth because, simply, no one could offer more. Under Yeltsin, business and the state became so closely related that it was often hard to tell the two apart. Yes, elections were held, and they were done so more liberally than at any moment in the seventy some-odd years of Soviet history (having more than one party on the ballot was a decent start). A select group of unelected citizens nonetheless held decisive sway over policy, using the state as a private investment portfolio. It created some pretty tough times for a lot of Russians and made the '90s a weird blend of political optimism yet an economic wild west. A decade and a half on, a couple of those businessmen are dead. A couple are still active, living in Russia. Some were arrested; some are in exile.[5]

It was into this situation that Putin stepped – and in ways surprisingly accidental. Now, the man wasn't *un*ambitious; he had had foreign postings with the KGB (he was in East Germany when the wall came down) and he then worked for Anatoly Sobchak, former mayor of St. Petersburg and a major player in Russia's liberalization process. However, it wasn't precisely Dr. Evil scheming his way to the top, as is sometimes portrayed in the West. Many weren't sure who Putin *was* when he first hit the national scene, and he might not have gotten enough name recognition to win the presidency had he not gotten oligarch help – Boris Berezovsky being of particular importance.[6] At the moment Putin *achieved* power, though, things changed fast. For reasons that are hard to pin-down short of pop-psychological guessing, Putin near-immediately clamped down on nearly every possible threat to his preeminence and appeared willing to stop at little to ensure he couldn't be knocked off the top.[7] It's hard not to notice, for example, that Putin has run the show for eighteen years, except for the small Medvedev interlude (again, 2008–12). And, indeed, apropos that interlude, in

---

5 An excellent account of the entire post-Soviet period can be found in Arkady Ostrovsky's *Inventing Russia: From Gorbachev's Freedom to Putin's War* (New York: Viking, 2015).
6 An excellent documentary of the move from the Yeltsin to Putin years chronicling much of this may be seen in Alexander Gentelev (director), *The Rise and Fall of the Russian Oligarchs* (Paris: Point du Jour International, 2005).
7 See Steven Lee Myers, *The New Tsar: The Rise and Reign of Vladimir Putin* (New York: Vintage, 2015).

one of the most laugh-out-loud, obviously-Tammany-Hall maneuvers one can imagine, Putin simply stepped into Russia's number two spot for a few years (Prime Minister) to avoid issues with Russia's constitutionally-set term limits (à la the U.S., you're not allowed to do more than two in a row). Indeed, before *that*, in a stunning move, after earning election for the first time and feeling more comfortable in power, Putin called the oligarchs (the whole gang) into a televised meeting at the Kremlin and flat-out accused them of cheating the state; he went straight after them when he *knew* he had come to power in part due to some of their support. What happened when one oligarch (Mikhail Khodorkovsky) said, yes, there *was* corruption and the Russian system needed reform? In an arrest that looked more like an extraordinary rendition than a regular taking-into-custody, *Khodorkovsky* would be hustled off by military toughs and, in full view of TV cameras, shoved roughly into jail (images of him sitting in the docks of Russian courts are by now iconic).[8] Then, what to do in 2008 when one of the best-known Russians, chess champion and political liberal Garry Kasparov, exhibited presidential ambitions? Make sure the guy's hotel rooms are canceled, that campaign meetings are misannounced, and the man's flights can't get permission to land.[9] Fast-forward ten years. The European Court of Human Rights said that Alexei Navalny could run for the presidency in the elections just held (2018). Russia is part of the European Court, and is supposed to abide by its rulings. That was incidental to *Russian* courts, however, who disallowed Navalny to run – and, for good measure, Navalny might be arrested when calling for demonstrations to protest. Indeed, opponent-to-Russian-intervention-in-the-Ukraine-and-previous-Deputy-Prime-Minister-and-distinct-Putin-threat Boris Nemtsov may not have been murdered by Putin-hired henchmen. More than a few think that Putin's "shut down opposition at any price" attitude contributed to his body showing up in the area of the Kremlin, however, and that, at the least, Putin wasn't displeased to hear the news.[10]

---

8   Much of this is recounted well in Tina Burrett, *Television and Presidential Power in Putin's Russia* (London: Routledge, 2011). For the kind of images I'm talking about, see The Independent, "Mikhail Khodorkovsky to Vladimir Putin: You Owe Me Answers," *The Independent*, March 17, 2010, https://www.independent.co.uk/news/world/europe/mikhail-khodorkovsky-to-vladimir-putin-you-owe-me-answers-1922385.html.
9   See Gentelev; Myers, 346.
10 See David Satter, *The Less You Know, the Better You Sleep: Russia's Road to Terror and Dictatorship under Yeltsin and Putin* (New Haven: Yale University Press, 2016).

So, given all that, why isn't Putin *himself* in jail, or at least been chased out of office for self-serving corruption – off of which he's become remarkably rich?[11] Why haven't *Russians, à la* the end of the Soviet period, said, "we don't accept that *either*; we need to get someone else in instead"? It's both related to Putin's strong-arming and not – or perhaps related to his strong-arming in a couple of different ways. Point one is that it appears dangerous to oppose the man. No, Putin neither can nor does arrest everyone who runs against him, and there aren't enough police to crack down on *every* protest. Putin also wants to maintain an air of democratic legitimacy, wherein *someone* has to run against him, and parliamentary procedure has to partially play out. Still, scaring the pants off of and oppressing opponents at key moments eases the pressure on oneself; it can get others to think twice before throwing their hats in the ring. Making someone wonder what will happen next can make them swallow hard and take an extra beat before challenging the powers-that-be. One might think of it as extended gerrymandering. It's not fooling with electoral districts. It is, however, playing with the borders of the law to push others around. Indeed, it's not just Navalny or Garry Kasparov who have had difficulty getting opposition movements off the ground. It's also local figures like Andrei Osipenko, who have been victims of awful shmear campaigns, and leaders of movements such as Other Russia, who have been intimidated and undermined by operatives from Putin's party.[12]

One would also have to say that Putin's relationship with the media doesn't hurt. Now, I'll be careful here. It's not as though dissenting voices aren't allowed *anywhere* in Russia. Ksenia Sobchak, e.g., a talk show host who ran in this year's election (and, yes, the daughter of Putin's mentor), actually *assented* to the American position that the Russians meddled in the 2016 U.S. elections – an absolute no-no from the Kremlin's perspective.[13] Indeed, while there's not as much independent media as one might like, the television channel *Dozhd* has

---

11 See Mary Hanbury and Áine Cain, "No One Knows Putin's Net Worth, But Many Speculate He's the Wealthiest Person on the Planet," *Business Insider*, July 16, 2018, https://www.businessinsider.com/how-putin-spends-his-mysterious-fortune-2017-6.
12 See, e.g., Stephen White, ed., *Russia's Authoritarian Elections* (London: Routledge, 2012); Anthony J. McGann, Charles Anthony Smith, Michael Latner and Alex Keena, *Gerrymandering in America: The House of Representatives, the Supreme Court, and the Future of Popular Sovereignty* (Cambridge: Cambridge University Press, 2016); Clifford J. Levy, "Putin's Iron Grip on Russia Suffocates Opponents," *The New York Times*, February 24, 2008, https://www.nytimes.com/2008/02/24/world/europe/24putin.html.
13 Mick Krever, "Putin Challenger Apologizes for US Election Meddling," *CNN*, February 8, 2018, https://edition.cnn.com/2018/02/08/world/ksenia-sobchak-amanpour-2016-election-intl/index.html.

been a relatively constant Putin-critical voice, and journalists like Mikhail Zygar have made big splashes with books like *All the Kremlin's Men*.[14] There are critical newspapers – *Novaya Gazeta* comes to mind – and the Twitter- and Facebook-spheres, as with many places in the world, are active and involve plenty of criticism.[15] Still, as more than a few Russia observers point out, there's been heavy "securitization" of the Russian media; extensive maneuvers have been made to bring news and journalism under official influence if not state control – that often via the argument of "public safety" or resisting "foreign influence." Indeed, beyond attempting to tilt electoral news (an issue), of interest has been limiting coverage of anti-terrorism efforts as well as coverage of Russian military interventions – be they in Chechnya or Syria.[16] There has *not* been interest in having a Kremlin version of the Pentagon Papers, or journalism of the type that helped undermine American efforts in the Vietnam War.[17] Most ominous, though – and this *is* scary stuff – is that there has been a rash of journalist deaths, and they've nearly universally been critics of the Putin regime (figures like Yevgeny Khamaganov, Akhmednabi Akhmednabiyev, and Dmitry Popkov). Is there proof that the Kremlin is to blame? No. Grey zones and "edges of the law" seem to be where Putin lives. It's a lot of "*are* we on legal territory, and by what standard?"[18] Like the Nemtsov case, however, the issue might be an atmosphere or a level of authoritarianism Putin promotes leading to situations that make it dangerous to dissent; situations where actors feel empowered to go after regime opponents (or simply their own), and dynamics where it's clear that cases will remain unsolved. That's if patsies aren't indicted or authorities don't look the other way.[19]

---

14 See Mikhail Zygar, *All the Kremlin's Men: Inside the Court of Vladimir Putin* (New York: PublicAffairs, 2016).
15 See Alina Ryabovolova, "We Have Been to Bolotnya: Russian Protest, the Online Public Sphere and the Discourse of Division" in *Social Media and Politics in Central and Eastern Europe*, ed. Paweł Surowiec and Václav Štětka (London: Routledge, 2018).
16 See, e.g., Edwin Bacon, Bettina Renz, and Julian Cooper, *Securitising Russia: The Domestic Politics of Vladimir Putin* (Manchester: Manchester University Press, 2013).
17 Ibid., 84.
18 See Slater, *The Less You Know*. Timothy Snyder advances a thesis along these lines concerning not only Russia, but in fact Europe and the U.S. as well. See Snyder, *The Road to Unfreedom: Russia, Europe, America* (New York: Crown, 2018).
19 See, e.g., Andrew E. Kramer, "More of the Kremlin's Opponents Are Ending Up Dead," *The New York Times*, August 20, 2016, available at https://www.nytimes.

Now, that shouldn't undo senses that Putin maintains real popularity. Yeltsin was *not* well-liked by the time he left office in '99, and many felt he was a buffoon. "Lethargy and drinking," historian Archie Brown has written, came back to bite him (Yeltsin was famous for both), and, after a couple of years of stumbling out of automobiles and some odd press conferences, the nation seemed relieved to be led by someone new.[20] Indeed, the oligarchs were a contentious topic as some began to feel that the robber baron culture of the '90s had run out of control. Even if he needed oligarch backers to get to the top, Putin seemed to crack down on them – an attitude appreciated by many.[21] Then there was competition with the West. In fact, Putin's first move was to get *closer* to America and Europe. Tony Blair was President Putin's first official guest, and it initially appeared he got along well with George Bush, Jr. (we all remember Bush's bizarre statement that he had looked into Putin's "soul" and liked what he saw).[22] However, Putin and more than a small share of Russians felt betrayed when the West got behind the 2004–5 Orange Revolution in the Ukraine and sided with Saakashvili's Georgia in the South Ossetia conflict. Many Russians also weren't wild with the rapidity of NATO expansion, and, as it became unclear if Russia was to be seen as a partner the post-Soviet world, Putin drew back from Western-positive attitudes

---

com/2016/08/21/world/europe/moscow-kremlin-silence-critics-poison.html. See also Radio Free Europe, "Russian Journalist Dies in Unexplained Circumstances," March 17, 2017, http://www.worldaffairsjournal.org/content/russian-journalist-dies-unexplained-circumstances; Andrew Roth, "Journalist Assassinated in Violent Russian Republic," *The New York Times*, July 9, 2013, https://www.nytimes.com/2013/07/10/world/europe/journalist-assassinated-in-violent-russian-republic.html: Lucy Popescu, "Dmitry Popov," *Literary Review* 455, https://literaryreview.co.uk/dmitry-popkov. This is accompanied by ultra-conservative nationalist groups, such as the Cossack's prosecuting violence on the regime's behalf. See Oliver Carroll, "Meet the Nationalist Paramilitaries Set for an Official Role in Russia's World Cup," *The Independent*, May 12, 2018, https://www.independent.co.uk/news/world/europe/cossacks-russia-moscow-putin-rally-demonstration-world-cup-a8348221.html.

20 Archie Brown, "Transformational Leaders: Gorbachev and Yeltsin" in *Gorbachev, Yeltsin, and Putin: Political Leadership in Russia's Transition*, ed. Archie Brown and Lilla Shevtsova (Washington D.C.: Carnegie Endowment for International Peace), 30.
21 See Marshall I. Goldman, "Putin and the Oligarchs," *Foreign Affairs* 83, no. 6 (2004): 33–44.
22 See Steven Mufson, "Bush Saw Putin's Soul; Obama Wants to Appeal to His Brain," *The Washington Post*, December 1, 2015, https://www.washingtonpost.com/business/economy/bush-saw-putins-soul-obama-wants-to-appeal-to-his-brain/2015/12/01/264f0c7c-984b-11e5-8917-653b65c809eb_story.html.

and made increasing appeals to national pride. This led directly to the country's annexation of Crimea, support for separatists in the east of the Ukraine, and played into Russia's intervention in Syria on the side of Assad. What's to like about that? For many Russians, Putin has provided predictability, a sense of order, and the sense that the country need be reckoned with. He's suggested that Russia *is* a great power and that there's law and order, even if in but the figure of him. Putin has put Russia at the center of global discourse and posed it as a rival to Europe and America. It goes too far to say that Russians are simply caught up in a nostalgia for Soviet might. However, whereas, in Trump's America, not all may agree the country need be made "great again," there might have been greater consensus around the need for such a thing in the world's geographically largest state. As I've been able to determine it, most reporting on the issue suggests that whether as large as it looks or not, Putin's popularity stems from a sense of restoring national strength and the idea that the nation is being *led* – something his strongman persona helps facilitate.[23]

A few things strike me about this. Firstly, Russia's democratic deficit is troubling. Democracy is a relative concept, and more countries may have problems with it than don't. Let's take the U.S., Russia, China, Great Britain, and Germany as the world's most powerful states. One of those is distinctly undemocratic (China), another has significant trouble with the concept (Russia), and the world's supposed leader in things democratic, the U.S., was downgraded in the wake of its 2016 election by the Economist Intelligence Unit's Democracy Index from the status of "full democracy" to a "flawed" one.[24] Putin opponents end up in jail. However, Trump declares journalists the "enemy of the people" and suggests that protestors at his rallies should be "carried out on…stretcher[s]."[25] Xi Jinping has modified his country's constitution to essentially keep himself

---

23 See., e.g., Julia Ioffe, "Why Many Young Russians See and Hero in Putin," *National Geographic*, December, 2016, https://www.nationalgeographic.com/magazine/2016/12/putin-generation-russia-soviet-union/; NPR, "Pride, Patriotism and How Putin Helped Redefine What It Means to Be A 'True Russian,'" July 10, 2017, https://www.pbs.org/newshour/show/pride-patriotism-putin-helped-redefine-means-true-russian; Pew Research Center, "Chapter 3. Russia: Public Backs Putin, Crimea's Succession," May 8, 2014, http://www.pewglobal.org/2014/05/08/chapter-3-russia-public-backs-putin-crimeas-secession/.
24 The Economist Intelligence Unit, "Democracy Index 2017: Free Speech Under Attack" (2017), http://pages.eiu.com/rs/753-RIQ-438/images/Democracy_Index_2017.pdf.
25 Michael Grynbaum, "Trump Calls the News Media the 'Enemy of the People,'" *The New York Times*, February 17, 2017, https://www.nytimes.com/2017/02/17/business/

in power for life and, the idea of a free election in China? Forget it (wherein among the five named states, Germany and Great Britain become democracy's standard-bearers).²⁶ In the last years of the twenty-first century's second decade, democracy is under challenge.²⁷ That's nonetheless while it *is* a human right. I.e., whether one looks to the United Nation's Universal Declaration of Human Rights (1948) or more specific conventions such as those concerning human rights in Europe (in which, again, Russia technically participates), "everyone has the right to take part in the government of his country, directly or through freely chosen representatives."²⁸ The people are supposed to be the fount of political power – with the people allowed free exchange of ideas and the right to assemble as they wish. A "social order" in which one can realize rights should be *all* states' foundation, and that involves not only "liberty," but making people feel "secure."²⁹ One shouldn't feel "securitized," pushed around, vaguely discomforted, or discouraged to speak. Jailing people to limit competition shouldn't be politics' *raison d'être* and grabbing parts of other countries' territory shouldn't be how things go. Indeed, why participate in an organization like the European Court of Human Rights if you're not interested in its rulings (e.g., the Navalny ruling [Belarus,

---

trump-calls-the-news-media-the-enemy-of-the-people.html; Chris Deaton, "Protestor Would Be 'Carried Out on a Stretcher' in the Old Days, Trump Reminisces," *The Weekly Standard*, February 23, 2016, http://www.weeklystandard.com/protester-would-be-carried-out-on-a-stretcher-in-the-old-days-trump-reminisces/article/2001211.

26 Chris Buckley and Keith Bradsher, "China Moves to Let Xi Stay in Power by Abolishing Term Limits," February 25, 2018, https://www.nytimes.com/2018/02/25/world/asia/china-xi-jinping.html.

27 See Amanda Taub, "How Stable Are Democracies?: Warning Signs are Flashing Red," *The New York Times*, November 29, 2016, https://www.washingtonpost.com/business/economy/bush-saw-putins-soul-obama-wants-to-appeal-to-his-brain/2015/12/01/264f0c7c-984b-11e5-8917-653b65c809eb_story.html; Freedom House, "Democracy in the World: Democracy in Retreat" (2019), https://freedomhouse.org/report/freedom-world/freedom-world-2019/democracy-in-retreat.

28 United Nations, "The Universal Declaration of Human Rights" (1948, article 21), http://www.un.org/en/universal-declaration-human-rights/index.html. As concerns Europe, the primary human rights instrument is the European Convention on Human Rights, supported by the Council of Europe, and enforced through the European Court of Human Rights. Russia is party to all of those. See Lauri Mälksoo and Wolfgang Benedek, eds., *Russia and the European Court of Human Rights: The Strasbourg Effect* (Cambridge: Cambridge University Press, 2018).

29 See UDHR, article 28, 3.

e.g., doesn't even pretend; we at least know where they stand])? Ours are authoritarian times. From Warsaw to Washington to Manila, public figures are getting big payoffs for adopting the strongman pose. Macho and a lot of jutting one's chin are the political postures *de rigueur*.

Again, though, there *are* higher "moral precepts and political ideals."[30] That authoritarian posturing may be fashionable doesn't mean one *has* to choose the authoritarian path. Yes, power can come down the barrel of a gun and involve invocations of "law and order." Bullies *can* make rooms go silent, and a powerful presence can have a variety of effect. We shouldn't underestimate the power of *ideals*, however, or the meaning of setting an example. We shouldn't underestimate the authority that *moral* authority gives, or the significance of what it means to say "we tried to do right." Taking the high road *can* have meaning, including in international affairs. "Soft power" is a legitimate policy position and ranges of countries (take a Canada or a Sweden) have effect partly due to the concepts they stand for as much as gunboats or the number of fighters they can get in the air.[31] It could be an intriguing move. As a range of Western capitals struggle to keep democratic standards in place, Russia could look to exert more influence on the world stage by *heightening* democratic practice as opposed to undermining it. It could underline the importance of being a *liberal* state, and derive strength from providing examples of how *that's* done. Russia could pose itself as a rival to Europe as a *democratic* power and it could demonstrate that it's on par with America by providing lessons in civic discourse. Perhaps the country could win a *realpolitikal* war on the terrain of *ideals* – that by positing itself as *more* of a rights state than its major competitors. One imagines that Russia is laughing all the way to the bank with Brexit and the rise of Trump (those Western fools can't get out of their own way!). However, the country might be able to laugh even *harder* if it took democratic ideals to heart and promoted itself as a rights-first country. In today's political climate, Russia might stand out from the crowd.

That, however, is the rub: by *not* making that choice – and making some of the choices it does – Russia is participating, if not taking the lead, in something dark.

---

30 Samuel Moyn, *The Last Utopia: Human Rights in History* (Cambridge, MA: Harvard Belknap, 2010), 1.
31 See, e.g., Thomas Risse, Stephen C. Ropp and Kathryn Sikkink, *The Power of Human Rights: International Norms and Domestic Change* (Cambridge: Cambridge University Press, 1999); Joseph S. Nye, *Soft Power: The Means to Success in World Politics* (New York: PublicAffairs, 2009); Mai'a K. Davis and Cross, Jan Melissen, eds. *European Public Diplomacy: Soft Power at Work* (London: Palgrave Macmillan, 2013).

It's contributing to an atmosphere that *has* gripped the world – again, whether one is in New Delhi, Cairo, or the center of Ankara. It's furthering something present in both East and West, and which has a foothold in a range of places around the globe. That's an inward turn; something brooding and confrontational. It's a poo-pooing of idealism, and a banging of the drums of "sovereignty" and the "nation-state." It's an idea that memory (and often a concocted one) generally trumps progress, and a notion that inclusion matters less than "strength."[32] It's not "let's lift all boats" or show how boat-lifting is done. It's saying "this boat is mine," shooting each other in the foot while escaping the Titanic, and not caring as you run. Yes; though terribly violent, one could argue that the Ukrainian conflict hasn't wracked the *entire* country because Russia has supported eastern separatists. Perhaps Russia has prevented Kiev from just grabbing the power back, in the face of which perhaps resistance from ethnic separatists in the east might sharpen and the gates of hell might truly open. Maybe Russian support of Assad has helped beat back Islamic State, and maybe it's the right thing that there's stability as opposed to endless civil war. Perhaps liberal politics *don't* capture the people's will, and tough talk and military victories make people feel secure. Still, something's lost with that; something's diminished by endless Machiavellian schemes. Something is damaged with the shoving and strong-arming, and ongoing declarations as to who's "in charge." The ability to dissent slips away. So does the idea that we might one day disarm. We lose the notion that anything lies *beyond* the boundaries of the nation, and we lose concepts that we might not just think of the rights of nations, but the rights of *all*. We lose the idea that we might engage in a level of dignity it's our *shared* duty to inculcate, and we lose the idea that we might proffer beliefs that we might ask *all* nations to respect.

Now, I understand – Putin's not charged to think about more than Russians. He's the President of the Russian Federation, not UN Secretary-General. Also, be it UN decrees or institutions like European rights courts, the institutions of internationalism have no sanction unless *nations* agree to them. Russia can poo-poo international rulings – and, indeed, if enough nations do, they'll no longer be made. *I* can think it's ridiculous when Putin is photographed riding shirtless on a horse or when cameras capture him tramping with a rifle through the bush. Media – and some professional historians – can speculate on whether Putin's reign results from a Russian fascination with the *Vozhd*, or a centuries-long

---

32 See Derek Hastings, *Nationalism in Modern Europe: Politics, Identity, and Belonging since the French Revolution* (London: Bloomsbury, 2018), 231–58.

tradition of strongman rule.³³ International critics and cosmopolitans can belittle tough-guy postures all they want – and many, many do. Putin has to play to *his* national audience, though; it's *his* people to whom he has to speak. It's *Russians* who have to decide about Russia, and, indeed, if I, or we, try too hard to tell them how Russia should do things, perhaps *we're* meddling in *their* elections or undermining their sovereign will. For universalists and rights thinkers, it's a shame Trump got elected and that parties from Germany's *AfD* to Hungary's *Fidesz* are on the rise. It's startling to hear slogans like "Heimat statt Multikulti" ("Homeland instead of multiculturalism") in democratic countries and to watch neo-fascist marches in Debrecen or Budapest. Still, that's the primary place politics are made (in the nation). If internationalism *is* to win out, it'll have to win out there.

Nonetheless, let's not fool ourselves on what lies behind events like Russia's March 18ᵗʰ election – Putin's eighteenth year in power. Let's not say a rationale underpins that event which doesn't and let's have no illusions as to whether conditions for civil society and open discourse in the country straddling the Urals meets human rights standards. Let it not be suggested that it's not ok to look for change or hope for levels of authoritarianism to end, and let's not say that operating in grey zones is what rights states are supposed to be about. I get it: it can feel overcooked to hear "the Russians did this," "there's a problem in Russia," or "the Russians, oh my God!" If American Democrats can't beat their own strongman at the polls, they have some thinking to do. The ways of twenty-first-century politics, if not those of Russia specifically, are also complex – and, boy, did Russia's privatization program at the end of the Cold War not go well. Like with strongmen, or *Vozhd*, in other places, however – be it in Riyadh or Caracas – opposition parties *are* being squelched and dissidents keep being jailed. Laws are changed to leaders' benefit, and we see moves *away from*, as opposed to *towards*, basic rights standards. It'll be interesting to see how the next six years play out – with Presidential elections being held every six years as opposed to four another artifact of Putin's reign. At that point, Putin may be such

---

33 E.g., eminent Russian historian Richard Pipes has argued for an essential continuity between Russia's czarist period and the Soviet period because, simply, there was no tradition of "conceiving of sovereignty as something distinct from the person of the sovereign." Russia without a "terrible" or "awesome" Czar was "inconceivable." Roughly, Putin fits into this mold. Indeed, as Stephen White notes, he's not the only historian to adopt this perspective. See Richard Pipes, *The Russian Revolution* (New York: Vintage, 1990), 308; White, "Russia" in *European Political Cultures*, ed. Roger Eatwell (London: Routledge, 1997), 193.

a fixture that he can leave the shirtless propaganda behind; he might feel confident enough in power that he can leave the hunting rifle at home or say "no" to photographs in his Judo *gi*. Of course, it might be then that we really need worry; when the shirt comes *on*. That's because it might mean his grip on power so tight that it won't be necessary to put his manhood on display; he may be so assured no one's seriously coming for his office that he doesn't feel the need to be seen as the next Nicholas I. That's bad for those of us who enjoy kitschy jokes about strongmen. It's also bad for those of us who aren't wild about tough guy rule – a trend that it feels we've had more than enough of over recent years.

The Turning Point
When Will It Stop in Israel/Palestine?
(April 18, 2018)

Abstract: *The Israeli-Palestinian conflict has taken a turn for the worse. Palestinian demonstrators have been shot along the border with Gaza, and Israel retrenches itself in a "security first" position. Can we not somehow get some of the pressure relieved vis-à-vis Israel/Palestine? Human rights would demand that we find a way.*

Israel/Palestine. It's a misnomer – though also, perhaps not. Israel *is* a sovereign state – though not all of the UN's members recognize it (some thirty-one don't). The borders of the country have shifted, most noticeably after the 1967 Six-Day War, in which Israel took the West Bank, Gaza, and the Sinai (the latter being returned to Egypt in 1982). Of course, settlements have grown up extensively over the years, with the Gaza Strip largely standing in Palestinian hands while 60% of the West Bank is Israeli outposts – that while there's a question as to who the Palestinian government *is*, or at least who speaks for the bulk of the Palestinian people (Hamas largely runs Gaza; Fatah the West Bank). It's *also* while Palestinians seek the right to return to lands they were driven off of in Israel's 1948 War of Independence, or *al-Nakba*, as it's known to Palestinians ("the catastrophe"); that at the same time that more than a few Israelis would say that the 1948 war is a war they didn't want. Now, as concerns the latter point, the situation is more or less as follows: in 1947, the United Nations sought to partition what was then the "British Mandate in Palestine" via cutting the country in half and placing Jerusalem under international control; an intended compromise after decades of debate as to who had rights to the land, what parts, and why. The Jewish Agency for Palestine – the organization that would more or less become the Israeli state – accepted the plan; it'd take the larger part of the Negev desert and territory up the Mediterranean coast (Tel Aviv would be the capital). Arab authorities rejected the plan, however, as they

"Flags of Israel and Palestine painted on cracked wall" @ danielo / shutterstock.com 422767261

saw injustice in granting a state to a bunch of newcomers (the number of Jews in Israel/Palestine previous to the start of the twentieth century was small), and they were wary of the fact that few Jews would live in the new Palestine, but significant numbers of Palestinians would be partitioned into the new Israel. Out of the rejection came competing claims to sovereignty and the insistence that neither side would back down, wherein, when Israel declared independence on May 14th, 1948, war broke out essentially the next day.[1]

Unfortunately, things have little calmed down since. Despite the 1993 Oslo Accords in which the PLO (Palestinian Liberation Organization) and Israel *de facto* recognized one another, the number of days of peace throughout Israel and the Palestinian Territories – to say nothing of throughout neighboring states and borderlands – has been small. Of course, there are the famous conflicts from earlier in the twentieth century: the Suez War of '56, the Six-Day War of '67, the Yom Kippur War of 1973, and the Lebanon War of 1982. Many also know of the 1987 Intifada that led directly to the Oslo Accords: an uprising that captured world headlines due to the deeply violent clashes between the Israeli military and various stripes of Palestinian resistance.[2] *Another* Intifada emerged post-Oslo (between 2000 and 2005) and, since then, there have been intense bombing campaigns to push back against perceived militants and radicals, such as in Israel's 2006 war in Lebanon, the Gaza War of 2008–9, and IDF (Israeli Defense Forces) incursions into Gaza in 2012 and 2014. Of course, Israel bombing neighboring countries and conducting harsh crackdowns in the occupied territories isn't the whole picture. The *other* side concerns Hezbollah rocket attacks, Hamas and al-Aqsa Martyrs Brigade putting bombs on buses and blowing up discos and hotel lobbies (e.g., the Dolphinarium in 2001 and the Passover Massacre of 2002), and groups like Palestinian Islamic Jihad exploding suicide vests in marketplaces – that to say nothing of events like the murder of eleven Israelis at the 1972 Olympics, the 1976 hijacking of an Air France jet filled with Israeli Jews (leading to the famous Entebbe raid), and the fact that, at least the 1948 and 1973 wars featured Israel fighting back against multiple Arab neighbors that had invaded *it*. However, reprisals against attacks on Israel *have* been intense (the

---

1   See Benny Morris, *1948: A History of the First Arab-Israeli War* (New Haven: Yale University Press, 2008); Ilan Pappé, *The Making of the Arab-Israeli Conflict, 1947-1951* (London: I.B. Taurus, 2006).
2   See Robert Owen Freedman, *The Intifada: Its Impact on Israel, the Arab World, and the Superpowers* (Florida International University Press, 1989).

dramatic siege of Yasser Arafat's Ramallah compound or the absolute flattening Israel delivered to Jenin in 2002 are emblematic of this) and, in addition to the military incursions and crackdowns, Israel has retaliated with a not-small-number-of-assassination plots – plots that on a few occasions haven't always been carried out with pinpoint accuracy.[3] The upshot of all this is that, between 2000 and 2014, at least according to one rights agency, roughly 8100 were killed. Among those 8100, 7000 are thought to be Palestinian and 1100 Israeli.[4] Of course, that's after too many deaths from previous decades to easily count.

Violence has reared its head again. On March 30th, in what was supposed to be six weeks of peaceful protest on behalf of Palestinian right to return, things got rowdy on the Israeli-Gaza border. What happened in the most precise sense is a point of debate. *The New York Times*, for example, argued that after a build-up of some 30,000 individuals, some protestors became less than peaceful with, beyond the normal rocks, bottles, and Molotov cocktails sometimes lobbed at Israeli Defense Forces, two gunmen emerging from the crowd and firing at troops across the border. The paper reported fifteen dead and "some 1000 injured" as part of the Israeli response.[5] *Al-Jazeera* offered a different account. *Seventeen* Palestinians had died and more than *1400* were injured, and the outlet's initial reports didn't discuss gunmen or feature GIFs of demonstrators slinging rocks.[6] Of course, *Israel* claimed that Israelis live close to the areas where

---

3   See Mark Tessler, *A History of the Israeli-Palestinian Conflict* (Bloomington: Indiana University Press, 2009); Anthony H. Cordesman, *The Israeli-Palestinian War: Escalating to Nowhere* (Westport: Praeger, 2005). The most well-known Israeli assassination misfire concerned the killing of Salah Shehadeh, an important Hamas leader. Killed in 2002, Israeli forces dropped a one-ton bomb on a house in which he was located. It was overkill, killing fifteen in the area of the house, as well as within it.
4   See Adam Taylor, "The Lopsided Death Tolls in Israeli-Palestinian Conflicts," *The Washington Post*, July 11, 2014, https://www.washingtonpost.com/news/worldviews/wp/2014/07/11/the-lopsided-death-tolls-in-israel-palestinian-conflicts/?noredirect=on&utm_term=.06e7b8453f27; The Israeli Information Center for Human Rights in the Occupied Territories, "Statistics," https://www.btselem.org/statistics.
5   Isabel Kershner and Iyad Abuheweila, "Israeli Military Kills 15 Palestinians in Confrontations on Gaza Border," *The New York Times*, March 30, 2018, https://www.nytimes.com/2018/03/30/world/middleeast/gaza-israel-protest-clashes.html?mtrref=www.google.dk.
6   Al-Jazeera, "Israeli Army Kills 17 Palestinians in Gaza Protests," March 31, 2018, https://www.aljazeera.com/news/2018/03/israeli-forces-kill-3-palestinians-land-day-protests-180330100034136.html.

the conflict played out and that, as a sovereign state, its first job was to secure its citizens. And, I have to say: in a world where most of the thirty-one states *not* recognizing Israel are more or less next door and the organization governing Gaza (Hamas) doesn't recognize the country's right to *exist*, it might not be an illegitimate point. Israel has serious firepower. However, there's a question as to whether Israel has a right to be recognized, and if it's legitimate that regional players demand that it's not.[7]

Legitimacy. Battles over it lay at the heart of the Israeli-Palestinian conflict. Two peoples claim one land (hence "Israel/Palestine"), with one maintaining the backing of the world's wealthiest and most powerful states (those of North America and Europe), and the other supported by regional powers *yet* also deployed as a bargaining chip in those powers' geopolitical arguments.[8] The energy and urgency behind Israeli statehood came from the Holocaust, if not the entire history of Western anti-Semitism. From the Middle Ages through the twentieth century, the larger part of the world's Jews lived in Europe – an experience that didn't go well, the nadir being the murder of 6,000,000 at the hands of the Nazis and their collaborators. After that, what had been a relatively small movement for Israeli statehood became noticeably bigger.[9] The energy and urgency behind claims to *Palestinian* statehood (as well as Palestinian right to return) emerge from Arab peoples having been on the land now identified as

---

7 Regarding Hamas, the issue is complex. It has, apparently, accepted a Palestinian state within 1967 borders of the Palestinian territories. Its charter, however, argues that "Israel will exist and will continue to exist until Islam will obliterate it, just as it obliterated others before it." I.e., the organization is still committed to Israel's destruction, rejects the "Zionist entity" that is theoretically the Israeli state. See Yale Law School, "Hamas Covenant 1988" (1988), http://avalon.law.yale.edu/20th_century/hamas.asp; Deutsche Welle, "Hamas Recognizes 1967 Borders, Rejects Israel," May 1, 2017, http://www.dw.com/en/hamas-recognizes-1967-borders-rejects-israel/a-38656798.
8 See Judith Miller and David Samuels, "Now Way Home: The Tragedy of the Palestinian Diaspora," *The Independent*, October 22, 2009, https://www.independent.co.uk/news/world/middle-east/no-way-home-the-tragedy-of-the-palestinian-diaspora-1806790.html.
9 See Dave Vital, *A People Apart: A Political History of the Jews in Europe 1789-1939* (Oxford: Oxford University Press, 1999); John Edwards, *The Jews in Western Europe 1400-1600* (Manchester: Manchester University Press, 1994); Heiko Haumann, *A History of Eastern European Jews* (Budapest: Central European University Press, 2002); Walter Laqueur, *A History of Zionism: From the French Revolution to the Establishment of the State of Israel* (New York: Schocken, 2003).

Israel and the Palestinian Territories in numbers beyond that of other groups for hundreds of years previous to the '40s (specifically, in greater numbers than Jews) and the territory being *their* (Palestinians') ancestral homeland as much as anyone else's.[10] Now, all the big post-World War II powers (the United States, the USSR, Britain, and France) recognized Israeli independence. The British abstained from the partition vote (they were the reigning colonial power), but extended *de facto* recognition by the end of 1949.[11] Regional (read "Arab") powers did *not* recognize the new state, however, wherein Israel was left surrounded by countries distinctly less than enthusiastic about its existence; a situation in which under a million Jews faced an angry Syria, Jordan, Egypt, Lebanon, and Iraq – the nations who invaded on May 15th. However, having managed to win the 1948 war – a not unremarkable feat – the new nation jumped relatively gladly into efforts like Britain and France's attempt to reclaim the Suez Canal (the nationalization of which was an important strike for Arab nationalism), a range of covert actions against Arab enemies, and attempts to destabilize the newly formed Nasser government across the Sinai via terrorist actions of its own (e.g., the infamous "Lavon Affair").[12] Of course, on the *other* side, PLO and Palestinian guerilla shenanigans got so great that come 1970, the King of Jordan – *Jordan* (an Arab ally) – had to call on *Israeli* help lest he be overthrown by Yasser Arafat and Syria's Hafez al-Assad.[13] The PLO then moved its base of operations to Lebanon, where it engaged in not only military incursions into Israeli territory, but actions like the Coastal Road Massacre.[14] Dubious PLO tactics at certain moments aside, however (the Coastal Road Massacre was brutal), Israeli

---

10 See Dalia Ofer, *Escaping the Holocaust: Illegal Immigration to the Land of Israel* (New York: Oxford University Press, 1990); Gudrun Krämer, *A History of Palestine: From the Ottoman Conquest to the Founding of the State of Israel*, trans. Graham Harman and Gudrun Kramer (Princeton: Princeton University Press, 2008).
11 See David Cronin, *Balfour's Shadow: A Century of British Support for Zionism and Israel* (London: Pluto, 2017).
12 The Lavon Affair was the attempt to destabilize the Egyptian government, largely to *keep* British troops stationed along the Suez, by planting bombs in and around a range of sites in Egyptian cities. It was an "affair" because it was done without the consent of the Israeli government, instigated as a rogue operation by Pinhas Levon, Israeli Defense Minister at the time. See James P. Jankowski, *Nasser's Egypt, Arab Nationalism, and the United Arab Republic* (Boulder: Lynne Rienner, 2002).
13 See Jeffrey K. Sosland, *Cooperating Rivals: The Riparian Politics of the Jordan River Basin* (Albany: SUNY Press, 2007), 99.
14 The Coastal Road Massacre involved a bus hijackng that killed some thirty-eight Israelis, including thirteen children.

settlements have generally grown while, in principle, it's more than fifty years ago that Israel should have pulled back to borderlines that predate the Six-Day War.[15] It's worth noting that about 20% of the Israeli population is Arab, and the vast majority of Arabs in Israel (more than 80%) are Muslim. In neighboring *Muslim* states, there's nary a Jew to be found; they're simply not welcome.[16] That's at the same time that many Arab-Israelis feel treated like second-class citizens to the extent that, yes, Israel is a democratic and not necessarily *un*inclusive country. However, it's increasingly identifying itself as a Jewish state, and the *raison d'être* for the country *was* to provide a homeland for the world's Jews."[17] Put another way, there are a heck of a lot of ways to snipe at one another and a million ways to turn the conflict's kaleidoscope. Twist the Israeli-Palestinian conflict one way and one side appears virtuous. Twist it another way and it's the other side that commits the sins.

It's hard to make judgments in the middle of all this. Indeed, one could posit the confusion via human rights. It's undoubtedly a right to pursue national self-determination, for example; self-determination is a well-recognized *international* right. "All peoples have the right [to it]" (self-determination), assert documents like the United Nations' International Covenant on Civil and Political Rights (1966 [the Covenant on Economic, Social and Cultural Rights from the same years states the same]), and "by virtue of that right they [may] freely determine their political status and freely pursue their economic, social and cultural [goals]."[18] Peoples should be able to determine their futures in political and cultural senses; no one should be left homeless, and recognition should

---

15 See Omar M. Dajani, "Forty Years without Resolve: Tracing the Influence of Security Council Resolution 242 on the Middle East Peace Process," *Journal of Palestine Studies* 37, no. 1 (2007): 24–38.
16 There had been significant Jewish populations in Arab countries. However, upon Israeli independence, all essentially had to move to Israel as anti-Jewish sentiment in the Arab world welled high. See Malka Hillel Shulewitz, ed., *Forgotten Millions: The Modern Jewish Exodus from Arab Lands* (New York: Continuum, 2000). Exceptions of this are Turkey, with a Jewish community of 15–20,000 and, ironically, Iran, with a community of 9–10,000 Jews.
17 Nahshon Perez, "Israel's Law of Return: A Qualified Justification." *Modern Judaism* 31, no. 1 (2011): 59–84; Haaretz, "The Proposed Nation-state Law is Discriminatory and Nationalistic," February 21, 2018, https://www.haaretz.com/opinion/editorial/the-proposed-nation-state-law-is-discriminatory-and-nationalistic-1.5841526.
18 United Nations, "The International Covenant on Civil and Political Rights" (1966, article 1), http://www.ohchr.org/en/professionalinterest/pages/ccpr.aspx; United

be delivered on collective in addition to individual scales. As romantic nationalist revolutionary Giuseppe Mazzini once put it, nationhood was a way of being admitted to the "fellowship of Peoples." It was a mode of making one's presence felt, and a way of assuring that belonging intersected with rights.[19]

Still, all isn't so simple. As more than a few critics note, the "nation" and the "people" off of which it might be built can be "imagined" – they can be concepts valorized and advanced as much as truths real or concrete.[20] *Who* is the member of a nation, and are not only *we*, but the members of nations themselves, *always* sure what the terms of membership are? Does one stop being French, e.g., because one doesn't hold the passport (say a legal technicality demanded one change citizenship)? Or, conversely, is one *necessarily* French simply because one *has* the passport (say one only took a French passport for only legal or practical purposes)? Indeed, there might be something nebulous about Israeli or Palestinian identity *specifically. Must* an Israeli be a Jew, for example – part of the *ethnic* people the state was designed to support? Technically not. Still, the agency that established the first government in the country wasn't the Agency for Newly Arrived Immigrants in British Mandate Palestine. It was the *Jewish* Agency for Palestine, and it's *clearly* the notion that Israel should be *for* Jews that drives Israeli defensiveness over claims to a Palestinian right to return.[21] On the other hand, though, must *Palestinians* be descended from people originating on land that has at some point been a part of *Israel*? Would Palestinians in the West Bank *not* have been Palestinian had the territory remained under Jordanian control, wherein *Israeli* history determines who Palestinians are as opposed to Palestinians themselves?[22] In fact, Palestinians and Israelis themselves might respond differently to these kinds of issues. Christians and Muslims live in Israel and, for what it's worth, most Israeli Jews are secular. That's while one can't miss the Star of David on the Israeli flag in the same way that, go to the Scandinavian countries, and it's

---

Nations, "The International Covenant on Economic, Social and Cultural Rights" (1966), article 1), http://www.ohchr.org/EN/ProfessionalInterest/Pages/CESCR.aspx.

19 In John McKay, Bennett D. Hill and John Bucker, *A History of World Societies* (Boston: Houghton Mifflin, 1996), 841.
20 See Benedict Anderson, *Imagined Communities: Reflections on the Origin and Spread of Nationalism* (London: Verso, 1983).
21 In essence – though there are particularities – anyone with a Jewish grandparent, with proper documentation, can gain Israeli citizenship. See Perez, "Israel's Law of Return."
22 I simply point here to the problem of agency: who should control one's identity – others, or oneself? See Dorothy Holland, et. al., *Identity and Agency in Cultural Worlds* (Cambridge, MA: Harvard University Press, 1998).

hard not to notice that national standards bear the Christian cross.²³ Conversely, there are fair numbers of Christian Palestinians, and, in the PLO years, the group trod lightly around religion as a focus of the national struggle.²⁴ That's while the status of the Haram al-Sharif, containing Islam's third holiest site (the al-Aqsa Mosque), played a serious role in the breakdown of negotiations in the 2000 Camp David summit oriented partly towards creating a Palestinian state, and Hamas is *clearly* a religious movement, though its 1988 charter also refers to it as a "distinguished Palestinian movement" in the nationalist sense.²⁵ All in all, "the nation" might be a concept as wet as quicksand. That's while concrete claims to national identity play centrally in claims to states.²⁶

Still, that might be the point: one has, or at least *can* have, a sense of personhood vis-a-vis "nationality," and those sensibilities have meaning. The moment at which groups *feel* themselves to have identities may be the moment at which they become deserving of rights. When one or one's neighbors claim an "us," one or one's neighbors may have to listen. Now, the question is what that means. Take Spain. Sure, Catalonia has a distinctive culture, and independence may be popular. There's a distinct language, and perhaps even a distinct set of mores.²⁷ Still, as the plethorization of nations continues, one wonders how "micro" they'll

---

23 This is but simply to say that religion, politics and national identity can mix in interesting ways – and differently than we think. Do most Danes or Norwegians explicitly imagine themselves as religious? Evidence seems to say no. There is, however, a clear statement of institutionalized religion as central to the national culture and that, at the end of the day, the state, while providing all civil rights, prioritizes a particular set of beliefs. See Inger Furseth, ed., *Religious Complexity in the Public Sphere: Comparing Nordic Countries* (Basingstoke: Palgrave, 2017). See also Rashid Khalidi, *Palestinian Identity: The Construction of Modern National Consciousness* (New York: Columbia University Press, 1997). See also Muhammad Al-Atawneh and Nohad Ali, *Islam in Israel: Muslim Communities in Non-Muslim States* (Cambridge: Cambridge University Press, 2018); Pew Research Center, "Israel's Religiously Divided Society," March 8, 2016, http://www.pewforum.org/2016/03/08/israels-religiously-divided-society/.
24 See Gerhard Bowering, et al., eds., *The Princeton Encyclopedia of Islamic Political Thought* (Princeton: Princeton University Press, 2013), 406.
25 Hamas, "Hamas Covenant 1988" (1988), http://avalon.law.yale.edu/20th_century/hamas.asp.
26 See, e.g., Geoffrey Hosking and George Schöpflin, eds., *Myths and Nationhood* (New York: Routledge, 1997).
27 See Andrew Dowling, *The Rise of Catalan Independence: Spain's Territorial Crisis* (London: Routledge, 2018).

become. Yes, the world has diverse senses of personhood and many "we's" populate global geography. Still, how far into distinction is one willing to go before one says "we have to think in larger terms," or asks if the fracturing of "peoples" into such small units is a complete necessity. E.g., Jews often imagine themselves as a "people." They've also been *identified* as such, including for the purposes of discrimination.[28] However, would there have even been a *question* of Israeli statehood if Jews had been fully accepted in Europe, and if they weren't discriminated against within the cultures of European states? Perhaps the Israeli-Palestinian conflict could have been solved before it began – that by *not* creating the conditions under which identity needed to be thought on highly particularized terms because there wouldn't have been an issue with being a German Jew, Russian Jew, Polish Jew, and so on. That's in the same manner that one has to ask if it's *necessary* that there be histrionics about who can be part of the Israeli state or whether there *need* be a Palestinian homeland. Could it not be possible to simply say that Palestinians are part of the state of Israel – or perhaps to rename such a thing Israel-Palestine? There are a lot of peoples out there. How many nations do we want, however, and could the world afford the almost 200,000 countries we would have if all countries were the size of Liechtenstein?[29]

In this context, Israel and Palestine, or Israelis and Palestin*ians*, become caught in a deadly circle. Creating a Jewish homeland wasn't easy, nor is it easy to maintain. The first king of Saudi Arabia once said to the American President Franklin Roosevelt, for example, that he thought what happened to Jews during the Second World War was a tragedy; he hadn't the least bit of sympathy for the Holocaust. However, why take land from *Arabs*? Why not give the Jews the best part of *Germany* – something which had no chance to happen?[30] Still, if Israel had been *defeated* in the 1948 war, where would Jews have gone? If Palestine was returned to the Palestinians, would Jews have returned to *Europe*? Should *all* Jews be in America (yes, the U.S. has long had the largest Jewish population outside

---

28 See Susan A Glenn and Naomi B Sokoloff, eds., *Boundaries of Jewish Identity* (Seattle: University of Washington Press, 2010).
29 See Omar Dahbour, *Illusion of the Peoples: A Critique of National Self-Determination* (Lanham: Lexington, 2003).
30 For one, both the Western powers and the Soviet Union wanted to retain a foothold of influence as far into Europe as possible, and the middle of Germany was where the two sides met. Moreover, though thoroughly defeated, Germany remained one of Europe's most populous states with enormous economic potential – that thought its industrial base had to be rebuilt from the ground up. Finally, the simple *disbanding* of a major European nation was could have engendered significant resistance.

of Israel; however, is it really a Jewish *homeland*, and, until recently, had it really been less anti-Semitic than not)?[31] Indeed, it's distinctly unhelpful that, with a few exceptions, Israel is *not* recognized by the states around it. Recognition from Fatah, or the old PLO (brought by the 1993 Oslo Accords), is great. Still, what about Hamas in Gaza, or the phalanx of countries outside of Jordan, Turkey, and Egypt who officially refuse to say Israel should even be on a map? What about the constant proclamations about Zionism in manners that make it sound like nineteenth-century French or British imperialism (which it's not)?[32] Anti-Israeli vitriol, to say nothing of moments when it turns anti-*Semitic*, don't help. It doesn't encourage Israelis to lower their guard, moderates to pull back settlements, or anyone to ask for the building of "security barriers" to be stopped.[33]

Of course, that's in the same way that continued settlement and wall-building – to say nothing of the asymmetry of the Israeli military taking on Palestinian insurgents – drives *Palestinians* away. It's in the same manner that disdain for *Palestinian* claims to recognition and the dragging of Israeli feet vis-à-vis a Palestinian state *also* keeps tensions on edge. Who can forget the near glee with which Ariel Sharon stuck his finger in the eye of Palestinians by visiting the Temple Mount at a serious moment in the peace process in 2000, touching off a fresh wave of riots? Or, who can but help notice the way in which the Netanyahu government constantly refers to "Judea" and "Samaria" instead of discussing the "West Bank," driving Palestinian authorities nuts?[34] Who hasn't noticed that

---

31 On American anti-Semitism, see Robert Michael, *A Concise History of American Anti-Semitism* (Lanham: Rowman & Littlefield, 2005).

32 Without getting too heavily into a debate (again) about the rights and wrongs of various Israeli actions, I simply note that there are of course obvious distinctions in the territorial size to Zionist ambitions as opposed to major European imperialist projects, and that the origin of the Zionist idea lay in the search for a homeland – no the "civilization" or economic exploitation of vast tracts of the world's peoples. See Laqueur, *A History of Zionism*.

33 A recent Pew Research poll, e.g., notes that roughly 42% of Israelis believe that settlements help security. That's a significant number. In a country whose population has come to include an increasing number of religious conservatives, though, some 30% of Israelis continue to think that ongoing settlement worsens Israel's security. Ongoing violence gives one reason to think it's at least not becoming *better*. See Kelsey Jo Starr, "No Consensus among Israeli Jews on Settlements' Impact on Security," *Pew Research Center*, January 3, 2017, http://www.pewresearch.org/fact-tank/2017/01/03/no-consensus-among-israeli-jews-about-settlements-impact-on-security/.

34 See Suzanne Goldenberg, "Rioting as Sharon Visits Islam Holy Site," *The Guardian*, September 29, 2000, https://www.theguardian.com/world/2000/sep/29/israel. For

when Israel pulled out of Gaza, it proceeded to annex *new* territory by way of its West Bank border wall?³⁵ Indeed, given the state of West Bank settlements – they're all over the place – where *would* a viable Palestinian state or sovereign nation be? Histories of terrorism damage trust. The rhetorical venom that sometimes emanates from regional governments against Israel and Jews can sometimes make one cringe. However, it's 2018, not the 1970s, and Israel deals from a position of strength. Sudden attacks like in the '73 War are unlikely (they'd be universally condemned), and the bulk of the world nations backs the existence of two states. Few global players are interested in a return to hijackings, and few want suicide bombings deployed as a means of protest. Most thus get it – Israel is there to stay, and coming to terms with that is something everyone needs to do.³⁶

Indeed, it's also worth noting that the Israeli/Palestinian conflict throws fuel on the fire of *other* conflicts; it's a bolt whose loosening might relieve the pressure in a range of *further* global hot spots. In one of the rare formal interviews by Osama bin Laden, e.g., the terrorism *jefe* noted that "Americans" and "Jews" sat atop his global enemies list. "If the instigation for jihad against the Jews and the Americans in order to liberate Al-Aksa Mosque [sic.] and the Holy Ka'aba [sic.] is considered a crime," the 9/11 mastermind intoned, then "let history be a witness that I am a criminal."³⁷ Jewish-Arab tensions played into perhaps the twenty-first century's seminal event. Of course, being anti-Semitic and anti-Israel are not the same. However, the *Iranian* leadership loves to dance on the borderline, playing

---

    me, the issue isn't only the event. It's a particular, almost mercurial attitude, Sharon projected when he discussed his motivations in making the visit to al-Aqsa. This can be well seen in the Norma Percy documentary *Israel and the Arabs: Elusive Peace* (London: BBC, 2005) – late in part one, especially.

35 This was a dramatic moment in the Israeli-Palestinian conflict: the Sharon government pulled fully out of and tore down all settlements in Gaza, leaving the area fully to the Palestinians, in some ways giving the Palestinians precisely what they want. The corresponding move, however, was to expand settlement in the West Bank and continue with border wall construction, which in a number of areas steps several kilometers into West Bank territory (effectively annexing that land to Israel). See Tami Amanda Jacoby, *Bridging the Barrier: Israeli Unilateral Disengagement* (Burlington: Ashgate, 2007).

36 E.g., Amnesty International, "Jenin: Israel Must Answer Questions," April 29, 2002, https://www.amnesty.org/download/Documents/120000/mde150712002en.pdf; Human Rights Watch, "Erased In A Moment: Suicide Bombing Attacks against Israeli Civilians," October 15, 2002, https://www.hrw.org/report/2002/10/15/erased-moment/suicide-bombing-attacks-against-israeli-civilians.

37 See Rahimullah Yusufzai, "Conversation with Terror," *Time*, January 11, 1999, http://content.time.com/time/magazine/article/0,9171,17676,00.html.

to senses of non-distinction. "Zionists," they claim (Jewish nationalists?), have a *Protocols of the Elders of Zion*-like grip on world affairs, and the state *created by* Zionists should be destroyed – wherein, apparently, Iran gains the right to make mischief from Lebanon to Syria.[38] The Arab League has a position against Israeli occupations (fair enough). However, *Al-Shabaab* operatives in *Kenya* apparently feel that *they* have proclamations to make on the matter; the "Jews," the group notes, "routinely kill our Palestinian brothers." Al-Shabaab militantism partly concerns the Palestinian cause; the Israel-Palestine issue is part of the worldview involved in their attacks.[39] Indeed, returning to rights, one might note that in the Arab League's Charter on Human Rights – a "regional" rights instrument, as such things are called – "Zionism" is listed next to "racism" as a breach of basic liberty. "All forms of racism, Zionism and foreign occupation…constitute an impediment to human dignity and a…barrier to the exercise of the fundamental rights of peoples; all such practices must be condemned, and efforts must be deployed for their elimination," the Charter says.[40] We can agree with the statement on domination – conquest and making people subservient is no way to conduct politics. Still, anger towards Israel plays into a broad variety of militancies and aggressive national postures. The lack of resolution on the problem becomes a reason to abscond attitudes looking for concord.

Now, yes: rights involve sovereignty. Rights concern access to "life, liberty and security of person."[41] Rights involve legal recognition, political representation, and the sustenance of due process – all things it's questionable the

---

38 See Meir Litvak, "The Islamic Republic of Iran and the Holocaust: Anti-Semitism and Anti-Zionism," *Journal of Israeli History*, 25, no. 1 (2006): 267–84; Jeffrey Goldberg, "The Iranian Regime on Israel's Right to Exist," *The Atlantic*, March 9, 2015, https://www.theatlantic.com/international/archive/2015/03/Iranian-View-of-Israel/387085/. In terms of Iranian involvement in the region, I have in mind its role in supporting the Assad regime in Syria (brutal), it's involvement in the Yemeni civil war, its sponsoring of Hezbollah and role in Lebanese politics, as well as its deep entanglement in a *de facto* proxy war with Saudi Arabia in virtually near all further hotspots throughout the region. This is well-chronicled in David Fanning, Linda Hirsch and Martin Smith (producers), *Bitter Rivals: Iran and Saudi Arabia* (Boston: WGBH, 2018).
39 See Shaul Shay, *Somalia in Transition since 2006* (London: Routledge, 2017), 121.
40 League of Arab States, "Arab Charter on Human Rights" (2004, article 2), http://hrlibrary.umn.edu/instree/loas2005.html.
41 United Nations, "Universal Declaration of Human Rights" (1948, article 3), http://www.un.org/en/universal-declaration-human-rights/index.html. Hereafter UDHR.

Palestinians have.⁴² However, rights also involve *peace*. Rights also involve *amity* and *brotherhood* as social relations' goal. Rights involve helping people to lead *full* lives, and providing more than minimal guarantees.⁴³ Violence should be reduced, and expressive outlets should be created such that peoples *don't* have to resort to "rebellion."⁴⁴ Conditions of contentment should be established such that peoples needn't appeal to sacrifice or the nobility of martyrdom or loss. In relations between two parties, the more powerful actor shouldn't push the minority party around, and "security" shouldn't be grounds for mistreatment. Forget settlements; firing back with live ammunition, as happened at the recent demonstration, explodes peacemaking chances; it helps tensions boil over and keeps parties from the negotiating table. That's at the same time that one can *claim* that launching Qassam rockets into what remains a quite small state is a mode of legitimate protest, or that kidnapping someone you see as trespassing on your land and killing them is one's only means to fight back.⁴⁵ Taking such actions, however, while spouting vocabulary about a state or people's destruction, only shores up senses that, after hundreds of years of uncertainty, Jews had best defend themselves and using live ammo is legitimate. It justifies using settlement as a security measure, and it encourages disproportionate response in the name of assuring people "get the message."⁴⁶ It encourages the bullying tactics that one claims one is concerned to *resist*.

---

42 Yes, it's clear that Palestinian citizens of Israel maintain the same legal rights as any other Israeli, and the Palestinian Authority also provides rights and a legal framework for Palestinians in the context of the Palestinian proto-state (the State of Palestine, as the Palestinian Authority has named it). However, given the disputed status of the state *in toto*, and the confused situation concerning the status of Palestinians in general (never mind that, at the moment, Palestine is *de facto* two states), it is difficult to describe Palestinians as enjoying a full battery of essential human rights. See Ali Abunimah, *The Battle for Justice in Palestine* (Chicago: Haymarket, 2014).
43 The notion of "bare life" is taken from Giorgio Agamben, *Homo Sacer: Sovereign Power and Bare Life*, trans. Daniel Heller-Roazen (Stanford: Stanford University Press, 1998).
44 UDHR, preamble.
45 The reference here is to the 2014 kidnapping and murder of three Israeli teenagers hiking in the West Bank – the cause for another major outbreak of violence. One Hamas figure claimed the group was behind the action while the official stance of the group was that it was not. See Orlando Crowcroft, "Hamas Official: We Were Behind the Kidnapping of Three Israeli Teenagers," *The Guardian*, August 21, 2014, https://www.theguardian.com/world/2014/aug/21/hamas-kidnapping-three-israeli-teenagers-saleh-al-arouri-qassam-brigades.
46 E.g., Yotam Berger, "Netanyahu Vows to Never Remove Israeli Settlements from West Bank: 'We're Here to Stay, Forever,'" *Haaretz*, August 29, 2017, https://www.haaretz.

Now, it's not that things haven't changed. As I write, Palestinians *inside* Israel are *also* protesting for the right to return. They have been commemorating the *Nakba* and presenting an alternative view of Israeli history than that which will be portrayed by the state come the country's seventieth birthday (this May). Protestors are arguing that, even though they might be citizens, the past seventy years have looked different for them than it has for their Jewish neighbors. Theirs is not a history of *building* a home, but wondering where long-term homes *went*. Nonetheless, as Arab member of the Israeli Knesset Ahmed Tibi noted, police and military presence at the demonstration was noticeably less than usual. Despite what was happening on the border with Gaza, *within* Israel, it was a matter of democratic course that protests might take place. It's also the case that proximal neighbors *do* recognize Israel (again Egypt and Jordan [Turkey is also close by]), and though Hamas is a problem, Mahmoud Abbas, the Palestinian Authority President, has consistently presented himself as interested in peace. Yes, evangelical zealots in the U.S. waiting for the rapture who have a fear of Islam have their viewpoints megaphoned by a shamelessly pandering Donald Trump.[47] Still, at least one American government has been willing to *criticize* Israel – the Obama Administration – and even George Bush, Jr. cast occasional doubts on settlement practices.[48] Not *every* American politician says "yes" to every Israeli action, and European governments, though generally supportive, are yet more willing to ask the Israelis to back down.[49]

Nonetheless, that's while, watching protestors descend on the Israel-Gaza border and soldiers establish their lines of defense, the scene didn't *feel* progressive. Events didn't *seem* to be moving forward when soldiers opened fire, and the violence, deaths, and injuries look like what peacemakers hope to avoid. On the

---

com/israel-news/netanyahu-vows-to-never-remove-west-bank-settlements-we-re-here-to-stay-1.5446461.
47 Allison Kaplan Sommer, "Armageddon?: Bring It On: The Evangelical Force Behind Trump's Jerusalem Speech," *Haaretz*, December 11, 2017, https://www.haaretz.com/israel-news/.premium-armageddon-bring-it-on-the-evangelical-force-behind-trumps-jerusalem-speech-1.5628081; Kate Davis, Franco Sacchi and David Heilbroner (directors), *Waiting for Armageddon* (Conroe: Q-Ball Productions, 2009).
48 Peter Baker, "For Obama and Netanyahu, a Final Clash after years of Conflict," *The York Times*, December 23, 2016, https://www.nytimes.com/2016/12/23/world/middleeast/israel-benjamin-netanyahu-barack-obama.html; Matt Spetalnick, "Bush: Israeli Settlement Expansion 'Impediment,'" *Reuters*, January 3, 2008, https://www.reuters.com/article/us-palestinians-israel-bush-idUSWAT00861920080103.
49 See Sharon Pardo and Joel Peders, *Uneasy Neighbors: Israel and the European Union* (Lanham: Lexington, 2010).

surface, it was the atmosphere we don't want; it was very much what one hopes to avoid. There was fear: fear of an oppressed "Other" returning for revenge. There was anger: seventy years of petitions for better conditions under-realized and a process that has *not* brought two states. There was angst: at what point *will* it be noted that Jews deserve security, and that, while past violences can't be undone, it's important that future strikes for Palestinian statehood are taken through non-violent means? There was lack of surety: when will *Palestinians* be secure, and when will the decades-long limbo status of millions of people end? There was death. Even if there *were* some riflemen among the demonstrators, Israel can't have been surprised. It *knows* potshots will be taken over its borders and somebody's going to hurl some rocks and bottles. It knows that until it relaxes certain policies, someone will shoot rockets off of rooftops. It's also very clear from experience that live rounds kill.

For me, then, the situation is like this: there's a question as to how cooler heads will prevail and, in tense situations, who might take a step back. In situations like those playing out on the border with Gaza, there's a question of at what moment someone takes the move to stand down and says that at least *parts* of this conflict are parts they no longer want. Yes, as long as groups like Hamas hold sway, we'll have a problem. Even if it wasn't "directing" the protests (something the Israelis claim), as long as its charter includes vocabularies like "the Jews' usurpation of Palestine," any Israeli government offering anything but a staunch defense of the nation will suffer serious political damage.[50] It also can't be *that* hard for regional governments to ask protestors to give it a rest with the "death to the Jews" chants, and organizations like the Arab League *could* tone down some of their proclamations against "Zionism." Still, those who have the backing of America and the West need to realize it, and if a country wants to claim its lifeblood in democracy – which Israel does – it shouldn't appear authoritarian. There's a question of who holds the cards in concrete situations, and there's a question as to whether even large-scale demonstrations with some violence are the same as the '48 or '73 invasions. I take my model from the first Gulf War. There, Saddam Hussein, convinced he was going to show his people that the Jews and Americans were going to "get theirs," fired rockets at Tel Aviv and Haifa. Even though *Israel*

---

50 The Economist, "Politics in Israel Increasingly Nationalist: Israel's Politicians Promote Religion and Intolerance," March 20, 2017, https://www.economist.com/news/special-report/21722031-israels-politicians-promote-religion-and-intolerance-politics-israel-increasingly; Aluf Benn, "Netanyahu Deployed the Politics of Fear; It Worked," *The Guardian*, March 18, 2015, https://www.theguardian.com/commentisfree/2015/mar/18/netanyahu-politics-of-fear-israel-arab.

wasn't invading his country and there's an *Israeli* side to the Israeli-Palestinian conflict, they'd be made to pay for their injustices towards the Arabs and their allegiance with the Americans. It took massive restraint on Yitzhak Shamir's part not to respond; though ready to send jets to strike back, he didn't – and, in not doing so, he prevented regional tensions from getting worse. I.e., even if at American prompting, Shamir may have helped the Gulf War from turning into a full-blown regional conflict. One can't know for sure. However, maybe in ratcheting down its responses to things like last month's demonstrations, Israel might *defuse* some of the arguments of Hezbollah and Hamas. Perhaps the country can provide an example for better regional relations and find points of cooperation with a greater number of regional players. Indeed, instead of extending Israeli territory *out* for security reasons, if the country is concerned for its citizens' safety, perhaps it might evacuate a few houses on demonstration days or, perhaps more reasonably, create a buffer zone *inside* a specific border fence. Such things might make it less of a debate as to whether Israel fundamentally supports humanitarianism and whether it seeks peace with neighboring countries. Keeping one's finger *off* the trigger might help it be understood that Israel isn't just a "homeland," but a state concerned with concord and the basic rights of all. It might help it be understood that Israel is an inclusive state and maintains basically benevolent goals. That's because short of that, we just have killing. Short of that, we only have marginalization and the quashing of dissent. In the absence of restraint, we have but dubious security actions and endless inquiries from the UN. We have the inflammation of tensions in a geopolitical turning point – a conflict at the heart of *other* struggles, where we find *more* shooting, terrorism, and death. For any humanitarian or rights activist, that's the last thing anyone wants. And, with all respect for security, it's also something that the states with the resources and right international backing need to do their part to stop. Certain elements from the world of 1948 haven't changed. Some well seem to have, though, and in the face of rising tensions, it may be time for actors who really *do* hold the upper hand in specific situations to realize that's the case.

Tossin' Bombs and Sayin' "Uncle Tom"
Where Michelle Wolf Got it Wrong
(April 30, 2018)

Abstract: *At the White House Correspondents Association Dinner in April, comedienne Michelle Wolf engaged the Trump administration in a full-frontal and sometimes quite harsh attack. One can comprehend the upset in view of the administration's war on civility if not civil rights norms. Was her strategy the best, though? Human rights ideas unfortunately suggest not.*

It was a big deal yesterday; a *really* big deal. Writer for the American political satire show *The Daily Show*, Michelle Wolf, headlined the White House Correspondents' Association Dinner and, using what has become recent parlance, she "went there." Reacting to what's been a tough couple of years for the American press vis-à-vis the country's decided culture wars (the American media establishment, President Trump has intoned, is the "enemy of the people"), Wolf slugged back at the culture of derision emanating from the White House by getting in her own Sopwith Camel and dumping her own bag of bombs right over the side. The President of the United States engaging in everything from ridiculing journalists to demeaning fellow politicians' genitalia to making racist slurs about members of Congress (e.g., calling Massachusetts Senator Elizabeth Warren "Pocahontas")? "Like a porn star says when she's about to have sex with a Trump, let's get this over with," Wolf declared as she took the rostrum – a reference to the accusations of sexual harassment and extra-marital affairs leveled at Trump by least one Playboy Playmate and a woman who has come out as an adult film star.[1] Continually pound the drum that it's

"Video recording activity, television cameras in a row broadcasting a live media even" @i viewfinder / shutterstock.com 1292396602

---

1   See, e.g., Callum Borchers, "Why Efforts to Silence Stormy Daniels and Karen McDougal Are Failing," *The Washington Post*, March 21, 2016, https://www.washingtonpost.com/news/the-fix/wp/2018/03/21/why-are-stormy-daniels-and-karen-mcdougal-not-afraid-to-talk-about-trump/?utm_term=.4b7977a78642.

"elitist" to suggest that there's anything but two ways to view a particular social issue, as did Trump advisor Kellyanne Conway when she proposed it was fine for the President to offer up "alternative facts" (recognized untruths)? "Man," offered Wolf, "she has the perfect name for what she does. Conway. It's like if my last name was Michelle-tells-jokes-frizzy-hair-small-tits" – a reference to Wolf's diminutive appearance and the sense that the current administration has replaced evidence with fraud.[2] Get a free pass on breaking norms for which other Presidents would have been *eviscerated* – from *bragging* about sexual harassment to not showing up at events like the Correspondents' Dinner itself? "I would drag him here [myself]," Wolf said of Trump. "[However], it turns out that the president of the United States is the one pussy you're not allowed to grab" – a reference to the now-infamous pre-election *Access Hollywood* tape.[3] Claim to be interested in *empowering* women while remaining mum on the sexist comments not-infrequently emanating from the President's mouth – as is often the case with "Assistant to the President" *Ivanka* Trump? "She was supposed to be an advocate for women," Wolf maintained. "But it turns out she's about as helpful to women as an empty box of tampons. She's done nothing to satisfy [us]."[4] Then came the *coup de grâce*; the *pièce de résistance* – the "Tom Bomb," as I call it. Show up in front of the press *every day* and defend the right to non-truth in the name of vindicating "the people?" Declaim the President's propensity towards exaggeration and misinformation as somehow *ok*? "I'm never really sure what to call Sarah Huckabee Sanders, you know?" puzzled Wolf vis-à-vis the President's Press Secretary – the oft-public face of the administration. "Is it Sarah Sanders? Is it Sarah Huckabee Sanders? Is it Cousin Huckabee? Is it Auntie Huckabee Sanders? Like, what is Uncle Tom but for white women who disappoint other white women? I know… Aunt Coulter." The latter is the name of one of the U.S.'

---

2   See David Smith, "White House Correspondents Dinner: Michelle Wolf Shocks Media with Sarah Sanders Attack," *The Guardian*, April 29, 2018, https://www.theguardian.com/us-news/2018/apr/29/white-house-correspondents-dinner-michelle-wolf-stuns-media-with-sarah-sanders-attack.

3   See, e.g., David A. Farenthold, "Trump Recorded Having Extremely Lewd Conversation about Women in 2005," *The Washington Post*, October 8, 2016, https://www.washingtonpost.com/politics/trump-recorded-having-extremely-lewd-conversation-about-women-in-2005/2016/10/07/3b9ce776-8cb4-11e6-bf8a-3d26847eeed4_story.html?utm_term=.16028ca04f6d.

4   Smith, "White House Correspondents."

more abrasive conservative commentators (Ann Coulter). "Uncle Tom" is a derogatory term for those who grovel in the face of oppression, if not engage in apologies for those conducting the oppression themselves.

I'm not sure we can characterize Wolf's actions as un*fair*. The recent atmosphere around American politics *is* hard to capture, and we might note that portions of American society *have* felt ignored as mainstream values *have* become more liberal and there might be less *de facto* room in the national culture for returns to fundamentalist opinions reinvigorating traditionalisms that, though seen as God-fearing by some, have often marginalized groups from national life. As one recent article put it, "inequality" *qua* problem may have become so heavily imprinted on the American psyche that a certain momentum from mid-twentieth century civil rights movements may not to be done away with.[5] The same goes for gender. Yes, feminism may have become a "dirty word." The gains that the feminist movements brought for society at large, though? No one but the most extreme arch-conservative would suggest women as deserving of any less a degree of social opportunity than men or dispute women's equal worth.[6] Still, the backlash *has been* massive. Self-proclaimed "deplorables" bark that conservatives are ignored in the American press – that despite the fact that the cable news

---

5   Peter Beinart, "Why America is Moving Left," *The Atlantic*, January/February 2016, https://www.theatlantic.com/magazine/archive/2016/01/why-america-is-moving-left/419112/.

6   A few points. First, regarding civil rights, this isn't just a matter of general impressions of political discourse. A 2014 CBS poll suggested that 81% of Americans thought that the 1964 Civil Rights Act had been good for the country – and more to the point, only 1% thought it had been *bad* for the country. Americans accept and are favorable about civil rights, even if there's significant debate about what being "pro-civil rights" might mean. Regarding the issue of women's rights, my point is that we're in a strange, dual situation. On one hand, there's no doubt that the effects of feminist movements are felt. There is little advocating women's inequality anymore, regardless of whether *de facto* inequality persists. Still, there apparently remains significant resistance to the idea of feminism as a political concept – in part, some argue, because there is wide perception that the goals of women's equality have been met (something more than open to debate). Andi Zeisler gets at some of this when she notes that feminism doesn't necessarily have a position *outside* society anymore – in opposition to it. Instead, despite the extensive number of challenges facing women in contemporary society, many core principles of feminism – not the least of which is at least theoretical gender equality – have been bought *within* everyday culture (though sometimes to the effect of commercializing feminism, or promoting feminism as style as opposed to a mode of social critique). See Zeisler, *We Were Feminists Once: From Riot Grrrl to Covergirl®, The Buying and Selling of a Political Movement* (New York: PublicAffairs, 2016).

network with the highest TV ratings is Fox, conservative America's near-official mouthpiece.[7] For the duration of his presidency, there were insistences that the previous Commander-in-Chief – Barak Obama, partly of African descent and bearing a politics roughly in accordance with Western European norms – was either a "socialist" or a "Nazi;" that when he wasn't faced with whisper campaigns that he was either a "Muslim" or perhaps not even American at all (campaigns led by the man who is *now* President, and more than once using Fox News).[8] There have been insistences that, even *after* conservatives' 2016 win, Trump challenger Hillary Clinton be "locked up" – that because she ostensibly did something shady with classified emails, but really, one suspects, because she sometimes advocated for a secular society and occasionally suggested that *human* standards might be invoked over national ones (unpatriotic).[9] It's manna from heaven for Trump. Go after "elites" with a vengeance? Sure! Because some *imagine* that liberal snobs are out to destroy America (a sentiment Trump loves to drum up), it's fine to say

---

7   Jon Otterson, "Rachel Maddow Tops Sean Hannity in March, Fox News Host Tops 2018 Q1," *Variety*, April 5, 2018, http://variety.com/2018/tv/news/rachel-maddow-ratings-sean-hannity-1202745403/.
8   See, e.g., Fox News, "Donald Trump on 'Hannity,'" March 16, 2011, https://video.foxnews.com/v/4645819/#sp=show-clips; Fox New Insider, "Donald Trump Takes on Whoopi, 'The View' Over Obama's Birth Certificate," March 28, 2011, https://www.youtube.com/watch?v=yfZixqYuL58; Fox News, "Trump's Hunt for Obama's Birth Certificate," May 1, 2011, https://video.foxnews.com/v/4633594/#sp=show-clips.
9   See Jennifer Rubin, "What is Clinton Willing to Do on Human Rights?" *The Washington Post*, August 17, 2016, https://www.washingtonpost.com/blogs/right-turn/wp/2016/08/17/what-is-clinton-willing-to-do-on-human-rights/?utm_term=.f43e90f180fc; Sophie Tatum, "Trump after 'Lock Her Up' Chant: Talk to Jeff Sessions," *CNN*, September 23, 2017, https://edition.cnn.com/2017/09/22/politics/donald-trump-alabama-hillary-clinton/index.html. Of course, part of the conservative right's argument with "Lock Clinton Up" also concerns the controversy over her handling of the Benghazi diplomatic outpost incident as Secretary of State, above and beyond the email controversy. However, in the same way that, as of the moment, there's no concrete proof of collusion between the Trump campaign and Russian operatives vis-à-vis the 2016 election, after an FBI investigation, there simply haven't been determinations of anything *criminal* on Clinton's part. Put another way, is the level of venom levied at Clinton *really* a matter of Benghazi or a sense of a miscarriage of justice concerning emails? Or, as with most things in the current political cycle, does it concern the politics-by-anger approach that Trump encourages? See Janet Reitman, "Hillary vs. the Hate Machine: How Clinton Became a Vessel for America's Fury," *Rolling Stone*, September 20, 2016, https://www.rollingstone.com/politics/features/how-hillary-clinton-became-a-vessel-for-americas-fury-w440914.

that's how it is. The question isn't how the battle is won – it's *that* the battle is won, damn the body count along the way.[10]

Such atmospheres aren't easy to combat. I.e., if one's *own* ideology involves a sense of fair play, fighting back means doing so vis-à-vis *some* concept of reasonable discourse and within at least *vague* boundaries of civil dialog. Resisting means resisting, yes. However, it *also* means finding room in that process to listen to *everyone's* opinions and *not* just shouting down those with whom one disagrees. Arguing involves taking *measured* tones – that such that the *bases* for one's opinion might be heard because one is cognizant that one's explanations have to play out in front of others and those others may maintain different points of departure than one maintains oneself. Yes, Trump gives liberals the hives, and media with a center-left lean (which most of it has) reflects that. Trump and his politics *have been* belittled by outlets like CNN, and there *can be* a tone-deafness towards not insignificant chunks of Americans saying "we're not understood!"[11] Still, *The New York Times*, invariably referred to by Trump as "the failing *New York Times*," has never run a headline belittling Trump as "the failing U.S. President," and networks like MSNBC state that it's their *opinion* that they're suspicious of Trump's agenda – not that it's a "fact" that the man is out to destroy America. When former FBI Director James Comey took a potshot at Trump's skin tone in his recent book, *A Higher Loyalty*, it was one of few examples of a Trump's opponent publicly doing something Trump does all the time – degrading someone he dislikes on a personal basis, or through the invocation of a physical or personality trait. *Ad hominem* attacks and conspiracy theory now

---

10 . A simple case in point, now noted in almost too many media sources to list, concerns divergent reactions to Donald Trump's supposed affairs and, by conservative standards, morally questionable behavior, and the same issues regarding Bill Clinton. In relation to Monica Lewinsky, Bill Clinton was *hammered* by the traditionalist right; he was flat-out attacked. Their support for Trump in the face of *Access Hollywood*, Stormy Daniels, and Karen McDougal, however, has been essentially unwavering. What does that concern? Political victories. Trump gives arch-conservatives what they want: dismantling governmental support for reproductive rights, support for few restrictions on gun ownership, support for less separation between church and state, and a willingness to dog whistle ideas that American multiculturalism has gone too far. See, e.g., Greg Price, "Evangelical Christians Support Trump Over Alleged Stormy Daniels Affair, Despite Slamming Bill Clinton Over Monica Lewinsky," *Newsweek*, January 29, 2018, http://www.newsweek.com/trump-evangelicals-stormy-daniels-clinton-793786.
11 William A. Galston and Clara Hendrickson, "The Educational Rift in the 2016 Election," *Brookings*, November 18, 2016, https://www.brookings.edu/blog/fixgov/2016/11/18/educational-rift-in-2016-election/.

sit centrally on the American tableau, and taking that tableau back may be no easy affair. It's an issue. If you're trying to successfully combat a declared war on civility, it's hard to know if one is going to win that fight by being civil or demonstrating much sensitivity oneself.[12]

Wolf thus came out guns blazing. She came to the WHCA with the attitude that, "if you've bombed others, I'll bomb you." She flew her plane right over Trump and his associates and, in the same manner that Trump and his people allow it to be thought that his opponents are but dangerous cretins, Wolf let the world know that she saw the Trump administration as the same. Trump and his people might not be "losers." They might not be "nothings," "failures" or "jokes." "Uncle Toms" *was* on the table, however, as was comparison to tampons and regrettable sex.

There's a number of reflections one might make on this – that in terms of both tactics and justification. Let's take justification first. In general, I'd suggest that Wolf's rhetoric can be understood in the same way that one might understand the Israeli response to the murder of eleven of the country's athletes at the 1972 Munich Olympics: fighting fire with fire and the stroke of one sword with the stroke of another. I.e., in the '70s, Israel said, "if you terrorize us, we'll terrorize you. You engage in killing? Fine. We'll do the same." The country then embarked on a campaign of retribution against Palestinian militants which did precisely that – terrorize. In response to assassination and degradation, *Israel* degraded and assassinated; in response to terror, *it* scared the pants off

---

12 This is a particularly contentious point. A significant claim of those pushing back on the liberal turn in American culture is that they are the forgotten *heart* of the country, and that shouldn't be taken lightly. Many heartland and traditionalist Americans who supported Trump don't see *themselves* as involved with conspiracy theories, even when things get as far out as questioning Obama's citizenship. Such claims need be heard. However, one also need ask if *that* – such vociferous insistence on the right to *hold* conspiratorial ideas (e.g., that immigrants are simply flowing unchecked over borders, that ISIS is to be found everywhere, or that the former President wasn't an American at all) – helps national discourse. For more commentary on this, see Jeff Guo, "A New Theory for Why Trump Voters are So Angry – That Actually Makes Sense," *The Washington Post*, November 8, 2016, https://www.washingtonpost.com/news/wonk/wp/2016/11/08/a-new-theory-for-why-trump-voters-are-so-angry-that-actually-makes-sense/?utm_term=.9a85b6fc2ae3; Max Ehrenfreund, "The Outlandish Conspiracy Theories Many of Donald Trump's Supporters Believe," *The Washington Post*, May 5, 2016, https://www.washingtonpost.com/news/wonk/wp/2016/05/05/the-outlandish-conspiracy-theories-many-of-donald-trumps-supporters-believe/?utm_term=.13a03c9be76e.

of people.[13] As one scholar notes, one might not *like* "eye for an eye" mentalities. One might not be fond of confronting being pushed by pushing back. The point was to level the playing field, however, and saying, "if you're going to do wrong, don't expect us to play by rules more pristine than you."[14]

Still, that's while people *got* hurt. It's while people *were* killed and families were made to grieve. It's while lives *were* destroyed, and murder was avenged via putting *more* lives to an end. "Fighting fire with fire" is *not* just an innocent act; hurting someone is hurting someone and, as with all things done, one can't just take it "back."[15] Now, clearly: this is an incongruent comparison. Wolf didn't murder anyone and wars of words aren't physical acts of terrorism. A cultural controversy isn't a military attack. There's something hyperbolic here. Nonetheless, Wolf *didn't* take the high road, and she turned no other cheek. Instead, Wolf pointed at the red mark where she felt she'd been hit and she delivered a haymaker right back. It *was* eye for an eye justice – and the ethics of such things are open to debate.

Indeed, in terms of *tactics*, one can raise similar questions. Is it *fair* that Trump can insult with impunity or talk ridiculous smack? Is it *just* that the President can call a Senator "Pocahontas" or question the previous President's citizenship while seeking the President's chair himself? Is it *ok* that Trump can call people attempting to do their jobs (journalists) "enemies of the people" – that while the level of untruth the man is involved with himself might make *him* susceptible to such attacks?[16] No. It's frustrating and mind-blowing; one wonders why

---

13 See Aaron J. Klein, *Striking Back: The 1972 Munich Olympics Massacre and Israel's Deadly Response* (New York: Random House, 2007).
14 See David Clay Large, *Munich 1972: Tragedy, Terror, and Triumph at the Olympic Games* (Lanham: Rowman & Littlefield, 2012), 240.
15 See, e.g., Bryan Brophy-Baermann and John A. C. Conybeare, "Retaliating against Terrorism: Rational Expectations and the Optimality of Rules versus Discretion," *American Journal of Political Science* 38, no. 1 (1994): 196–210; Ariel Merari, "Deterring Fear: Government Responses to Terrorist Attacks," *Harvard International Review* 23, no. 4 (2002): 26–31; Jens Ryberg, *The Ethics of Proportionate Punishment: A Critical Investigation* (Dordrecht: Kluwer, 2004); Klaus Neumann and Janna Thompson, eds., *Historical Justice and Memory* (Madison: University of Wisconsin Press, 2015).
16 Of course, Trump supporters nor the media outlets that support him tend to view him as involved in untruths. Still, the level of exaggeration and flat-out falsehood involved in many of his public pronouncements is well-chronicled. See Glenn Kessler and Meg Kelly, "President Trump Has Made More Than 2000 False or Misleading Claims in 355 Days," *The Washington Post*, January 10, 2018, https://www.washingtonpost.com/news/fact-checker/wp/2018/01/10/president-trump-has-made-more-than-2000-false-or-misleading-claims-over-355-days/?utm_term=.148891a03cff.

he gets away with it when equivalent moves by almost anyone else would have engendered immeasurable outrage (imagine if Obama had questioned *George Bush, Jr.'s* citizenship or used a slur against Native Americans; try, for a moment, to imagine that). Still, a claim of the 40% of Americans who support Trump is that "centrists and lefties hate us; they're blowhard bougies with nothing but disinterested in the common man. They're coastal elites who don't care about flyover America, and they're unsympathetic with how a real American lives." Wolf's speech *will* be thrown back at progressives to say, "we told you so; we're hated." It'll be used as evidence that the average Joe *is* pushed around and that, for all their talk about inclusion, cosmopolitans are as dictatorial as anyone else. Wolf's bombs may put shrapnel into the leg of the *anti-*Trump movement – and if press reports are right, they may already have.[17]

So – fair enough: Wolf might have tactical problems. Extracting a pound of flesh might not be the best approach to combatting the politics of revenge. Hitting back may unleash a new flurry of roundhouse punches, with the melee trudging on. Wolf might also have a *justification* problem – that to the extent that it can at least be *complex* to see how one improves societies in conflict by contributing to conflict oneself. (Did Israel's tactics after Munich contribute to peace in the Middle East? I'm not sure.)[18] Still, the *deepest* problem with Wolf's approach may concern *human rights*. The most fundamental issue with Wolf's tack may concern our most fundamental ideals. What's the reason to combat Trumpism? Because of that – in accepting, supporting, and deploying the vocabularies of the President, we have an administration that appears to accept *not* recognizing all human beings as deserving of "inherent dignity," and which accepts *not* according people the equal worth that should be every society's guiding light.[19]

---

17 "Enough of elites mocking us," tweeted conservative activist Matt Schlapp, who was present at the dinner. Schlapp and his wife walked out, and other conservative figures joined in the accusations of cultural elitism on the part of Wolf, the national media, and the supposed liberal ruling class' part. See Martina Stewart, "Comedian Faces Criticism After Controversial Remarks at D.C. Gala," *NPR*, April 29, 2018, https://www.npr.org/2018/04/29/606834453/comedian-faces-criticism-after-controversial-remarks-at-d-c-gala. See also Ed Pilkington, "Michelle Wolf White House Routine Ignites Backlash and Defence of Sanders," *The Guardian*, April 30, 2018, https://www.theguardian.com/us-news/2018/apr/29/michelle-wolf-white-house-correspondents-dinner-sarah-sanders.

18 See Kline, *Striking Back*; Kameel B. Nasser, *Arab and Israeli Terrorism: The Causes and Effects of Political Violence, 1936-1993* (Jefferson: MacFarland, 1997).

19 United Nations, "The Universal Declaration of Human Rights" (1948, preamble), http://www.un.org/en/documents/udhr/. Hereafter UDHR. I do recognize that the Trump

In allowing *ad hominem* attacks and fanning the flames of conspiracy theory, we have a government and sector of the public that has allowed revenge to gain franchise as politics' *modus operandi* and accepted personal degradation as the currency of public affairs. In a universe in which Trump sits at the center, politics don't concern *inculcating* "freedom from fear" or creating "security of person."[20] They concern cultivating "outrages" of "conscience" and the abrogations of "brotherhood" that were the basis for institutionalizing rights in the *first* place.[21] Politics has become about making individuals feel *in*secure, and establishing cultures of "who knows what will come next?" The point becomes not *what* one tries to win.[22] It's finding a way to the top while belittling standards as for "losers" and ideals as symbols of "weakness" or a nation unwilling to "stand up for itself."

Now, I haven't the least interest in defending Trumpism. The politics of anger and fear don't excite me whether they're in Mississippi, Germany's eastern provinces or the Hungarian countryside – places where "elites are out to get us" has become a more than occasional refrain.[23] I don't like conspiracy theories leading to heightened securitization, and, if I had my druthers, I'd take some fences down as opposed to putting more up.[24] Still, it appears the case that, at a crucial

---

administration itself would likely say that it's not out to undo basic dignity (and in fact has). Again, though, how insult politics contributes to any kind of rights-based atmosphere – and doesn't risk making those one insults feel marginalized – is something very hard to see. See, e.g., Ronald C. Arnett and Pat Arneson, *Dialogic Civility in a Cynical Age: Community, Hope and Interpersonal Relationships* (Albany: SUNY Press, 1999), 74. See also Charles P. Pierce, "Who the Hell is Kellyanne Conway to Call for 'Civility'? *Esquire*, October 10, 2018, https://www.esquire.com/news-politics/politics/a23708512/chaz-tk/.

20 Ibid., preamble, article 3.
21 Ibid., preamble, article 1.
22 One can of course debate means and ends in an abstract sense. However, e.g., the Nazis may have *won* the invasion of Poland in 1939. Was that good? See, e.g., Mark R. Amstutz, *International Ethics: Concepts, Theories, and Cases in Global Politics* (Lanham: Rowman & Littlefield, 2005).
23 See Philip Oltermann, "'Revenge of the East?: How Anger in the Former GDR Helped the AfD," *The Guardian*, September 28, 2017, https://www.theguardian.com/world/2017/sep/28/is-germanys-election-result-the-revenge-of-the-east; Dariusz Kalan, "Hungary's Strongman has a Weak Spot," *Foreign Policy*, April 9, 2018, https://foreignpolicy.com/2018/04/09/hungarys-strongman-has-a-weak-spot/; Philip Alston, "The Populist Challenge to Human Rights," *Journal of Human Rights Practice* 9, no. 1 (2017): 1–15.
24 This isn't an absolute truth. Michael Walzer argues that a "politics of fear" or "negative politics" can have value when they defend values worth defending. Constant states of

moment in ongoing political debate – at a moment at which many are fighting to keep rights ideals *within* the spectrum of everyday discourse – Wolf suffered a minor brain fog. The comedienne momentarily lost her orientation and seemed to forget that, in taking an undignified approach to presenting *her* own views, she risked dinging dignity at-large. Wolf seemed to not remember that, in getting pulled into anti-humanitarian games, she risked broadening the circles of anger in which irrational tones become deepened and "we told you so" continues as the hymn of the week. It seems that Wolf didn't look at her *own* goals and consider where *humor* should go – towards *deeper* cultural understanding and bird's eye views of the issues we face. Again, that some Americans are upset doesn't give Trump license to act like a turkey or revel in drumming-up fevers of revenge. Just because American *Wutbürger* might exist in some numbers (*Wutbürger* being the German term for angry citizens on the right) doesn't mean that *Wut* (anger) should be the sentiment of the day. Still – we can only assure that we aren't governed by anger when we don't allow anger to govern *us*. We can only dial down irrationality when we bake our cakes with a measure of rationality ourselves. We can only claim victory for higher ideals when, even if we offer a few well-timed quips or jokes, it's higher ideals that *we* practice, and "I'm pissed off" becomes left at the door. One *might* posit this as a matter of tactics – the pragmatics of handling this or that situation. One could posit it as a matter of *justification* – whether "eye for an eye" is the ethics we want. For me, however, the question is the vision of the societies that we seek to *create*. The question is where we want to *go*, and staking out futures of "freedom, justice and peace."[25] The issue is *reclaiming* rights trajectories, and *stabilizing* systems that are inclusive of all. I understand that Wolf's upset may have come from surveying her atmosphere; that it may have come from senses that basic rights *are* under attack. I get that her barbs may have come from feeling barbed herself, and that she may have been wondering why "barbs" are the coinage of the day. At the *end* of the day, however, I'm not sure that Wolf captured any of rights' territory *back*; I'm not sure she conquered the high ground where we at least hope battles are won. I'm not sure she took the fight that would win the war, or that she found the lever that would bring down acrimony's walls. And, in times like these, that's what we need: victories for the "human family" as opposed to fanning flames that may chase some

---

anger, blaming and conspiracy mongering are not what Walzer had in mind, though. See Walzer, "On Negative Politics" in *Liberalism without Illusions: Essays on Liberal Theory and the Political Vision of Judith N. Shklar*, ed. Bernard Yack (Chicago: University of Chicago Press, 1996), 17–24.

25 UDHR, preamble.

of the family out. We need senses that we're out to "develop" personalities, as opposed to tearing some down. No doubt; throwing a couple of bombs can be fun. Lord knows I enjoy throwing a few myself. Carpet bombing leaves a pretty brutal landscape, however, and, at the next WHCA dinner, I'd suggest that the headline act keep a few grenades in their Sopwith. That's so that we're not all running for cover, and we can keep the focus on bringing the war to an end.[26]

---

26 The vocabularies of "human family," the development of "personality," and aspiration are from the UDHR, preamble and article 22.

June in Singapore
When Militant Authoritarians Make Peace
(May 15, 2018)

Abstract: *A bizarre but important peace summit is about to take place in Singapore: the meeting of Donald Trump and Kim Jong-un. It's a boon; from any human rights perspective, peace is important. It's tough to know how to react to peace-making processes, though, when they're engaged in by individuals who don't seem interested in peace as an idea. We have to wish Trump all possible success (and it's largely on Trump that I'll focus). It would be helpful if he believed in peace, however, and made it a higher priority in international affairs.*

It will officially be one of the more bizarre political meetings we've seen in a while: the unpredictable and bombastic if not race-insensitive and misogynistic American President, Donald Trump, with his reality show, bread and circus politics, and Kim Jong-un, the North Korean dictator who dresses like it's 1956 and leads a country where it might still be. I've done a bit of writing on North Korea in the past – in part a year or two ago in relation to its nuclear program, which I ridiculed – and it turns out that the country's nuclear technology is more evolved than I thought. Evidence seems to suggest that DPRK (Democratic People's Republic of Korea [North Korea]) is in fact on the cusp of nuclear weapons, if it doesn't already have them, and that may be accompanied by the ICBM power to deliver them.[1] There have been spectacular failures along the way: rockets falling into oceans, missiles crashing into the DPRK's own towns, anchormen- and women on state-sponsored

"USA and North Korean flags. Relations between the countries, the threat of war. that is hidden" @Andrii Spy_k/ shutterstock. com 472362958

---

1   See BBC, "North Korea's Nuclear Weapons Programme: How Advanced is It?" August 10, 2017, https://www.bbc.com/news/world-asia-pacific-11813699; Al-Jazeera, "North Korea's Nuclear Weapons: What We Know," February 20, 2018, https://www.aljazeera.com/news/2017/05/north-korea-testing-nuclear-weapons-170504072226461.html.

television delivering high-octane, belligerent proclamations *as* rockets have fallen into oceans and crashed into towns, and a lot of posturing that seemed to be just that – posturing, more or less. Things took off over the past couple of years, however, and it now seems that North Korea must be dealt with in a more definitive sense.²

Therein, in the wake of the April 27th meeting between Jong-un and Moon Jae-in, the President of South Korea, Jong-un and the *American* President will meet in Singapore in June to see what *they* might accomplish. It's a shocking turn of events. Firstly, as part of his "I don't back down from anyone" *schtick*, Trump made headlines in 2017 by suggesting that he'd be willing to rain "fire and fury" down on North Korea if they didn't back off their nuclear program – a provocative vocabulary in relation to one of the most heavily armed areas in the world (the demilitarized zone between the Koreas simply bristles with weapons).³ Trump then went before the UN (yes, the UN) and referred to the North Korean leader as "little rocket man" – reminiscent of the name-calling in which Trump engaged during the 2016 presidential campaign, yet in one of the global locales that sets the highest premium on diplomatic discourse.⁴ Of course, North Korea engaged in name-calling in response, terming Trump a "dotard," or a bumbling old man – their use of a little-used English term being

---

2   See Sung Chull Kim and Michael D. Cohen, eds., *North Korea and Nuclear Weapons: Entering the New Era of Deterrence* (Washington, DC: Georgetown University Press, 2017). See also Sofie Lotto Persio, "North Korea Test Fail Sent Missile Crashing Over One of Its Own Cities, Report Says," *Newsweek*, January 4, 2018, http://www.newsweek.com/north-korea-test-fail-sent-missile-crashing-over-one-its-own-cities-report-770392; BBC, "North Korea Rocket Launch Fails," April 13, 2012, http://www.bbc.com/news/world-asia-17698438.

3   See Peter Baker and Choe Sang-Hun, "Trump Threatens 'Fire and Fury' Against North Korea if It Endangers U.S.," *The New York Times*, August 8, 2017, https://www.nytimes.com/2017/08/08/world/asia/north-korea-un-sanctions-nuclear-missile-united-nations.html.

4   Fiona Keating, "Donald Trump Calls Kim Jong-un 'Little Rocket Man' as He Again Threatens North Korea," *The Independent*, September 23, 2017, https://www.independent.co.uk/news/world/americas/donald-trump-kim-Jong-un-little-rocket-man-north-korea-alabama-senator-luther-strange-nuclear-a7962771.html. See also Matt Flegenheimer, "Band of the Insulted: The Nicknames of Trump's Adversaries," *The New York Times*, January 5, 2018, https://www.nytimes.com/2018/01/05/us/politics/trump-nicknames.html.

the grounds for some tittering in the press.⁵ The larger point, however, seemed to be two. Firstly, on one side stood a neophyte politician representing a base of opinion in American politics that is virulently anti-communist (though one wonders if that base is always clear what communism *is*), intensely pro-military (they seem to know what *that* is), and often *very* committed to the idea that, come hell or high water, America's enemies are its enemies and those who oppose America are to be *defeated* – not tarried with at the negotiating table.⁶ On the other side is a country that, regardless of ideology, has spent the better part of its history painting the United States as the worst of villains and bases nearly its entire existence around the idea that foreign powers are out to get it.⁷ I.e., in *theory*, the people Trump represents have no tolerance for the North Koreas of the world and believe that its ideals represent a godless crime. Conversely, *Trump* represents the kind of religion-infused hyper-capitalist belief system that regimes like North Korea were founded to oppose. Of course, North Korea was never going to "defeat" the United States. It *might* carve out room for the Kims to continue as what amounts to hereditary monarchs (and *that* may be the point).⁸ Still, North Korea has been full of largess: releasing Americans held captive in the country, talking peace treaties with the Republic of Korea, sending a joint Olympic team with its southern neighbors to the 2018 Seoul games, and giving its diplomats license to use a bit more charm and pizzazz.⁹ Trump seems to have not been able to resist. Grabbing onto the North Korea "thaw" maw, he'll meet with Jong-un to discuss disarmament and, if all goes well, he's promised to

---

5   See Austin Ramzy, "Kim Jong-un Called Trump a 'Dotard.' What Does That Even Mean?" *The New York Times*, September 22, 2017, https://www.nytimes.com/2017/09/22/world/asia/trump-north-korea-dotard.html.
6   See Stephan Chan, *Out of Evil: New International Politics and Old Doctrines of War* (New York: I.B. Taurus, 2005); Peter Hay Gries, *The Politics of American Foreign Policy: How Ideology Divides Liberals and conservatives on Foreign Affairs* (Stanford: Stanford University Press, 2014).
7   See Paul French, *North Korea: The Paranoid Peninsula: A Modern History* (London: Zed, 2007).
8   See Yongho Kim, *North Korean Foreign Policy: Security Dilemma and Succession* (Lanham: Lexington, 2011). Kim's book predates Kim Jong-un's regime. The basic dynamics it illustrates, however, are those many think to be at work in the Kim regime: stirring the foreign policy pot as part of keeping loyalty to the regime intact.
9   See Motoko Rich and Choe Sang-Hun, "Kim Jong-un's Sister Turns on the Charm, Taking Spence's Spotlight," *The New York Times*, February 11, 2018, https://www.nytimes.com/2018/02/11/world/asia/kim-yo-jong-mike-pence-olympics.html.

help the DPRK get back on its feet.[10] Suddenly, the North Korean leader is "honorable" and, despite the conservative base that Trump speaks for, the attitude is no longer "no quarter to evil communists unless they renounce their godless ways." After a pretty intense amount of bluster, we find ourselves in a relatively pragmatic, "let's-start-the-negotiating-process-and-see-what-comes-out-of-it" kind of place.[11]

Now, no one who abhors war, heightened levels of global militarism, or weapons of mass destruction can be upset about this. Anyone who hopes for tensions between peoples and states to be lowered can only wish this peace process the greatest success. The Trump–Jong-un meeting, UN Secretary-General António Guterres has offered, is in the "interest of all stakeholders."[12] Regardless of whatever has come out of Trump's mouth, if the 38th parallel could become something *less* than the most militarized place on earth, peace activists should be pleased. The question of North Korean's civil rights must be brought up at the summit, Amnesty International has intoned. However, the two countries meeting need be considered "historic;" "Trump-Jong-un, the Handshake" could be a meaningful moment in the search for international concord.[13] Still, for those of us who have been committed to peace as a life-long goal, the meeting *does* raise the question of whether peace matters or "counts" the same when its processes are not only guided by people who don't seem much invested in the idea as a *belief* (peace), but who appear to enjoy trading in militancy as central to the national posture. I.e., if the American President isn't interested in concord as a *principle* and he thinks the point is American *power* – a point he frequently makes – does he deserve *credit* for any peace deal which might emerge? Or, need such a thing be dismissed as an anomaly intended to keep Trump in front of TV cameras and suggest that the world hinges on what he does? I'll focus less on the

---

10 The Guardian, "Mike Pompeo Offers Aid to North Korea in Exchange for Forfeiting Nukes," *The Guardian*, May 11, 2018, https://www.theguardian.com/us-news/2018/may/11/mike-pompeo-north-korea-aid-nuclear-weapons.
11 Quint Forgey, "Trump Praises Kim as 'Very Honorable,'" *Politico*, April 24, 2018, https://www.politico.com/story/2018/04/24/trump-praise-kim-Jong-un-547610.
12 Nick Wadhams, "UN Chief Says 'Straitjacket' on North Korea Makes Deal Possible," *Bloomberg*, May 11, 2018, https://www.bloomberg.com/news/articles/2018-05-11/un-chief-says-straitjacket-on-north-korea-makes-deal-possible-jh1fo594.
13 Amnesty International, "North Korea/US Summit: Horrific Human Rights Situation Must Not Be Ignored at Historic Summit," June 8, 2018, https://www.amnesty.org/en/press-releases/2018/06/north-korea-us-summit-horrific-human-rights-situation-must-not-be-ignored/.

DPRK. However, the same might be asked of Chairman Kim – does it matter if the guy is at all concerned about lowering global tensions, or is it ok for someone who has a history of nasty rights violations and pouring petrol on international relations to get credit for what might be an important moment in international affairs?

Such things are hard to judge. Never mind who facilitated bringing the parties to the table (many point to President Moon); peace involves making odd bedfellows.[14] Watch Richard Nixon shake hands with Mao Tse-Tung and one gets the idea – outside of Trump and Jong-un, one couldn't have seen a more divergent blend of ideologies and styles: the obsequious-to-the-point-of-smarmy Nixon, defending conservative America's "silent majority," and the hardened revolutionary and committed Marxist Tse-Tung, veteran of the "Long March."[15] Barak Obama got together with some interesting characters during his time in the Oval Office, first vis-à-vis trying to get Syria to give up its chemical weapons (a deal cut between the U.S., Russia, and the Assad regime), and then again in trying to slow Iran's progress towards its own nuclear bomb (the 2015 nuclear deal).[16] The Yitzhak Rabin-Yasser Arafat handshake was an interesting one (a couple of guys who had near-literally been at each other's throats), and who could forget Nelson Mandela breaking bread with F.W. de Klerk – the anti-Apartheid revolutionary and the former defender of the white minority rule system?[17] Those are long ways to go; middle ground is peace's territory. Of course, the concept of "middle ground" only makes sense if parties have stood on genuinely different sides.[18]

---

14 See Daniel Levy, "Trump is Following, Not Leading," *Foreign Policy*, May 11, 2018, http://foreignpolicy.com/2018/05/11/trump-is-leading-from-behind-if-hes-leading-at-all/; The New York Times, "The Daily: The Prospect of Peace with North Korea," March 14, 2018, https://www.nytimes.com/2018/05/14/podcasts/the-daily/donald-trump-north-korea-summit.html.
15 The "Long March" was highly arduous, year-long retreat over 1934-5 by the communists in the Chinese civil war which extended over thousands of kilometers around a great deal of the Chinese landmass which saved communist forces. It's legendary in communist lore. See Sun Shuyun, *The Long March* (New York: Harper, 2006).
16 See Kilic Bugra Kanat, *A Tale of Four Augusts: Obama's Syria Policy* (Istanbul: Seta, 2015); Trita Parsi, *Losing an Enemy: Obama, Iran, and the Triumph of Diplomacy* New Haven: Yale University Press, 2017).
17 See Bruce Jentelson, *The Peacemakers: Leadership Lessons from Twentieth Century Statesmanship* (New York: W.W. Norton, 2018).
18 See, e.g., Susan Allen Nan, Zachariah Cherian Mampilly and Andrea Bartoli, eds., *Peacemaking: From Practice to Theory*, 2 vols. (Denver: Praeger, 2011).

That is while there *are* differences in attitude that paint some of the above scenarios in different tones than Trump's meeting with Jong-un. If one looks carefully, e.g., Obama placed a consistently high premium on the judicious use of force. That's a way to understand what in the U.S. are often seen as his most significant foreign policy *blunders*: his non-enforcement of the 2012 "red line" concerning Bashar al-Assad's use of chemical weapons, and his announcement of an exit date for the troops sent in the 2009 Afghanistan "surge." I.e., after roughly a decade of war and charges of a "clash of civilizations" prosecuted by the Bush, Jr. administration, Obama sought to tone the situation down. He took policy routes via which America might not only be understood as the global "heavy," but a country that sought *reasonable* relations with multiple actors and took a variety of perspectives into account.[19] Of course, Nixon drove the Vietnam War to its absolute height. He was a villain to the popular movements that opposed Western involvement in Southeast Asia. Still, there was a tradition in the Cold War of various sides claiming they were interested in concord as socialists and liberals *both* claimed their ideologies as grounded in attempts to find the better world. Both claimed that they sought social progress, and both argued that that freedom is what one gained when their systems worked as they should. Yes, "national strength" played into various sides' rhetoric: Mao, the Soviets, the Viet Minh, the United States – all appealed to the national ideal. Something larger was *also* supposedly at play, however – something that involved liberation, natural freedom, and the idea that, from time to time, despite the turmoil, such "larger" things might become real.[20]

With Trump, there have been very few overtures to "larger things." Generally, his philosophy has been that America is best when it's strong, and that's it. "America First!" Trump proclaims, and whatever happens with the world around the United States is *its* business. Waterboarding? A crime against humanity, but let's bring it back![21]

---

19 See, e.g., Michelle Bentley and Jack Holland, eds., *The Obama Doctrine: A Legacy of Continuity in US Foreign Policy?* (London: Routledge, 2017); Michael Clarke and Anthony Ricketts, "Did Obama Have a Grand Strategy?" *Journal of Strategic Studies* 40, no. 1–2 (2017): 295–324.

20 See David C. Engerman, "Ideology and the Origins of the Cold War: 1917–1962" in *The Cambridge History of the Cold War: Volume 1: Origins*, ed. Melvyn P. Leffler and Odd Arne Westad (Cambridge: Cambridge University Press, 2010), 20–43.

21 BBC News, "Donald Trump Says He Believes Waterboarding Works," January 26, 2017, https://www.bbc.com/news/world-us-canada-38753000.

Islamic State? "Bomb the shit out of 'em!" – a direct quote.[22] Afghanistan? Maybe we should pull out. However, not before using the deadliest non-nuclear weapon in the American arsenal – a weapon no Commander-in-Chief had been willing to use before.[23] Iran upholding its end of the nuclear deal? Not good enough – punish them whether America's allies agree or not. North Korea *before* Trump's turn? My nuclear button is "bigger and more powerful" than "his," tweeted Trump; no puny Cold War leftover would suggest it could take down the twenty-first century's global behemoth (and, yes, we all caught the phallic reference).[24] Leave liberalism versus communism aside – the world is a mano-a-mano face-off in which it's a national shame if Trump doesn't come out on top. It's hard to know where in that one can read, "if they step down, we'll back off too." It's hard to know where in there we hear, "we might be interested in strength, but it's strength for a purpose – peace and rights." Of course, such things would demand a different slogan. "America First!" would have to be replaced with "America for a Reason!"

In a way, none of this surprises. *Massive* dimensions of Trump's popularity stems from him saying out loud what it seems more than a few Americans think. The larger portion of the nation appears to see the stick as opposed to the carrot as the answer to dealing with the bulk of its opponents; previous to Trump's decision to go to Singapore, e.g., the Pew Research Center noted 61% of Americans as viewing sanctions as opposed to negotiation as the way to deal with the Jong-un regime. Americans tend not to like North Korea, and most think the U.S. shouldn't be doing it favors (wherein, one wonders what the public reaction would be if *Obama*, and not Trump, had decided to meet with Jong-un).[25] Those on the American *left* (for the purposes of the survey, supporters of the Democratic Party) tend to view peacemaking organizations like the UN

---

22 See, e.g., Bob Dreyfuss, "The World is Getting a Taste of the Trump Doctrine," *Rolling Stone*, April 14, 2017, https://www.rollingstone.com/politics/features/the-world-is-getting-a-taste-of-the-trump-doctrine-w476839.
23 This is the co-called "MOAB" – Mother of All Bombs. See Robin Wright, "Trump Drops the Mother of All Bombs on Afghanistan," *The New Yorker*, April 14, 2017, https://www.newyorker.com/news/news-desk/trump-drops-the-mother-of-all-bombs-on-afghanistan.
24 Lauren Gambino, "Donald Trump Boasts That His Nuclear Button is Bigger than Kim Jong-un's," *The Guardian*, January 3, 2018, https://www.theguardian.com/us-news/2018/jan/03/donald-trump-boasts-nuclear-button-bigger-kim-jong-un..
25 See Jacob Poushter, "Americans Hold Very Negative Views of North Korea Amid Nuclear Tensions," *Pew Research Center*, April 5, 2017, http://www.

positively (81%); many *would* be interested in negotiations with North Korea and see the institutions of peace as the way forward. Those identifying themselves as *Republicans*, however (the vast majority of whom supported Trump [93%]), take a much dimmer view of organizations such as the UN (only 44% of Republicans view it positively), and 68% of Republicans – again, Trump's party – believe that using military force preemptively (before one is attacked oneself) is for the most part ok.[26] It's also the case that the number of Republicans who think it essential to be open to people outside the U.S. comes in at around 50% – that as opposed to the 85% or so of Democrats who see foreigners in a positive light.[27] On today's American right – from where the bulk of Trump's support comes – no one was going to garner much support with policies of internationalism and peace at the head of the agenda. Trump captured something in his economic-populist appeal to blue-collar voters. He also hit a note on foreign affairs, however, as the average Republican wants tough talk about the country's enemies, is skeptical of those not carrying American passports, and isn't wild about internationalism *qua* ideal. Be it withdrawal from the TPP, the Paris Climate Accord, or the Iran nuclear deal, Trump's played to these beliefs. The posture has been, "we don't care what others think; we have a national strategy, not a global one, and it's ok to provoke as a means of promoting a level of strength the United States has supposedly lost."[28]

What, then, is the North Korean summit about? How does entering negotiations with someone one disagrees with and *has* identified as a fiendish enemy help if one posits such moves as off the table in virtually all other areas?

---

pewresearch.org/fact-tank/2017/04/05/americans-hold-very-negative-views-of-north-korea-amid-nuclear-tensions/.
26 Pew Research Center, "The World Facing Trump: Public Sees ISIS, Cyberattacks, North Korea as Top Threats," January 12, 2017, http://www.people-press.org/2017/01/12/the-world-facing-trump-public-sees-isis-cyberattacks-north-korea-as-top-threats/. There also may be cases to make *for* preemptive strikes. As a general tactic, however, it doesn't usually fall as the preferred method for those seeking peace. See Richard J. Regan, *Just War: Principles and Cases* (Washington D.C.: Catholic University Press, 2013).
27 Samantha Neal, "Most Americans View Openness to Foreigners as 'Essential to Who We are as a Nation,'" *Pew Research Center*, August 4, 2017, http://www.pewresearch.org/fact-tank/2017/08/04/most-americans-view-openness-to-foreigners-as-essential-to-who-we-are-as-a-nation/.
28 See Robyn Wright, "Trump's New, Confrontational Foreign Policy and the End of the Iran Deal," *The New Yorker*, May 21, 2018, https://www.newyorker.com/magazine/2018/05/21/the-end-of-the-iran-deal-and-trumps-new-confrontational-foreign-policy.

Again, imagine that such negotiations were entered into by anyone *other* than Trump (again, Obama comes to mind). Would the 40–45% of American voters who *support* Trump have done anything but *eviscerated* such a move and declared it inimical to American interests? Would Obama, or a theoretical President Kerry, have been anything but tarred-and-feathered on Fox News and decried as a near-traitor by conservatives in Congress? And – more to the point – if peace *is* made across the 38th parallel, *can* we think as well of it if it comes from one, if not *two*, parties seemingly disinterested in conciliation, or, what do we do with concord if it comes from actors with not only little history of interest in finding it, but records of more or less *poo-pooing* the idea?

Point one is hard to answer. I can only speculate on why Trump is willing to deviate from his tough-guy stance in the case of the DPRK. My sense, though it's pure speculation, is that there's a need for one "mainstream" foreign policy victory so the administration can't be written off as just plain kooky. Somewhere, those around Trump need to indicate that he's not just a war-monger, and due to a range of cultural positions in his base (the intense support for him by Evangelicals generating an intensely pro-Israel and Arab- and Iranian-skeptical stance), it may be easier to make peace with an outdated commie than, say, to take the moves necessary to encourage peace in the Middle East. Yes, Trump will from time to time pose himself as a non-interventionist or say he wants out of places like Syria. Little he does, though, goes anywhere near defusing tensions in central conflicts, and he's essentially redeclared Bush's "War on Terror."[29]

Regarding point two, I'll turn to human rights. I.e., under *normal* circumstances, the gold standard for any political act is whether it accords with the standards established by the international community regarding baselines for socio-political behavior. The point is *supposed* to be whether foreign policy assists the ethics towards which all states should strive. The teleology of political action *should be* – and in terms of international reaction, often *is* – upholding ideas that *don't* rely on "social custom, judicial announcement or some act of

---

29 See Ishaan Tharoor, "Trump's Incoherence on North Korea and Iran," *The Washington Post*, April 30, 2018, https://www.washingtonpost.com/news/worldviews/wp/2018/04/30/trumps-incoherence-on-north-korea-and-iran/?utm_term=.af0b55658e84; Masood Farivar, "Trump Pledges War on Radical Islamic Terrorism," *VOA News*, January 18, 2017, https://www.voanews.com/a/donald-trump-pledges-war-radical-islamic-terrorism/3676303.html. Indeed, the Trump's use of the vocabulary "radical Islamic terrorism" has been key here. The Obama administration tried to stay away from such cultural identifiers. Trump's use of it has been designed to signal a new aggressiveness.

parliament;" ideas that reflect *some* level of humanitarianism and privileges that should be present for all.[30] As one scholar puts it, "in general, it should be possible to study a state's foreign policy and to evaluate it not just with respect to its commitment to promote human rights internationally...but also for the overall thrust of its policies in terms of their effect upon harmonious international relations."[31] *Generally*, the end of foreign affairs is supposed to be assisting the privileges and securities that all people are supposed to have.

Now, if one looks at international rights documents – the locales in which our supposed baselines are laid-out – the situation is clear: "freedom, justice and peace in the world" are the goal.[32] "Brotherhood" is the ethics by which we should treat one another.[33] "Understanding, tolerance and friendship among all nations, racial or religious groups" is what we seek.[34] Everyone's "inherent" worth should be sanctioned and everybody should see their dignity endorsed.[35] Amity is the endgame, and "getting along" is where global social bodies should end up. Yes, there are specifics. Rights entail democracy. We should have free speech and freedom of thought. People should have equality as concerns legal recognition, and the free flow of information should be part of everyday life. We should have access to health care, shelter, and the possibility of an education; indeed, we should even have "periodic holidays with pay" (i.e., there are certain socio-economic expectations we might maintain).[36] Still, putting down the guns and

---

30 Johannes Morsink, *Inherent Human Rights: Philosophical Roots of the Universal Declaration* (Philadelphia: University of Pennsylvania Press, 2009), 21.
31 James G. Murphy, *War's Ends: Human Rights, International Order, and the Ethics of Peace* (Washington DC: Georgetown University Press, 2014), 27.
32 United Nations, "The Universal Declaration of Human Rights" (1948, preamble), http://www.un.org/en/universal-declaration-human-rights/index.html. Hereafter UDHR.
33 Ibid., article 1.
34 Ibid., article 26.
35 Ibid., preamble.
36 Ibid., article 24. United Nations, "International Covenant on Economic, Social and Cultural Rights" (1966, article 7), http://www.ohchr.org/EN/ProfessionalInterest/Pages/CESCR.aspx. Hereafter ICESCR In the world of international human rights, the UDHR represents the principle declaration of rights *principles*. The ICESCR, along with the International Covenant on Civil and Political Rights, form the first two layers of legally binding documents in the international rights regime. That's while there are noticeable *non*-participants in the IESCR – the United States primary among them. It's an older article on the issue. However, the topic is addressed well in Philip Alston, "U.S. Ratification of the Covenant on Economic, Social and Cultural Rights: The Need for an Entirely New Strategy," *The American Journal of International Law* 84, no. 2 (1990): 365–93.

backing off of aggressivity with each other is a baseline. Reconciliation between peoples is human rights' *spirit*, and solving border conflicts and negotiating intercultural tensions are ground floor dimensions of what rights are about. Rights aren't fully pacifistic; they offer room for their enforcement.[37] "Enforcement" isn't what rights are after, however. They're rather concerned with equitable societies and fair balances of power on the international stage.[38]

That being said, however, those are *pragmatic* goals. Rights are supposed to be a baseline and peace sits centrally within them. Amity matters, and rights have no small part to do with that. Still, *nowhere* in rights documents does it say who the bringer of peace is supposed to *be*. No rights covenant describes the history of the peacemaker, nor provides a map of the peacemaker's heart. The bringer of concord doesn't submit blood for a purity test, and you don't have to be a saint to enter the negotiating room. Rights say what we're supposed to *do* – treat each other well – and they say what the human family *is* (a community of creatures of the same worth, maintaining the capacity for "reason and conscience"). Rights suggest how we should be valued (equally) and they suggest that we all should have dignity. True: to the extent that we have "reason and conscience," rights ask us to think internationally because "reason and conscience" know no bounds. There *is* a sense that we're best serviced by transnational attitudes because *as* humans, we share both foundations and interests.[39] Still, there's no statement that says, "if someone's not a nice guy, any peace they make is invalid." Nothing says, "if one has generally advocated war, we should stop that person from signing a denuclearization accord." There's also nothing that says, "there's no making peace in one of the world's most contested areas if you're not a fun fellow" or that "only internationalists can draw down tension in the world's most militarized zones." In an immediate sense, rights ask us to pass *no* judgment on such things. Rights rather ask us to *make* peace and *build* civil societies. They ask us to *establish* brotherhood, *raise* living standards, and *lower* levels of violence. Rights ask us to

---

37 See Cristina Gabriela Badescu, *Humanitarian Intervention and the Responsibility to Protect: Security and Human Rights* (London: Routledge, 2011).
38 See David P. Forsythe, *Human Rights and Peace: International and National Dimensions* (Lincoln: University of Nebraska Press, 1993).
39 Former UN Secretary General Kofi Annan, e.g., once noted that human rights should "cross any border, climb any wall, defy any force" – they shouldn't be wall-off by national borders or cultural tradition. See Annan, "Message by the United Nations Secretary-General" in *Reflections on the Universal Declaration of Human Rights: A Fiftieth Anniversary Anthology*, ed. Barend van der Heiden and Bahia Tahzib-Lie (The Hague: Martinus Nijhoff, 1998), 18.

give space to each other and to *try* to make things better. In general, rights criteria are contented when such things happen.

For people like myself, that adds up to the following. It can be difficult to credit political foes; it's hard to allow someone one just "knows" is a scoundrel to wear the mantel of virtue. It's difficult to watch people who seem like they're out to generate upset get credit for truces, and it's tough when something that feels like grandstanding generates positive results. It feels unfair when the classroom bully is voted most likable, and it stinks when the guy who throws elbows on the basketball court is constantly high-fived. In the most important ways, however, whether one is a "true believer" in humanitarianism is beside the point. Whether one "really" thinks that international justice matters or peacemaking institutions are good isn't the standard with which rights are concerned. Having fewer weapons of mass destruction pointed at each other – *that's* the point. Families separated for generations being in contact again – *that's* the point. A spirit of dialog in the air between long-term rivals – *that's* the point. More freedom of ideas for peoples intellectually oppressed – *those* are results we want. A poor country with low standards of living getting *better* standards of living – *that's* something we seek. A world-historical military power denuded of an object towards which to flex its muscle – *that* something with meaning. People in better communication is the point. Less demonization and stereotyping is the point. A better sharing of common space is the point, as is making more out of humanity's common wealth.[40]

That's at the same time, though, that it *is* no fun when such opportunities are brought by people who *don't* really seem to care. It's while it *doesn't* feel well when the classroom bully *is* voted Mr. Congeniality, or individuals committed to sowing discord get credit for the rare moment of extending a hand. It feels like heck when someone who's played dirty wins, and it doesn't feel good when a partner who's cheated on you also takes the good chairs when they move out. One might think of it this way: *precisely* the same point can be made about a potential North Korean pact as the Trump Administration has made – constantly – about the nuclear deal with Iran. All deals have limitations. There's no such thing as a full guarantee. Unless one is *not* going to reduce U.S. military presence and leave North Korea at least a *bit* more to itself – unless the country is going to *continue* to be the subject of militaristic discourse and remain militarily surrounded – there's no point to even sit down. If one isn't going to allow North Korea a *bit* more latitude, the point of peace becomes hard to understand. And there, it helps

---

40 See Forsythe, *Human Rights and Peace*.

to *believe* in negotiation. There, it's useful to *want* peace's success; it *can* be helpful to find meaning in peace as a priority. As I write, the opening of the American embassy in Jerusalem and concordant protests are plastered all over the news. It's another Trump provocation, bringing violence one could easily predict. While Trump's face is there, referencing the Bible and discussing Jewish destiny (another thing in which one has to wonder if he genuinely believes), Palestinians are being shot by the dozen and protests are being put down with live fire. This has been damaging; part of a peace worked on for more than twenty-five years has been near-totally thrown out; one of the world's most difficult situations is becoming demonstrably worse. This could be a problem with a Trump-North Korea deal: that the whole thing may involve a certain randomness except for pizazz, and that it doesn't emerge from a *culture* of peace-*qua*-goal. Let's leave the question of Kim's motives aside. I'd hate to rely on the *DPRK* to uphold a North Korean peace; I'd hate for it to be *their* dedication to an agreement that might hold the thing together through a tough moment or two. That's the situation we find ourselves in with Iran – that it's *they* who are discussing keeping the deal alive; that it's an "axis of evil" country and *not* the supposed bastion of leadership on the international stage that is attempting to establish a pacifistic tone.[41] Indeed, if this *is* a PR stunt, I worry that's what we'll have – an opportunistic peace on the side of the Americans with Jong-un expected to play the principled part. And, indeed, such problems might not be at stake not only in Singapore, but *anywhere* authoritarians, militants, ultra-patriots, and nationalists sit at the negotiating table. Sure: peace lovers take the chance for concord when it's offered and they'll always applaud fewer bombs and less shooting. Still, we hunger for people who *believe* in disarmament and thirst for people who *believe* in processes. We feel best about peace when actors indicate by *ranges* of actions that amity is their priority, and peace feels best when it's made by people who craft it into their vocabularies and speak about it with their supporters. That's because we want people who will *keep* peace and look after it. We're not so wild about people who enter into it on a whim, or because it's but politically expedient.

---

41 See Erin Cunningham, "Iran to Negotiate with Europeans, Russia and China about Remaining in Nuclear Deal," *The Washington Post*, May 8, 2018, https://www.washingtonpost.com/world/middle_east/iran-prepared-for-all-scenarios-if-trump-nixes-nuclear-deal-officials-say/2018/05/08/531047a0-5241-11e8-a6d4-ca1d035642ce_story.html.

When It Goes Too Far
Venezuela
(May 23, 2018)

Abstract: *Venezuela has been in crisis for some years now: controversial elections, clashes in the streets, debates over the legacies of Chavismo, and controversies around the figure of Nicolás Maduro. The anti-socialist attitudes of America and the West are unfair; they represent unsophisticated understandings of what the Chávez movement was about. Maduro's gone too far, though, tipping the balance in ways that can't be excused in the face of international rights standards.*

Venezuela held an election yesterday – "election," I say, with quotes around it, as the larger part of significant opposition leaders weren't allowed to run, and the country teetered between participation and non-participation as it was largely Maduro supporters who showed up at the polls because opposition parties urged their voters to stay away. The results, such as they were, were clear. Maduro scored 68% of the poll. The one opposition candidate who *did* run – Henri Falcón – scored 21%. This meant that, yes, opposition votes *registered*. However, the results looked a lot like those coming out of what The Economist Intelligence Unit labels "hybrid" political regimes: countries like Turkey or Russia where, yes, people vote, and there's not *no* exchange of ideas. The clamps can come down awfully quickly on dissent, however, and there's more than a small amount of danger in finding oneself at odds with the regime.¹

"Venezuela" @ Tudoran Andrei / shutterstock.com 507491968

The background for the elections concerns the crisis in the coastal South American country that's been welling for several years now – a crisis organized partly around political strife and confrontation, but also the legacies of oil, class

---

1   The Economist Intelligence Unit, "Democracy Index 2017: Free Speech under Attack" (2017), http://pages.eiu.com/rs/753-RIQ-438/images/Democracy_Index_2017.pdf.

division, and the inheritances of Hugo Chávez's populism (with Chávez's eyes still peering out from innumerable wall murals around the country's larger cities [Chávez died in 2013]). Venezuela has had an interesting journey. In the 1970s, people talked about "Venezuela Saudita [Saudi Venezuela]" as, rather like their fellow oil power in the Middle East, the destiny of the country bordering Colombia, Brazil, and Guyana changed dramatically with the early twentieth-century discovery of what's perhaps the world's most precious resource (oil was found in Venezuela in 1914; Saudi Arabia in 1932). Now, dictators got rich off the discovery, and, as happened virtually everywhere else in the world oil appeared, the big players moved in as soon as the first well was built (Standard Oil, British Petroleum, Shell, etc.). This quickly made how to use the society's oil wealth and *who* would make decisions about such things central issues as, while oil profits brought upward mobility for some, the country's working class continued to struggle. Democracy movements thus became important, and Venezuela had some serious ones. From '58 on, *Acción Democratica* and *COPEI* (*Comité de Organización Política Electoral Independiente*, the country's Christian Democratic party) ran governments that took both political liberalism and economic welfare at least somewhat seriously, wherein a decent chunk of Venezuelans experienced improved living standards while democracy and free expression functioned reasonably well.[2] Centrist governments overspent, though (high capital cronyism also never fully disappeared from relations between the government and the oil sector), wherein a late-'80s economic crash emerged that gave way to rioting and an attempted coup. The coup came in '92 and was the event that put Hugo Chávez on the map. Telling especially Venezuela's working class that an attempt to take power in the people's name hadn't worked "for now" (his initial grab for power failed), Chávez would remain a focus in national politics over the coming years and become the elected leader of the country by 1998. Chávez was bold. Socialism may not have taken quite the hit in Latin America that it took in Europe during the 1990s as forces with left-wing bents remained meaningful players throughout the region. Still, Chávez's embrace of the Castros in Cuba, his unabashed use of oil wealth

---

2   This is a contentious topic. Search the literature on Venezuela and democracy and one sees an intense split between those who think that the Chávez regime *ended* decades of relative success with centrist democracy, and those who think that Chávez instituted a new, exciting democratic experiment. I refer readers to one of the standard histories of the country in English, taking a roughly middle of the road view (written at the start of the Chávez years). See H. Michael Tarver and Julia C. Frederick, *The History of Venezuela* (Westport, CT: Greenwood, 2005).

for broad-based social programs, and, perhaps most importantly, his *nationalization* of oil production, provided a lot of the base color for the "pink wave" that swept Latin America at the start the twenty-first century.[3] There's no doubt Chávez could be *jefe*-like; he engaged in some serious public theatrics (his *Aló Presidente* shows were legendary), and his regime also hardly always respected civil rights.[4] People liked Chávez for a reason, however. There are some real arguments that he brought working people more power, he may have provided working people with a *sense* that they had more power, and, in both political and economic senses, he provided more than a few Venezuelans with the feeling that the country was suddenly *theirs*. Many who for decades had felt pushed to the side by the country's socio-political dynamics felt all of a sudden noticed. Chávez was given a lot of credit for that.

For better or worse (worse, really), things haven't gone so well for Chávez's successor, Nicolás Maduro. When the economy bottomed out again – which it did through 2013-4 – many felt the pinch as the highly regulated *Chavismo* system wasn't well set-up to absorb the fluctuations that global markets can bring (simply put, Venezuela was near-bankrupt when the rest of the global economy

---

[3] The feature figures in this were clearly Chávez, Evo Morales of Bolivia, and Lula da Silva in Brazil. However, at its height around the end of the twenty-first century's first decade, all South American governments leaned left except for Colombia's and Chile's, and Nicaragua and El Salvador featured left-leaning governments in Central America (above and beyond socialist stalwart Cuba). See María del Rosario Queirolo, *The Success of the Left in Latin America: Untainted Parties, Market Reforms, and Voting Behavior* (South Bend: University of Notre Dame Press, 2013); Geraldine Lievesly and Steve Ludlam, eds., *Reclaiming Latin America: Experiments in Radical Social Democracy* (New York: Zed, 2013).

[4] As Michael Shifter noted in 2006, "dissent [was] permitted" and there were clearly critics of Chávez as part of Venezuela's political tapestry. A number of telltale signs of something less-than-democratic were well part of the picture, however: Chávez remaining a military officer while in power, passing laws against criticizing the person of the president, imposing "administrative restrictions" on TV and radio broadcasts, putting the military in a central role in national governance, expanding the supreme court so he could stuff it full of judges sympathetic to his cause and, of course (*à la* Putin in Russia or Xi in China) extending the number of terms he might serve as president. We'll see that I'm not at all opposed to many of Chávez's reforms – including ways in which he may have sometimes brought *more* people into the political system. That doesn't prevent issues around civil rights, however, of which Chávez had some. See Michael Shifter, "In Search of Hugo Chávez," *Foreign Affairs* 85, no. 3 (2006): 45–59; Daniel H. Levine, "The Decline and Fall of Democracy in Venezuela: Ten Theses," *Bulletin of Latin American Research* 21, no. 2 (2002): 248–69.

was starting to recover from the 2008 slump).⁵ The political opposition – an admittedly more middle-class movement than the working class support behind Chávez – won 2/3 of the seats in the country's 2015 parliamentary election, leading Maduro to channel his inner you-name-the-neo-authoritarian-dictator and claim that power *really* belonged to something called the "National Communal Parliament," which was *his* people, more or less.⁶ Then the real tumult began. Somewhere in the area of two hundred died in clashes between demonstrators and authorities as the government declined compromise, and anti-Chavismo demonstrators took forcefully to the streets. Maduro won a number of victories in subsequent gubernatorial elections, and his PSUV (*Partido Socialista Unido de Venezuela*) continues to retain support. To ensure that the most recent presidential elections would be a slam dunk, however, three opposition parties, including one of the traditional powers in the center, *Acción Democratica*, were banned from running – that coming after Maduro declared that whatever power was left with the National Assembly now lay in the hands of a judiciary stacked full of *Chavismo* men.⁷ Maduro got his win. However, as shown in a post-election video that went viral yesterday, Maduro might be waving to crowds that don't exist (apparently, there's some raw footage of Maduro waving that was intended to be doctored [i.e., crowds put in]; no one got around to the photoshopping, where Maduro seems to be waving to empty streets]). Again, the PSUV has its backers. It's not the *only* political option, however, and it looks like Maduro and his party are trying to force people to that say it is.⁸

---

5   See Max Fisher and Amanda Taub, "How Venezuela Went from the Richest Economy in South America to the Brink of Financial Ruin," *The Independent*, May 21, 2017, https://www.independent.co.uk/news/long_reads/how-venezuela-went-from-the-richest-economy-in-south-america-to-the-brink-of-financial-ruin-a7740616.html.
6   See Daniel Lansber-Rodríguez, "President Maduro and His Imaginary Parliament," *Foreign Policy*, December 22, 2015, http://foreignpolicy.com/2015/12/22/president-maduro-and-his-imaginary-parliament-venezuela-elections/.
7   See Jonathan Watts, "Venezuela Opposition Allege Coup as Supreme Court Seizes Power," *The Guardian*, March 20, 2017, https://www.theguardian.com/world/2017/mar/30/venezuela-president-nicolas-maduro-national-assembly. See also Kirk Semple, "Venezuela's Two Legislatures Duel, But Only One Has the Ammunition," *The New York Times*, November 3, 2017, https://www.nytimes.com/2017/11/03/world/americas/venezuela-national-assembly-maduro.html.
8   See John Lee Anderson, "How Long Can Nicolás Maduro Hang On to Power in Venezuela?" *The New Yorker*, May 22, 2018, https://www.newyorker.com/news/news-desk/how-long-can-Nicolás-Maduro-hang-on-to-power-in-venezuela.

Now, one can hear it: "here we go again." Latin America is known for its turbulent politics and, be it the conflict between the government and *FARC* rebels in Colombia from the 1960s on, the civil wars that dominated Central America through the '70s and '80s, or simply the broad range of strongman regimes peppering modern Latin American history, political calm seems to have been hard to find throughout the region. I wanted to determine how many *coup d'états* Latin America has had, say, since the Second World War, and ran across a 1967 article noting that Latin American countries had had no less than one hundred and five coups since 1907.[9] Of course, 1967 doesn't take into account some *major* events in Latin American history: the overthrow of Salvador Allende in Chile (1973), the inculcation of the Bordaberry dictatorship in Uruguay (also in '73), the overthrow of Alfredo Stroessner in Paraguay in 1989 (though that was good for democracy), or the overthrow of Juan Peron's third wife Isabel in Argentina in 1976 (perhaps not good for democracy, but, then again, it's not clear *Peronismo* was either).[10] Now, throwing Venezuelan history unthinkingly into the bin of "tumult" would be unfair. Democratic forces *were* overthrown in a 1948 coup after which the military reigned for a decade. With the election of Rómulo Betancourt in 1958 and the signing of the Punto Fijo Pact, however (a kind of centrist political concord), there was a relatively stable consensus in Venezuelan politics that led to an essential level of prosperity providing the lens through which the latter decades of the twentieth century up to the financial collapse in the late-'80s are often seen (the so-called "Punto Fijo Years").[11]

With all that in mind, the current situation evokes a series of thoughts. One is that Latin American stability remains an issue, even though one wants to take care with stereotypes. Colombia is ramping up for a general election at the same time that Venezuela experiences turmoil, and there's a good chance that the 2016 pact via which the *FARC* entered the political process might be

---

9 Egil Fossum, "Factors Influencing the Occurrence of Military Coups d'Etat in Latin America," *Journal of Peace Research* 4, no. 4 (1967): 228–51.
10 See Frederick C. Turner and José Enrique Miguens, eds., *Juan Perón and the Reshaping of Argentina* (Pittsburgh: University of Pittsburgh Press, 1983). There are extensive debates about the degree to which Peronism was authoritarian, which it's often assumed to be. Regarding Isabel Peron's overthrow, the *junta* that took over was clearly authoritarian, leading to several years of dictatorship in Argentinian history.
11 See Jennifer L. McCoy and David J. Meyers, eds., *The Unraveling of Representative Democracy in Venezuela* (Baltimore: Johns Hopkins University Press, 2004).

undone. Right-wing candidate Ivan Duque wants to toss out amnesty for a serious section of the old *FARC* leadership – a plan which could lead to renewed tension.[12] Corruption has been an ongoing theme in Brazil, with former (and once-popular) presidents Lula da Silva and Dilma Rousseff indicted for different varieties of financial malfeasance – a disappointment for center-left forces as the da Silva presidency was often seen as a force for positive change.[13] Nicaragua has seen conflict as one-time revolutionary Daniel Ortega has sought to cut welfare benefits and demonstrators have resisted him in force, and Honduras has also been in turmoil as protestors have questioned the legitimacy of the election of President Juan Orlando Hernández, making their presence felt in the streets.[14] The NGO The Fund for Peace publishes a frequently used index of fragile states, and in its most recent version, it notes Argentina, Chile, Panama, and Uruguay as on par with countries such as Poland and Spain (i.e., not infinitely stable, but within generally accepted norms). Brazil represents a grey zone, however, and, outside of Costa Rica, a good chunk of others fit into categories with decided problems.[15]

A second point that comes to mind is that, regional tranquility or not, the outrage expressed by both the current American administration and Europe vis-à-vis the Maduro/Venezuela situation is not disconnected to valid points – free elections are free elections and Venezuela's not having them. However, it's an outrage that also rings a bit hollow. Let's ignore the problems with democratic practice in places like Hungary and Poland (parts of the supposed democratic stronghold of the EU); the President of the *United States* has flat-out indicted his country's free press as "the enemy of the people" and claimed that protestors

---

12 See Francesco Manetto, "Iván Duque: 'No hay que hacer trizas los acuerdos con las FARC, pero sí modificaciones importantes,'" *El País*, January 18, 2018, https://elpais.com/internacional/2018/01/17/colombia/1516162343_892303.html.

13 Reuters, "Brazil Former Presidents Lula and Rouseff Charged in Corruption Case," September 6, 2017, https://www.reuters.com/article/us-brazil-corruption/brazil-former-presidents-lula-and-rousseff-charged-in-corruption-case-idUSKCN1BH013. See also, e.g., Nicholas Lemann, "The Anointed," *The New Yorker*, November 27, 2011, https://www.newyorker.com/magazine/2011/12/05/the-anointed.

14 See Elisabeth Malkin, "Political Unrest Grips Honduras after Contested Election," *The New York Times*, November 30, 2017, https://www.nytimes.com/2017/11/30/world/americas/honduras-vote-political-crisis.html; Frances Robles, "In Just a Week, 'Nicaragua Changed' as Protestors Cracked a Leader's Grip," *The New York Times*, April 26, 2018, https://www.nytimes.com/2018/04/26/world/americas/nicaragua-uprising-protesters.html.

15 See Fund for Peace, "Fragile States Index" (2018), http://fundforpeace.org/fsi/.

at his rallies should be taken out on "stretchers" (a variety of strongmanism the U.S. generally hasn't seen).¹⁶ One also need be clear on the idea that the U.S. and its European allies spend some serious time *not* complaining about regimes who engage in some *very* dubious practices (I mean, Saudi Arabia? Come on!), and the U.S., especially, has a history of going guns blazing after popular movements in Latin America with any kind of left-wing bent (see Cuba, 1961, Chile, 1973, Nicaragua, 1980s, El Salvador, 1980s, and the entirety of "Operation Condor" – an explicit, multi-year attempt to go after opponents of the U.S.' anti-communist [and sometimes pseudo-fascist] allies).¹⁷ Now, the Obama administration was the first American administration to at least *somewhat* back off of the U.S.' "Latin American socialism must be defeated at every turn" stance. Obama reestablished diplomatic relations with Cuba (something the Trump administration seeks to undo), and both Obama and Secretary of State Hillary Clinton were at least *willing* to engage in some light conversation with Chávez – something unheard of up to that point.¹⁸ With the shift back to politics-as-usual come Trump, however, the "Yanqui go home" mantra is back in place in Latin American politics because "Yanquis" seem to be saying if not doing the same old thing.¹⁹ The problem with socialist movements south of the border? They question the idea

---

16 Michael Grynbaum, "Trump Calls the News Media 'the Enemy of the American People,'" *The New York Times*, February 27, 2017, https://www.nytimes.com/2017/02/17/business/trump-calls-the-news-media-the-enemy-of-the-people.html. A potential exception might be the Nixon years, with not only the administration's involvement with Watergate, but issues like the President keeping an "enemies" list. I.e., we're discussing an attitude of relative authoritarianism and the personalization of politics.
17 See Lars Schoultz, *Beneath the United States: A History of U.S. Policy towards Latin America* (Cambridge, MA: Harvard University Press, 2009); J. Patrice McSherry, *Predatory States: Operation Condor and Covert War in Latin America* (Lanham: Roman & Littlefield, 2005); Grace Livingstone, *America's Backyard: The United States and Latin America from the Monroe Doctrine to the War on Terror* (London: Zed, 2009).
18 UPI, "Hillary Bumps into Hugo Chavez in Brazil," January 2, 2011, https://www.upi.com/Hillary-bumps-into-Hugo-Chavez-in-Brazil/19601293994589/; Steve Holland, "What's in an Obama-Chavez Handshake?" *Reuters*, April 20, 2009, https://www.reuters.com/article/us-obama-handshake-analysis/whats-in-an-obama-chavez-handshake-idUSTRE53J6EK20090420; Peter Baker, "U.S. to Restore Full Relations with Cuba, Erasing Last Trace of Cold War Hostility," *The New York Times*, December 17, 2014, https://www.nytimes.com/2014/12/18/world/americas/us-cuba-relations.html.
19 See Ted Piccone, "U.S.-Cuba Relations are about to Get Worse," *Brookings*, April 16, 2018, https://www.brookings.edu/blog/order-from-chaos/2018/04/16/u-s-cuban-relations-are-about-to-get-worse/.

that capitalism alone is the global way forward, and they *very* much question the idea that U.S. involvement in the region has been much except exploitative for the larger part of Latin Americans. The present U.S. administration isn't interested to repair such legacies, and despite differences in other areas, Europe is little concerned to challenge America in its dealings from the Rio Grande south.[20]

To all of that, I'd add a last point, which is it can be curious why, though recent troubles in Venezuela *have* gotten attention (and Chávez was not shy about making an issue out of *himself*), the crisis in Venezuela doesn't get *more* notice than it does. I.e., as dire as things have been, what is a serious situation always seems to come out second banana in a survey of global media coverage. Now, sure: Venezuela doesn't involve the drama of "civilizational" conflict that clashes with Islamic State or the Taliban bring. There also isn't the sense of a rising power challenging American dominance, as colors news concerning China.[21] There isn't the mano-a-mano face-off between the world's military behemoths, as features in U.S. relations with Russia, or the belly-bumping of belligerent egos, as dominates dealings between Washington and Pyongyang.[22] Still, vis-à-vis Venezuela, one *is* discussing a country that sits on the greatest amount of the world's most valuable natural resource reserve – oil (no one has more of it than Venezuela) – and one is also talking about inflation rates the likes of which the world has rarely seen (they recently reached over 13,000%).[23] One is discussing a country that, with Chávez's coming, became one of the great locales for "stick it in America's eye" rhetoric, and one is considering a nation that features one of the most precipitous drops from relative prosperity to near-total collapse in recent memory (Venezuela's also not small; it's got some 32 million people).[24] Perhaps – perhaps – the fine points of political-philosophical debates

---

20 Christopher Sabatini and William Naylor, "Trump Riles Latin America," *Foreign Affairs*, November 8, 2017, https://www.foreignaffairs.com/articles/south-america/2017-11-08/trump-riles-latin-america.
21 See, e.g., Martin Jacques, *When China Rules the World: The End of the Western World and the Birth of a New Global Order* (New York: Penguin, 2009).
22 E.g., Kate Samuelson, "Here Are All the Times Kim Jong Un and Donald Trump Insulted Each Other," *Time*, September 22, 2018, http://time.com/4953283/kim-Jong-un-donald-trump-insults/.
23 International Monetary Fund, "Inflation Rate, Average Consumer Prices," June 1, 2018, http://www.imf.org/external/datamapper/PCPIPCH@WEO/WEOWORLD/VEN.
24 See Jon Kelly, "Hugo Chavez and the Era of the Anti-American Bogeyman," *BBC*, March 7, 2013, http://www.bbc.com/news/magazine-20977849; Ray Sanchez, "Venezuela: How Paradise Got Lost," *CNN*, July 27, 2017, https://edition.cnn.com/2017/04/21/americas/venezuela-crisis-explained/index.html.

concerning liberalism versus socialism just feel like something which belong to the Reagan era as opposed to something for our times; maybe the whole notion of "Bolivarian revolutions" just doesn't feel right in the post-ideological era of the first couple of decades following the supposed "end of history."[25]

Still, I wonder if the conflicts involved with Venezuela's political-economic turmoil grab fewer of the headlines than, say, upheavals in the Middle East, because they are "southern." I.e., there is a serious bias towards viewing both long-term and recent historical trends through the lenses of Europe first, and then those of the United States. Put another way, modernity's great powers dominate modern times' historical narratives, and we expect news cycles to revolve around the powers of the West. Now, I over-simplify. Go to most countries and have a discussion on global trends, and many will discuss their national situation first; "all politics is local," it's been said, and one might say the same about social and historical knowledge.[26] Still, it's no coincidence that, pick up near any world history textbook, and events surrounding Europe and North America take center stage. If Canada were in the throes of national collapse, e.g. – a nation of with roughly the same population as Venezuela – I can't imagine anything other than it would be a constant headline in global news. Again, I speculate. However, I'd suggest that we can be *very* concerned about Mid-East crises because they're framed in terms of cultural clashes affecting North Americans and Europeans, and that there's a question as to what "Northerners" or "Westerners" are going to "do." Other narratives get shaded out – governmental collapse in Africa or Latin America, or regime changes in Southeast Asia? We've got a place in the

---

25 Of course, the "end of history" was Francis Fukuyama's great thesis that the ideological battle between communism and capitalism, or at least liberalism, had come to a close with the conclusion of the Cold War. See Fukuyama, *The End of History and the Last Man* (New York: Penguin, 1992).

Regarding media coverage and Venezuela, looking at the indices of *The New York Times* as one of the largest circulation global dailies, since January 1, 2017 (to June 1, 2018), there were 811 articles on Venezuela and 2956 on Islamic State. In *The Times of India*, as the world's largest circulated English language daily, Venezuela was mentioned in 1231 articles between June 1, 2017 and June 1, 2018. Islamic State – in a period where the Venezuelan crisis was at its height and the conflict with Islamic State had begun to tone down – Islamic State was mentioned in 2915 times. This is taken from the advanced search function on both newspapers' online sites.

26 Though a commonplace observation now, the specific wordplay is often attributed to former Speaker of the House for the American Congress Tip O'Neill. See O'Neill, *All Politics is Local* (New York: Random House, 1995).

newspaper in the "international section" for you at the bottom of page one, or perhaps at the bottom of page two.[27]

Now, that's of course all interesting. Yes, "southern" narratives can get shaded out of history, and there can be hypocrisy in American criticisms of Latin American political movements. One wonders if Europeans should worry more about the *Alternative für Deutschland* or Italy's *Lega Nord* than getting worked up about events in a South American country some thousands of miles away.[28] That doesn't mean, though, that people's fates aren't at stake as street fighting erupts in Caracas and they're offered shaky participation in elections. It doesn't mean that there's not meaning in individuals finding it difficult to afford medicine and foodstuffs, and it doesn't mean that elections are coming off the right way or that the right to engage in free speech hasn't become impinged. I.e., the *most* fundamental issue concerning Maduro and the Venezuelan crisis may involve human rights. The most fundamental problem concerns what are supposed to be our most fundamental principles, or our "Magna Carta" ideals.[29] There *is* a question as to whether people can constitute their own governments, and there's a question as to whether the institutions exist that would carry such rights forward. That's compounded by the question as to whether or not, materially, people have access to the essential goods that they're supposed to have.

Now, I have to put a massive caveat on all this. Chávez, in his way, actually put some serious emphasis on human rights. A rights scholar named Rhoda Howard-Hassmann correctly notes that Chávez put an especially heavy emphasis on concepts like the right to food.[30] It's interesting: in terms of core international human rights instruments – the rights documents and treaties of the UN, but

---

27 See, e.g., Richard C. Stanton, *All News is Local: The Failure of the Media to Reflect World Events in a Globalized Age* (Jefferson: McFarland & Co., 2007).
28 Among other things, the EU charged that "a constituent assembly, elected under doubtful and often violent circumstances, cannot be part of [Venezuela's] solution," in relation to parliamentary elections over the past years, and has threatened sanctions on the Maduro regime in relation to the most recent poll. See The Guardian, "Venezuela Poll: EU Condemns Violence as Turnout Figures Disputed," July 31, 2017, https://www.theguardian.com/world/2017/jul/31/venezuela-poll-eu-condemns-violence-as-turnout-figure-disputed; Al-Jazeera, "EU Prepares to Hit Venezuela with New Sanctions," May 28, 2018, https://www.aljazeera.com/news/2018/05/eu-prepares-hit-venezuela-sanctions-180528140548981.html.
29 See Micheline R. Ishay, *The History of Human Rights: From Ancient Times to the Globalization Era* (Berkeley: University of California Press, 2008), 218.
30 See Rhoda E. Howard-Hassmann, "The Right to Food under Hugo Chávez," *Human Rights Quarterly* 37, no. 4 (2015): 1024–45.

also those of regional organizations – food *can* escape attention. I.e., there's general recognition of the right to what's termed an "adequate standard of living" vis-à-vis the notion of welfare, as well as access to a doctor and medical care. Shelter is noted as a human right, and the right to an education is oft-discussed. So too are socio-economic concepts like equal pay for equal work.[31] Search the discussion on human rights for the right to food, however, and, yes, results come in. That's often of a relatively specialized kind, however, and in fewer numbers than one might expect.[32]

There are reasons for this. Firstly, food might be such an essential right that many assume that it goes without saying. *No one* would say that one will survive if you starve yet can see a doctor. *No one* would imagine that an "adequate standard of living" *doesn't* involve a chicken in one's pot or at least enough square meals for one's family to get by. No one imagines that welfare doesn't mean people *not* starving, or at least *trying* to make sure they don't. That's a potential reason why Chávez's emphasis on food may escape attention yet is clearly worth noting: because it goes to such a fundamental level. It's easy to forget – that at the same time that, absent full bellies, there's little to discuss.

Another problem, though, is that, think of human rights, and it's usually the realm of *civil and political rights* that comes to mind: prisoners of conscience (Amnesty International's traditional area of concern), denials of minority rights, governments' use of torture, the right to have space for one's personal thoughts, and the right to freedom of conscience. Economic, social and cultural rights *are* embedded in the larger space of human rights concepts – economic, social and cultural rights being again the category under which something like the right to food falls.[33] Such rights are institutionalized to a noticeably lesser degree,

---

31 See, e.g., Samantha Power and Graham Allison, *Realizing Human Rights: Moving from Inspiration to Impact* (New York: Palgrave, 2006).
32 There are clearly many articles and books addressing the right to food – and that's not just recently (the academic article search engine JSTOR notes 1393 articles on the issue, dating from the 1960s on). It's drowned by discussion of other rights, though – e.g., the right to education (3595 articles), the right to health (3098), or simply socio-economic rights generally (over 5800) (the most frequent place one sees the right to food mentioned [though, again, together with ranges of other socio-economic rights]). For one of the more thorough overviews of the right to food, see George Kent, *Freedom from Want: The Human Rights to Adequate Food* (Washington DC: Georgetown University Press, 2005).
33 See Food and Agricultural Organization of the United Nations, *The Right to Food: In Theory and Practice* (FAO Information Division: Rome, 1998).

however, than things like free speech and legal equality, and they're less in discourse than concepts like freedom of mind or the right to say one's piece. Some scholars note that has much to do with liberal powers having dominated the international discussion of rights issues, while others have noted that it concerns the difficulty in institutionalizing economic equality (it's tough to demand how countries are supposed to use their wealth).[34] Both might be right. Civil and political rights are *de facto* prioritized globally partly because they're the ones that gain consensus – yet it's also true that there is serious difficulty in asserting that countries *must* use their monies in specific ways. I.e., outside of national law, it isn't easy to find mechanisms for socio-economic rights' enforcement.[35]

That is, though, while socio-economic rights *should* have equal status within the panoply of human rights. Be it medical care, welfare *or* food, one *shouldn't* have to scratch out a living. A roof over one's head *should* be a minimum, and basic nutrition should be on the table for everyone. It should be possible to get to school and get a decent education, and healthcare shouldn't be but for the rich. Here, *Chavismo* leaves a significant legacy. Yes, nationalizing oil wealth brought Chávez popularity. However, the point with nationalization was to ensure that oil wealth served *Venezuelans* as well as guaranteeing that national wealth went not just to *some* Venezuelans, but to *all*. Oil revenues and government expenditures were used to make major investment in housing, free medical clinics, combatting illiteracy, providing land to poorer farmers, and assuring that pupils finished

---

34 Koen Raes, "The Philosophical Basis of Social, Economic and Cultural Rights" in *Social, Economic and Cultural Rights: An Appraisal of Current European and International Developments*, ed. Peter van der Auweraert, et al. (Antwerp: Maklu, 2002), 43–55.

35 The literature on this issue is vast. However, to quote an oft referred-to volume, Isfahan Merali and Valerie Oosterveld note that "a lack of political will...to protect and advance economic, social and cultural rights remains apparent today." "Within the international system, and at domestic levels," they contend, "the eloquent statement made by the UN General Assembly in 1948, that economic, social, cultural, civil and political rights are indivisible and interrelated, has not yet been translated into reality." As Kenneth Roth, director of Human Rights Watch notes, issues involve enforceability because at issue is the allocation of resources, which in some cases can be "scarce" (wherein, one in fact needs a *global* reallocation of resources). This collides immediately with state sovereignty, and opens questions as to how much wealth one person or group should have access to as opposed to another. See Merali and Oosterveld, "Introduction" in *Giving Meaning to Economic, Social and Cultural Rights*, ed. Isfahan Merali and Valerie Oosterveld (Philadelphia: University of Pennsylvania Press, 2011), 1; Roth, "Defending Economic, Social and Cultural Rights: Practical Issues Faced by an International Human Rights Organization," *Human Rights Quarterly* 26, no. 1 (2004): 65.

high school. It was used for adult education programs and beefing-up infrastructure. It was used to better the spaces used by communities in Venezuela's cities and, indeed, grouped under the heading of "Bolivarian Missions" (various areas of social investment), the most important program may have been "Mission Mercal," providing price-controlled food in what amounted to thousands of supermarkets collected into a government chain – that in addition to thousands of soup kitchens. As Howard-Hassmann suggests, there are debates to be had about whether strict price controls ended up accomplishing their goals. Statistics regarding many social indicators under Chávez's rule clearly improved: poverty dropped, malnutrition fell, illiteracy shrunk, and life expectancy increased (that without getting into the idea of who in fact *owns* a state's wealth).[36] Still, funding such initiatives near-exclusively out of a single source – oil wealth, and oil's price on the international market – risked setting such initiatives up for failure when prices in said sector dropped. They did, and it hurt: money ran out, *especially* hitting the food subsidies provided by the government. Social policy and economic dynamics didn't match each other well, and nationalization policies isolated Venezuela in the global economy by making the country less attractive for investment. Therein, once the floor went out from underneath the national wealth source, there were few ways of subsidizing programs without simply printing money – which is what the government did.[37]

---

36 This also translated into some meaningful international appreciation of certain of Chávez's moves, despite recognition of civil rights issues. Joseph Stiglitz offered praise for Chávez's attempt to provide locally based economic power, Jeremy Corbyn was supportive of Chávez anti-imperialist stance, and Human Rights Watch noted meaningful improvements in women's rights, indigenous rights, and the "potential benefits of cooperatives for economic development" (again, despite civil rights issues). See Rory Carroll, "Nobel Economist Endorses Chávez Regional Bank Plan," *The Guardian*, October 12, 2007, https://www.theguardian.com/business/2007/oct/12/venezuela.banking; Al-Jazeera, "How Will the World Remember Hugo Chavez?" March 7, 2013, https://www.aljazeera.com/programmes/insidestory/2013/03/20133791253883508.html; Human Rights Watch, *A Decade under Chávez: Political Intolerance and Lost Opportunities for Advancing Human Rights in Venezuela* (New York: Human Rights Watch, 2008).
37 Rachelle Krygier and Anthony Faiola, "Venezuela Hopes to Tackle the World's Worst Inflation by Deleting Zeros from Its Currency," *The Washington Post*, March 23, 2018, https://www.washingtonpost.com/news/worldviews/wp/2018/03/23/venezuela-hopes-to-tackle-the-worlds-worst-inflation-by-deleting-zeros-from-its-currency/?utm_term=.f6386fded6a7.

Now, that's a complex story – one of success, but also failure. It indicates a bold and potentially honest vision – yet one overly insistent on ideology as national economies have to be able to play ball with the world around them. This perhaps leads to a couple of points. Firstly, as we approach the legacies of *Chavismo* as well as Venezuela's ongoing crisis, we're faced with two conceptions of rights. The first conception suggests that one must get life's necessities and, in fact, no one deserves more access to necessities than others. Bread, water, and housing *are* supposed to be available to everyone, and potentially in equal amounts. Whether one likes it or not, this is a principle of socialism. "From each according to their ability, to each according to their needs," as Marx put it, and, indeed, lest we forget, more than half the world's people had such ideas as grounding elements in their political-economic systems around halfway through the twentieth century.[38] An "alternative…society" in which emancipation was "truly 'universal' because all were given sufficient, if not equal, material means," historian Eric Hobsbawm argued, was the *raison d'être* for the socialist world.[39] Philosophically, the idea was that all types of labor relied on each other, wherein one couldn't say that one kind of work was of *less* worth, or should be compensated radically differently, than any kind of *other* work (indeed, even the unemployed, Marx suggested, had a role as the "reserve labor army" – available labor when economies expand).[40] In that context, notions that that which one "tills, plants, improves [or] cultivates" *belongs* to one, as liberal forefather John Locke put it, are false.[41] When you get something from the ground by "tilling it," socialism suggests, you violate basic fairness if you don't share your produce with the man or woman who made your spade or hoe. Indeed, socialism also suggests that, hog the results of using your hoe too long, and the men and women who made it may get annoyed and *ask* for something in return. Deny them *that* request and, well, workers weren't outside their rights in breaking down your door and simply hauling their fair share home.[42]

---

38 Karl Marx, *Critique of the Gotha Program* (New York: International, 1966), 82.
39 Eric Hobsbawm, *The Age of Extremes: A History of the World, 1914-1991* (New York: Vintage, 1996), 72.
40 See Marx, *Capital, vol. 1*, trans. Ben Fowkes (New York: Penguin, 1976), 781.
41 See John Locke, *Second Treatise of Government and a Letter Concerning Toleration*, ed. Mark Goldie (Oxford: Oxford University Press, 2016), 17.
42 Oppression, wrote Marx and Engels in *The Communist Manifesto*, can lead the proletariat (working class) to organize itself *into* a class and, "by means of a revolution… [sweep] away by force the old conditions of production," including sweeping away "class antagonisms" – antagonisms which came when some reaped more profits from

Of course, that presents an angry socialism – a socialism, as Marx put it, in which all history is the history of "class conflict."[43] It portrays a scenario in which disadvantaged classes have the right to take revenge on those who hold the advantage – and, in certain circumstances, likely will.[44] However, one *could* suggest that such ideas represent an invitation to *democracy*. One *could* say that such scenarios concern working people's right to self-determination and making sure that what are in fact *most* people are included in decisions about their lives. It suggests inculcating frameworks in which people, including the proletariat that most of us are, are charged to look after themselves, and in which it's underlined that the voices of the many shouldn't be drowned out by those of the few. Indeed, *Chavismo* provides impressive examples of this. E.g., there was a short coup against Chávez in 2002. Unsuccessful (Chávez was back in power within a day or so), moneyed powers got the state-run oil company, PDVSA (*Petróleos de Venezuela, S.A.*), to lock its doors, meaning that workers were disallowed from doing their jobs, including refining the product responsible for the larger part of national wealth. Tankers remained in port, trucks were locked in shipping bays, and garages and gates were bolted shut. The workers' response? To take the power back. Working people demonstrated, attempted to report to work, and tried to restart production. They insisted on doing work *they* found valuable and partly felt that they owned. With Chávez's help, they succeeded; corrupt managers were thrown out, and production resumed. That's not ballot box voting. It's making *social space* a voting booth, however, and insisting that power is *always* in people's hands. It suggests that it's up to the people to decide when to activate their agency and that, as concerns using one's own power, it's always one's right to decide.[45]

---

society's productive force than others. See Marx and Friedrich Engels, *Manifesto of the Communist Party* (New York: Cosimo, 2006), 74–5.
43 Ibid., 39.
44 The Marxist thesis is that, in essence, once living standards become untenable, classes would take action against those who oppress them to remake the social relations feeding into those living standards. See, e.g., F.R. Hansen, *The Breakdown of Capitalism: A History of the Idea in Western Marxism, 1883-1983* (London: Routledge, 1985).
45 Anthony Spanakos argues that, especially in its early years, Chávez movement was constituted of "micropublics" that were not necessarily "self-conscious" – i.e., it was more or less a spontaneous political movement born of coalescing interests opposing the previous regime and engaging a range of liberation agendas. This might be thought of as a kind of "multitudinous" political organization – the production of common cause not

Now, that's all well and good. It's a concept of rights that's left its mark on documents like the Universal Declaration of Human Rights when they note that one should seek political systems in which people won't *need* to take recourse to "rebellion" in the face of "oppression." You can feel the presence of socialism in rights ideals when they suggest that democracy is likely to be pulled off better when people *have* acceptable living standards because those who should participate in civil society aren't shoved to "bare minimum" status or somehow pushed to the side.[46] It's a way of suggesting that societies function best when everyone *has* a full belly, and that it's even better if you don't have a class of fat cats while some do but a hair better than starve. Now, human rights concepts, or at least central human rights *covenants*, don't say that all should have the same. International rights documents don't advocate the *maximal* levels of equality that one *might* espouse as the best conditions for equal rights. Still, they advocate a sharing of the wealth, not only in the name of dignity, but in the name of social peace and inclusive public cultures. They suggest spreading the wealth around a bit so that most are within *some* zone of decent living standards, and that most do more than just barely make it by.[47]

However, there's the rub: what happens if you dissent against *that*? What happens if you find *those* ideas problematic? Let's leave libertarianism to the side. Let's say that you're sympathetic towards looking out for the people's welfare, but you see dangers in radical economic shifts. Let's say that, regardless of political philosophy, you worried that what *did* happen to the Venezuelan economy in fact *would*, and that Chávez was putting the economy in the tank. Or, what if one believes that labor *doesn't* produce collective ownership, but rights for the

---

    directed by "some central point of command," as phrased by political theorists Michael Hardt and Antonio Negri, nor the result of "spontaneous harmony among individuals," but a "space between" concerning "collaborative social interactions" concerning strategic though-not-necessarily-unified acts for liberation generating a specific result. See Spanakos, "Citizen Chávez: The State, Social Movements, and Publics," *Latin American Perspectives* 38, no. 1 (2011): 18; Hart and Negri, *Multitude: War and Democracy in the Age of Empire* (New York: Penguin, 2004), 222.

46 United Nations, "The Universal Declaration of Human Rights" (1948, preamble), http://www.un.org/en/documents/udhr/. Hereafter UDHR.

47 As social theorist David Harvey notes, minimum guarantee of socio-economic rights demands "massive" effort – in fact beyond the designs of the current global economic system. Still, the practices involved in human rights missives on socio-economic standards are part of the human rights spectrum, and the intention is fuller, more sovereign individuals on a global basis. See Harvey, *Spaces of Hope* (Berkeley: University of California Press, 2000), 90.

individual – that private ownership *is* something one deserves as a product of hard work, and that hard work is hard work, and reward should go to the one who *does* the work in whatever terms that's valued? What if you think that Chávez (or Maduro) have manipulated popular sentiment for their own gain, and that they're wolves in sheep's clothing? What happens if you're convinced that most people *don't* support *Chavismo*, even if it seems like many do? Indeed, say you're *truly* conservative and believe that some people *don't* deserve the same rights as others and that societies are better off with a landed class that's educated to rule? Should your opinions just be shut down? Should you have *no* room to express yourself or to speak your mind? Should you be censored and told you haven't the right to think that, or make your case out loud? I'd put it this way: let's also put aristocratic conservatism to the side. Should law and the mechanisms of state *not* provide ways for people to express that they have doubts about what's going on around them, or that they'd like different reforms than those that are unfolding? Even if it might be interpreted as unsolidaric, should not people be able to say that they wonder about an economic program, or argue that the duty of government is to secure freedom of opportunity over the guarantee of ends? Party lines might make sense – massive public investment and the nationalizing of resource wealth based on the equal value of all labor isn't an *un*reasonable idea. Still, if economic empowerment should be accompanied by democracy, can one *really* dissolve parliament, or use military power to do street battle with protestors?

No. Now, a part of me wishes I could say different because economic inequality, never mind people's lack of access to basic resources, drives me crazy. We have to at least *ask* whether legal equality in the marketplace (capitalism) is equality as such, and whether saying that the right to *try* to do what one wants constitutes fairness in a social system.[48] The level of grassroots organizing needed to make the poor heard is noticeably harder than purchasing political megaphones via personal wealth, and it is *much* harder to start making your way with nothing than, say, the millions inherited by Donald Trump.[49] Indeed, I oppose philosopher John Rawls' idea of a "veil of ignorance." If justice is correctly practiced, Rawls argued, it should be from a position in which no one knows how the results of one's decisions will turn out (wherein the "process" in "decision-making process" become primary). One should behave as a neutral "citizen," and one's identity

---

48 See, e.g., John E. Roemer, *Equality of Opportunity* (Cambridge, MA: Harvard University Press, 1998); Shlomi Segall, *Equality and Opportunity* (Oxford: Oxford University Press, 2013).
49 The Economist, "Thanks, Pop: Donald Trump's Inheritance," October 6, 2018, https://www.economist.com/united-states/2018/10/06/donald-trumps-inheritance.

should be put to the side.⁵⁰ Is that possible, though? Can one really discard experiences of oppression or marginalization, or the feeling of being pushed to the side? Can one really ignore the feeling of having had little or having watched others have wealth and the privileges that wealth brings? Can one really forget what it's felt like to not get a fair shot, or to see others use society's resources largely for their ends? Or can one forget what it's like to *have* – sometimes more than others, or in a way where your existence is secure while others' are not? Can one forget what it's like to *feel* privilege, or be part of a privileged clique oneself?⁵¹

I wonder. Experience might drive us to things, including advocating for change. Oppression may drive the search for a way out or to concretely change one's circumstance. Still, we don't know *what* way out one will want and we don't know *what* change an individual might seek. We don't know who will have sympathy for transformation, or be willing to risk what they have in order to join the fight. We're not automatons. One set of experiences *needn't* result in but *one* solution and there's not anywhere history is supposed to go. Some might ask for certain solutions, while others might ask for something else. In fact, I'd argue, a purer socialism recognizes that. "Workers of the world, unite!" wrote Marx; the oppressed need to organize themselves and take action. Now, yes, Marx *himself* had ideas about what social action should be and *he* had visions of how communist society should work. *He* had senses of historical necessity and ideas of how history should progress. Still, we should be *exalted* to see each other. We needed to be *encouraged* to work together and overthrow oppressive powers. *We* needed to recognize our conditions and *we* needed to feel them and lay out plans for their change. It was *our* revolution that we should lead – one that emerged because *we* wanted it, and *we* might chart its course. This involved *debate* – how does one create the better society? It involves reflection: what's wrong, and what's the *best* way out? And, if reflection was *really* going to be critical, Marx noted, one had to "doubt everything;" one had to look critically at *every* received truth.⁵² That meant

---

50 See John Rawls, *A Theory of Justice* (Cambridge, MA: Harvard Belknap, 1971), 136–7.
51 Political philosopher and economist Amartya Sen notes that the "significance of history…lies…in the more general understanding that established traditions continue to exert some influence on people's ideas." This is a deep debate within approaches to justice – should they be blind or should they be historical, and is justice a bar to be jumped over, or a bar whose height we set? I'm pointing to the latter idea – a notion which will need its own work to fully flesh out. See Sen, *The Idea of Justice* (Cambridge, MA: Harvard Belknap, 2009), 332.
52 Karl Marx, "Bekentnisse" in *Karl Marx Friedrich Engels Werke 31* (Berlin: Dietz, 1965), 597.

free speech. It meant freedom of opinion, including freedom of opinions towards which one was skeptical. It suggested a free media, freedom of assembly, and the reaffirmation of the people as the source of government. "Doubting everything" meant accepting that there might be unity on given issues. It also meant accepting, however, that, in some areas, there might not.[53]

Not recognizing such things helped destroy the socialist world. While many ingredients were part of that phenomenon, resistance to thought police and the demand that one follow party lines was part of the events of '89-'91. From Moscow to Prague, come the late 1980s, there was interest in more democracy and forcing the elections that, though not necessarily intended that way, would result in regimes' end.[54] While it's the case that communism involved its own iterations of critical thought – questioning capitalism and imperialism were central to the socialist cause – schools were nonetheless packed with propaganda and orthodoxy, regime opponents were derided, and "freedom of conscience, freedom of thought, and freedom of religion or belief [were] perceived as having vast subversive potential for national…stability and security."[55] Is that how things are in Venezuela? Maybe not precisely. As with the Russian elections a couple of months ago, there *was an* opposition candidate; *somebody* ran against Maduro. The country has media outlets that the government doesn't control, and there are broadcast and print outlets opposing the regime. Indeed, in a move representing the best of democratic socialism, *Chávez* founded thousands of "communes" – grassroots communities intended to exercise control over economic production and the use of government monies. Now, has Maduro engaged in democratic backsliding? Yes. Barring electoral candidates, making people feel threatened, and changing the rules along the way is *not* democracy. Sending out too many

---

53 This is not a point of unity in Marxist theory. There are interpreters of Marx's work, or at least Marxism, who see him and it as antithetical to democracy. That is hardly the only understanding of Marxism however, as there is a massive tradition interpreting socialism and communism as highly democratic ideas, at least at the theoretical level. See, e.g., Alexandros Chrysis, *'True Democracy' as a Prelude to Communism: The Marx of Democracy* (London: Palgrave, 2018); Richard Wolff, *Democracy at Work: A Cure for Capitalism* (Chicago: Haymarket, 2012). See also Joseph V. Femia, *Marxism and Democracy* (London: Clarendon, 1993).
54 For an excellent overview of the events of '89, see Vladimir Tismaneanu, ed., *The Revolutions of the 1989* (London: Routledge, 1999).
55 Thomas M. Krapf, "Lossed Opportunities and Missed Targets: Notes on Freedom of Religion or Belief in the Organization of Security and Co-operation in Europe" in *The Changing Nature of Religious Rights under International Law*, ed. Malcolm Evans, Peter Petkoff and Julian Rivers (Oxford: Oxford University Press, 2015), 132.

riot police isn't allowing free thought, and loading people into paddy wagons isn't allowing people to speak. Waving to empty streets is waving to no one and it isn't engaging in dialog with the public body. That's at the same time that there *are* arguments that *Chavismo* involved policies that brought more people into the political process and did so in genuinely powerful ways. Chávez may have forced Venezuelan politics to surpass the normal clique of people expected to exert high levels of influence, and he may have encouraged real levels of popular activism on the part of everyday Venezuelans across the national scene.

Therein may lie the point: that something has changed from the heyday of "let-the-people-work" protests against PDVSA lockout and the "take the power back" *élan* of the "Bolivarian revolution's" early days. There may be a change in attitude via which an imperfect regime became not just imperfect but ugly and in which policies may have gone from something one could debate to flat-out wrong. Something may have crossed the zero threshold between plus one and minus one and something provocative may have become something that oppresses. Now, Venezuela isn't the East Bloc and *Chavismo* is based on ideologies that pursue less (much less) centralized governance than anything that emerged from Soviet socialism. There was no Henri Falcón in Soviet elections and the USSR had no news agency but TASS. Brezhnev didn't feel the need to *debate* about the Prague Spring – he just ran over it with tanks (Maduro spends a lot of time on the back and forth with opposition forces).[56] Still, the "let's-keep-as-much-of-the-oppostion-as-possible-off-the-electoral-slate" attitude (indeed, policies) of Venezuela's most recent election resemble *Putin's* Russia, and, as opposition grows, the number of outlets for alternative voices shrinks.[57] Opposition leaders *have been* jailed on dubious charges, and one can no longer claim that it's only the middle class and the educated protesting against the government.

---

56 Many are also clear on the post-colonialist, decentralized, indigenous rights and, dare it be said, postmodern dimensions of not only Chávez's movement, but a number of the popular social-progressive movements in Latin America. See Barry Cannon, *Hugo Chávez and the Bolivarian Revolution: Populism and Democracy in a Globalized Age* (Manchester: Manchester University Press, 2009), 207; Spanakos, "Citizen Chávez," 21.

57 Currently, Reporters without Borders ranks Venezuela 143rd out of 180 ranked countries for press freedom. See Reporters without Borders, "2018 Press Freedom Index" (2018), https://rsf.org/en/ranking. Of course, this involves the relationship between media and the state, wherein the use of social media cutting around mainstream media channels is lesser taken into account. However, that gets at the point: that one must find unofficial, non-traditional media channels because the mainstream outlets for civil discussion are increasingly less open.

Indeed, the government isn't any longer shy about deploying the military against demonstrators or using methods verging on torture to squash dissent. These are the images we see: riot squads and the national guard running over activists, and dissidents being handcuffed and hauled off. Not just water cannons but live fire are aimed at demonstrators, and the UN reports some pretty brutal methods in obtaining confessions from opposition activists and the organizers of various protests.[58] No, Venezuela might not be Erich Honecker's East Germany; its system isn't a Soviet-style monolith. The country's social dynamics might not be unlike East Germany in '89, however, where, as demonstrators began to express discontent, the government reaction was to suppress. A *Washington Post* reporter in Berlin in October 1989 wrote, "when police ordered the protesters to leave a street near a church that has been a center for pro-reform groups, the crowd shouted, 'We are the people!' Security forces began to pull protesters away from the march and hit them on the head with truncheons as other demonstrators chanted 'No violence,' and residents threw raw eggs at police who were trying to block part of the street."[59] It was the classic picture of a regime being a *regime*, strong-arming people into place. It was the bullying that comes with authoritarianism and the use of force to maintain order. Look at scenes from Caracas and other Venezuelan cities over the past year and *The Post*'s images strike a chord. That's except to the extent that East Germany at the end of the '80s was probably in better economic shape than Venezuela is today – that despite the GDR having nothing like the natural resources that Venezuela holds.[60]

---

58 See Rachelle Krygier, "Chávez Yes, Maduro, No. The Growing Split in Venezuela," *Americas Quarterly* September 14, 2016, http://www.americasquarterly.org/content/chavez-yes-maduro-no-growing-split-venezuela; Joshua Partlow and Rachelle Krygier, "Venezuela's Slide into Chaos is Splintering the Chávez Movement," *The Washington Post*, June 14, 2017, https://www.washingtonpost.com/world/the_americas/venezuelas-slide-into-chaos-is-splintering-the-chavez-movement/2017/06/13/4a72055c-4d33-11e7-987c-42ab5745db2e_story.html?noredirect=on&utm_term=.65b89ab9dc4a; BBC, "UN Warns Venezuela over 'Use of Excessive Force,'" August 8, 2017, https://www.bbc.com/news/world-latin-america-40861095.
59 David Remnick, "Police Beat Protestors in E. Berlin," *The New York Times*, October 9, 1989, https://www.washingtonpost.com/archive/politics/1989/10/09/police-beat-protesters-in-e-berlin/f7e899d2-7406-422c-988a-ce3d7e57237e/?utm_term=.f4a792967911.
60 See, e.g., Hartmut Berghoff and Uta Andrea Balbier, eds., *The East German Economy, 1945-2010: Falling Behind or Catching Up?* (Cambridge: Cambridge University Press, 2010).

That's when things go too far. It's when things become wrong and difficult to understand. It's when events cross a line, and someone need say "stop." There's much that's been admirable about *Chavismo* populism, and it's *had* a spontaneous nature that can give it a sympathetic sheen. Though one can always ask if movements should be so contingent on a single figure – and *Chavismo* was sometimes that – Chávez appears to have tried to shift the power down and offer greater control of wealth and politics to larger numbers of people. Chávez asked if a just society doesn't feed everyone, and suggested that the little man should hold meaningful sway. Still, can one understand undemocratic crackdowns when the *raison d'être* behind a movement was supposed to be *greater* democracy and *more* power in the people's hands? Can one understand rigging elections and jailing opposition leaders when *socialism* should involve critique and dialog with those with whom one disagrees? Can one understand quashing dissent while people sit in misery, asking for more solutions than just declaiming American and capitalist "plots?" Not as I see it. Such practices eat at the *reason* to advocate for "a standard of living adequate for the health and well-being of [oneself] and [one's] family," and the recognition that progressive societies seek. Such approaches undermine the purpose of the search for more social parity and the purpose of putting more wealth into people's hands. Such approaches undermine the reason for *some* level of economic parity and making sure that there's not only a chicken in everyone's pot, but some celery and a couple of carrots too. That's freedom, pure and simple. It's more enfranchisement, not less. It's greater participation in the society around one, and *in fact* assuring that many voices are heard and not only those of a select few. I wonder: if Maduro stepped out onto a Caracas street and looked into Chávez's eyes in one of the murals bearing his visage, would he see approval or reproach? Would *Chávez* look at Maduro and say that what's going on is ok? It seems to me that if the point of *Chavismo* really *was* democracy, the answer has to be "no." You can't support the people and crack down on them at the same time – a clarity Maduro seems to lack.

Nuremberg
The Center of the Vortex
(September 17, 2018)

Abstract: *Nuremberg sits in the center of Europe and houses some of the continent's most important sites in terms of human rights. The experience of being there, however, and specifically at the city's Nazi party rally grounds and the site of the Nuremberg Trials, makes one reflect on the interplay between history and memory and the meanings, narratives, and stories we tell ourselves surrounding justice in the modern world. Meaning might be the most important of those categories. There are debates to be had about historical facts, and Nuremberg invokes many observations regarding German history and international affairs. The city's ultimate significance nonetheless concerns confrontations with concepts of justice that we've built up over time and the power of the site of historical memory in conveying such ideas.*

It's a wild town, somehow, Nuremberg. It's at the heart, the actual heart, of Europe. Come to the city from the north and you pass through the great plains of Northern Europe – the farmland and fields that define so much of the geographic culture from Denmark to the Netherlands to the north of France over to rural Poland. Come at it from the south, and one descends from the Alps – the roof of Europe, and the great divide between a continent connected to the warm seas of the Mediterranean and the noticeably colder waters of the Baltic and North Seas. Come at the city from the east, and one's on one's way to France, and Spain – the behemoths of Europe's West, whose blocky square shapes can't be missed on any world map. Come at it from the west and one is moving towards Slavic lands; the close bunching of former medieval kingdoms that have configured and reconfigured themselves in relation to any manner of empires and whose emergence from the Soviet orbit may be the defining component of

Photo of *Justizpalast* and *Kongresshalle* by author.

their modern history.¹ Nuremberg is itself a medieval city with a skyline dominated by the enormous *Nürnberger Burg*, one of the imperial centers of the Holy Roman Empire, and the picture of what many have in mind when they think of the fortresses of the thirteenth and fourteenth centuries. Albrecht Dürer is perhaps the city's most famous son – the paradigm of early German Renaissance painting, printmaking, and art. The city is awash with the timber-framed buildings that tourists love to ooh and aah at – yet another artifact of the imagination of an aristocratic era when Europe was beginning to develop a middle class and the modern world was fresh on the horizon. Unlike its sister city in Bavaria, Munich, things can be just the smallest touch shabby. While filled with sightseers and home to some three-quarters of a million people (well, Nuremberg and a few of the towns around it), you get the feeling that the area needs investment. It's dusty – a touch unkempt; like a solid Victorian house that's worth buying, yet will take a few summers of hard work to get into shape.

Of course, Nuremberg is also home to some of the indelible scenes that bookended either side of World War II. In the ultimate act of Nazi homage, e.g., Leni Riefenstahl memorialized the city in *Triumph of the Will*, the 1935 piece of ur-propaganda that both innovated filmmaking yet stands today as a clarion call to how spooky things can get when brainwashing is effective and you get people hooked like cocaine on the national ideal. Rows of be-uniformed young men wielding spades like rifles and uttering to Hitler how they have a sacred mission to build the country like soldiers on the battlefield, yet only on construction sites and farms, makes for a spine-shivering scene. So too do the scenes with seas of brownshirts marching in endless rows with flags and standards and Hitler egging on their mind-numbing obedience with half yelled rants about how the nation was cheated, yet now Germany was somehow "back." Speaker after speaker from the Nazi pantheon – Goebbels, Ley, Röhm – all of that was filmed

---

1 Of course, Yugoslavia, whose break-up provided one of the worst of the post-Soviet conflicts, was not part of the Soviet sphere; it was determined to create its own socialist path. It isn't atypical to discuss a universe of "post-Soviet conflicts," however, in which wars from the Balkans to the Caucuses fit – part of the governing logic being that, part of the Soviet sphere or not, the end of communism in Europe helped let the genie of ethnic conflict out of the bottle that socialism had generally held down. See Christoph Zürcher, *The Post-Soviet Wars: Rebellion, Ethnic Conflict, and Nationhood in the Caucuses* (New York: New York University Press, 2007), x, 36, 219; Reneo Lukic and Allen Lynch, *Europe from the Balkans to the Urals: The Disintegration of Yugoslavia and the Soviet Union* (Oxford: Oxford University Press, 1996).

in Nuremberg, in the shadow of the *Burg* and at the "party days" (*Parteitage*) the Nazis put on through the 1930s. They're scenes with which we're well-familiar; they're used again and again in documentaries about the Third Reich. In one of the well-read works on fascism, political scientist Alan Cassels once posited Nazism as selling an "exciting romance" – a national culture the wealthy could claim they were uplifting, yet a project of strength to which the "maladjusted" could belong.[2] He had a point. The Nazis looked to put the absolute coordination of the nation on display, and their "party days" at Nuremberg were where they chose to do so.[3]

Of course, we know the "Thousand Year Reich" lasted a grand twelve years, and once Nazi Germany was overrun by the Americans, British, and Soviets (and Hitler had shot himself), there was a price to be paid. The heavens had "darkened," one historian has written, and, after tens of millions of deaths – genocides included – something had to be done.[4] In fact, "something" began up the road in Lüneburg in the form of the Belsen Trials. That's to say that when the allies liberated the Bergen-Belsen concentration camp, they thought it important to not only punish those who organized the bestiality, but do so in accordance with the letter of some kind of law. It was important. While the notion of "crimes against humanity" and "human rights violations" didn't come into play, the notion of "war crimes" did, and it was forwarded that *some* variety of international justice should be deployed.[5] At Nuremberg, things went further. Addressing a broader array of atrocities than was tackled at Lüneburg, a grander display of international justice had to be made, wherein the trials introduced the idea of "crimes against humanity" and the notion of not only breaking the laws of war, but violating a sense of human rights. That happened in Nuremberg's Palace of Justice (*Justizpalast*), chosen because it was relatively intact compared to buildings in many of Germany's main towns as well as the city's symbolic value vis-à-vis the party rallies. Of course, this

---

2 Alan Cassels, *Fascism* (Arlington Heights: Harlan Davidson, 1975), 124–5.
3 See Stephen Brockmann, *Nuremberg: The Imaginary Capital* (Rochester: Camden House, 2006).
4 I here paraphrase Arno Mayer, *Why Did the Heavens Not Darken?: The Final Solution in History* (London: Verso, 2012).
5 See Donald Bloxham, *Genocide on Trial: War Crimes Trials and the Formation of Holocaust History and Memory* (Oxford: Oxford University Press, 2001), 97–101.

was the Nuremberg Trials – maybe the most famous moment in the history of international justice.

It is like stepping into another era. The Nazi party rally grounds, where Hitler and his cronies made their overbearing displays, still sit there, just beyond the southeast of the main city, maintained as a museum, yet also falling into disrepair (the city debates with itself to what degree it should maintain the site).[6] The grounds are in fact a complex (not one simple parade ground), and the buildings and plazas are overbearing and huge. Fascist architecture was not about emphasizing people's individuality; as it's been noted, the point was uniformity and subsumption to a larger whole – and the party rally grounds most certainly did that (subsume).[7] Constituted of several parts, it's hard to grasp the scale of the thing. Today, the main features are the so-called Zeppelin Field (*Zeppelinfeld*), the Congress Hall (*Kongresshalle*), and the Great Road (*Große Straße*) – areas that remain in a rough kind of tact. More was planned, however. A so-called *Märzfeld* (Marching Grounds) was supposed to have room for more than 150,000 soldiers, taking up land equivalent to eighty American football fields (gigantic), and the world's largest sports stadium was also planned as part of the grounds – a monument to the physical superhuman Hitler hoped to create. There were to be accommodations for the many workers and citizens who were hoped to come rally for the Nazi cause wherein, if plans had been followed through (the war stopped them), it would have been one of the most massive building projects the world had ever seen. What's there is nonetheless crazy. While some parts of the complex, such as the Luitpoldarena (also a massive parade ground) are overgrown, the outlines of the Zeppelin Field remain. It's there that many of the most famous images of Nazi rallies were shot, with phalanxes of leather-booted military columns surrounded by tens of thousands of Hitler-salute offering Germans. The Congress Hall looks like a gigantic landed mothership rising from the foliage and the area's ponds; it's like an insane Colosseum dominated by a lack of ornamentation. The Great Road appears like a crypto-fascist Champs-Élysées – a massive boulevard denuded of anything but the grey concrete squares designed to facilitate the boots of endless armed columns. At the Zeppelin Field,

---

6   See Ton Paterson, "Nuremberg: Germany's Dilemma over the Nazis' Field of Dreams," *The Independent*, January 1, 2016, https://www.independent.co.uk/news/world/europe/nuremberg-germanys-dilemma-over-the-nazis-field-of-dreams-a6793276.html; Deutsche Welle, "Bad Buildings: Nazi Architecture and Tourism," May 6, 2016, https://www.dw.com/en/bad-buildings-nazi-architecture-and-tourism/a-19239123.

7   Leland M. Roth, *Understanding Architecture: Its Elements, History, and Meaning* (London: Routledge, 2018), 566.

one can walk onto the rostrum where Hitler held his speeches and imagine what it would have been like to look out over extensive fascist hordes. I didn't.

The site of the Nuremberg Trials is totally different. It isn't small – it's today a working administration building for the regional court system, and Nuremberg isn't the smallest of cities. Still, you come across the building like you would any other administrative office block in a mid-sized town – sort of by chance, amidst the rest of the city's scenery and in a manner that says business is the agenda, not the remaking of the national "folk." Then the room where the trials were held (Courtroom 600) is pretty but in many ways unremarkable. The first thing one notices is a massive Catholic cross sitting over the justices' benches. It had been removed in preparation for the Nuremberg Trials, but was put back into place after the building was returned to local authorities. There's an ornate doorway featuring a figure holding a sword and another a fasces – the symbols of German and Roman law (in photographs from the Nuremberg Trial, one will often notice that). However, the room is plain; wooden – solid. Today, the orientation is rotated ninety degrees from how it was set up for the Trials themselves. If one imagines the room as a square, whereas the judges now sit at its top side, for the Trials, they sat on the left, with defendants sitting on what today is the bottom. The whole thing is quiet; on the day of my visit, the sunlight filtered through the window and you could almost hear the sound of the landing dust. It was hard to imagine Hermann Göring, Alfred Rosenberg, Rudolf Hess and a dozen or so others who had contributed to such destruction and mayhem sitting in the same place. It's ethereal; ghost-like – like returning decades later to a place on a playground where you might have been pushed around or beaten as a schoolchild, yet that moment when the abuse was finally seen and, with no real joy to anyone, the bully was hauled off by the teacher and the child's parents called.

Ghosts. They obviously have little meaning unless they speak to the present. In an essay written in 1874, the philosopher Nietzsche discussed the notion of the past as functioning like "one giant call[ing] to another across the bleak intervals of [the] ages," and perhaps he's right.[8] The past is the past, and there's nothing to do about it. There is no recovering actions completed, or undoing them, wherein (though Nietzsche had a politics I don't particularly like), the point may be that history should be used "for life." As he wrote, the "ideal condition cannot be achieved by dreaming;" rather, "we must fight and struggle to achieve it."[9]

---

8   Friedrich Nietzsche, *On the Advantage and Disadvantage of History of Life*, trans Peter Preuss (Indianapolis: Hackett, 1980), 53.
9   Ibid.

Whatever whispers or giant-like hollers the past has to give to us, they dissolve into emptiness unless someone is there to hear them. It's the meaning we take from sceneries like Courtroom 600 where Göring and company were tried or the crumbling relics of Nuremberg's gargantuan rally grounds that imbue them with significance, and it's the importance that *we* invest in the *lieux de mémoire*, as historian Pierre Nora put it – our "sites of memory" – that make them what they are.[10] When we stand in places like Nuremberg, we tangle and string together pieces of information, visual cues, and things we think we know like mad collage painters running out of time. We create a picture, set of sensibilities, and atmosphere, if not a story, from the multiple, sometimes disparate, parts of what we see and what's available around us to grasp.[11]

One of those stories – one that's hard not to feel when one is imposed upon by objects so *large* (the rally grounds are like asking for a piece of birthday cake and being handed three whole cakes instead) – is that there was simply something sick at play; that Germany *must* have been gripped by a fever by which it goosestepped itself into the netherworlds of the political soul – though perhaps a fever laying long-dormant under the surface, waiting to break through. A recent film, *The White Ribbon* (*Das weiße Band* [2009]), picks up on this idea. In the sinews of Christian Europe, it argues – especially protestant Europe, with its culture of deference and "keep your emotions to yourself" (never mind what the sociologist Max Weber termed the "Protestant work ethic") – there was simply a streak of evil; a kind of meanness that sat in the air, ground in by hundreds of years of repressive ideas. No country may have done more to condemn the evils of its past than modern Germany; I, anyway, have never quite seen a country go as far out of its way, in deadly serious manners, to say it was wrong and it's sorry. However, a *White Ribbon*-esque atmosphere is something one can almost imagine oneself into in driving through a northern German town on a cold day with the sun behind the clouds in which things are eerily quiet, the windows of houses are shuttered, and you know people are there, but you wonder where they've gone. One almost gets the sense that the histrionics of the right nationalist, or the smooth, ironic tones of the right propaganda minister, could have

---

10 See Pierre Nora, et al., *Realms of Memory: The Construction of the French Past*, trans. Arthur Goldhammer (New York: Columbia University Press, 1996). Goldhammer uses the term "realms" for *lieux*. My sense is that "sites," or "places" – where one sees something – is better.

11 This is a complex notion. However, I provide a fleshing-out of it in Ben Dorfman, "History Phenomenology: An Outline," *Ideas in History* 3, no. 1 (2008): 107–36.

the effect of loosing a Freudian scream – a "look at us! We're here! I'm tired of having to hold so much back!" In such a story, Germany couldn't stop itself. It took its sense of formality and *fleißigkeit* (industriousness) and weaponized it – it turned it to kill. The massive monuments of the rally grounds were to guide this catharsis – insisting that what was really madness was the revitalization of something "great" and that mayhem was mayhem with a purpose, or raw power signaling a kind of strength. In this story, the Nuremberg Trials play the doctor – the psychologist come to the cell after the patient is subdued to make his or her mentality "right." They're an operation or balm applied to an infected sore – a scalpel scraping out a cancerous tumor, or a lobotomy not damaging the brain, yet removing those parts that make the patient run amok. The Nuremberg Trials are the rain pellets one shoots into the air over Beijing, cleansing the sky and taking away the stink.[12]

Of course, the line between madness and murderous sanity can be thin, and such things have been brought up in various ways by books like Daniel Goldhagen's *Hitler's Willing Executioners* (1996), dimensions of the German "historian's debate" (a kind of sniping at each other about the Nazi period engaged in by German academics in the '80s), as well as the notion that there might be

---

12 We need to be very clear about a number of points. Firstly, as evidenced by contemporary political debate, any kind of trying to abscond Germany from guilt regarding the events of the Second World War is enormously controversial within the country; members of the far-right *Alternative für Deutschland* have gotten themselves into significant hot water for doing just that. That is part of a larger reality around modern Germany – it is a democratic state (highly so), and it goes far (very far) out of its way to recognize what it did and to condemn its own past. Still, as Michael Haneke points to with his film (*The White Ribbon*), there's a question of putting yourself in a physical environment and trying to think backwards about how things may have felt – something, unfortunately, one is forced to do through the present and settings as they exist now. Of course, another point worth mentioning is that while there may be something to a "psychological" understanding of Nazism somehow involving notions of repression and perhaps Protestantism and the atmosphere of the country's north, the Nazi party concretely emerged out of Munich, in Germany's largely Catholic south. See Deutsche Welle, "AfD, On Course for Parliament, Says Germany Done with Nazi Past," September 15, 2017, https://www.dw.com/en/afd-on-course-for-parliament-says-germany-done-with-nazi-past/a-40519573; Mary Corliss, "White Ribbon: Poisonous Seeds of Hitler's Germany," *Time*, May 14, 2009, http://content.time.com/time/specials/packages/article/0,28804,1898196_1898204_1900375,00.html; Stuart Klawans, "Fascism, Repression and 'The White Ribbon,'" *The New York Times*, October 30, 2009, https://www.nytimes.com/2009/11/01/movies/01klaw.html.

a particularly unique "German path" through modern history (the *Sonderweg* thesis, historians call it [special path thesis]). I'll start with the latter. As eminent German historian Jürgen Kocka argues, the primary question is why, in contrast to comparable, developed countries in the West and North, "Germany became fascist and/or totalitarian in the crisis of the 1920s and 1930s."[13] I.e., despite the histrionics of Oswald Mosely and even faced with a world-wide depression, the British didn't turn to Nazism, and, though we know of French collaborationism during the War and interwar France was perhaps nearly as unstable as interwar Germany, neither did the French. America didn't head down that path, despite a flare shot up by the German-American Bund (Google "American Nazis Madison Square Garden 1939") – so why Germany? How can we explain fascism *there*?[14]

There have been a lot of answers: illiberal dimensions of German political culture, a determination to romanticize the country's past because of Germany coming *de facto* late to the table of unified nations (modern Germany only dates to 1871), the persistence of a pre-industrial landed culture in a rapidly industrializing world, the skepticism of certain members of traditional classes towards parliamentarianism, and an intense militarism brought by a Prussian military class embodied in Otto von Bismarck's assertions that the nation would be unified through "blood and iron" are some of the explanations proffered vis-à-vis some of the country's radical right tendencies.[15] Central to understandings like this has been a famous book among social scientists by a German historian named Fritz Fischer who, though addressing World War I, also seemed to be speaking to tendencies that would manifest themselves in World War II, or would show up later, somehow. In Fischer's words, "the German Empire created by Bismarck in 1871 was a partnership between the Prussian military and authoritarian state and the leading circles of the new industrial and commercial liberal bourgeoisie." Unified Germany was formed by men fervently informed by national ambition and who were willing to use new technologies to advance the power of the nation all the

---

13 Jürgen Kocka, "Germany Before Hitler: The Debate about the German Sonderweg," *Journal of Contemporary History* 23, no. 1 (1988): 4.
14 The German-American Bund represents a minor historical episode, though it caused controversy at the time. Led by Fritz Julius Kuhn, it was a kind of neo-Nazi organization that, not unlike today's white nationalist movements, sought to pass itself off as "patriotic." It was eventually shut down come the start of the war. Its 1939 event at Madison Square Garden attracted some 20,000 people, however, wherein it got some attention. See Anrie Bernstein, *Swastika Nation: The Rise and Fall of the German-American Bund* (New York: St. Martin's, 2013).
15 Ibid.

while believing wholeheartedly in a "wishful and emotional content to volkisch and racial conceptions."[16] Perhaps Germany wasn't involved in psychosis in a psychological sense. The country suffered from a *parvenu's* complex, however, which, mixed with the authoritarianism of the country's landed classes and a romanticization of the national *volk*, translated into a decided anti-liberalism and attitudes organized around crushing the country's perceived enemies. And, as Fischer notes, those enemies could be found at home as well as abroad. That was in the form of minorities, political opponents, or, of course, Jews.[17]

Certain dimensions of the so-called "historians' debate" (*Historikerstreit*) echo this. Was the Nazi period something which might be explained by the political machinations of a particular clique – the property of a few well-placed deviant minds? Or, as historian Ernst Nolte suggested, were its "eliminationist" tendencies predicated by the *left* via certain of the "either you're with us or against us" tendencies of the *French* and *Russian* Revolutions and *their* totalitarian moments (i.e., maybe Nazism was less unique than we think)?[18] Not many who responded to Nolte, including philosopher Jürgen Habermas, suggested that German history was somehow infected with a "disease." They did, however, suggest that there was no line to be drawn under Germany's fascist doings and that there weren't excuses to be made for them in any way, shape, or form. The nation must bear responsibility for what it had done, and regardless of whether Stalin or Robespierre also murdered people, Germany must accept racist and marginalizing as part of what *it* had been. Anything else was "officious-conservative" narration, figures like Habermas argued, and those who suggested otherwise were simply not looking at the truth.[19]

Then there was the Goldhagen thesis. Now, a lot of historians were annoyed with the tone of Goldhagen's book – Goldhagen perhaps claiming to discover something "new" more than he actually had. Some felt he didn't give credit where credit was due and that his work built too much off of sources developed by

---

16 Fritz Fischer, *Germany's Aims in the First World War* (New York: W.W. Norton, 1967), 7.
17 Ibid.
18 Some of these views are well-explained in François Furet and Ernst Nolte, *Fascism and Communism*, trans. Katherine Golsan (Lincoln: University of Nebraska Press, 2001).
19 Jürgen Habermas, "A Kind of Settlement of Damages: The Apologetic Tendencies in German Historical Writing" in *Forever in the Shadow of Hitler: Original Documents of the Historikerstreit, the Controversy Concerning the Singularity of the Holocaust*, trans. James Knowlton and Truett Cates (Atlantic Highlands: Humanities Press, 1993), 39.

others.[20] Still, he advanced a convincing idea: *someone* killed Jews and millions of others in the Holocaust; it wasn't just officials and "policies," and it wasn't *but* deviants and miscreants or exceptional individuals divorced from everyone else – not when you're talking about murder in the tens of millions. A *society* was involved in the ordeal, and despite collaborators across Europe and SS divisions that included foreign troops, the society in question was *Germany*. *People* were anti-Semitic, *someone* was a racist, and *someone* was involved with illiberal beliefs. Regardless of the precise reason why, Goldhagen argued, the Holocaust happened because *Germans* assented to Nazism and *they* built the camps. And *that*, as one report from the Social Democratic party in Nazism's early days noted, *might* border on "psychosis." Perhaps Germany *was* a society that need be acknowledged as not well.[21]

It's hard to know what to say about such ideas. Again, walking through the Nazi party rally grounds means to feel something amiss. It's hard to see what *joy* could have been felt by anyone standing in those monumental structures with their blockish, unadorned, turn-up-the-volume-to-eleven-rip-off-of-Greco-Roman-architectural-convention aesthetics. It's hard to see who would have been excited by such an overblown presentation except those suffering angry discontent or who felt their possibilities for belonging cut off everywhere else. Still, at least one well-received book suggested that the most virulent strains of anti-Semitism emanated from the *East* – locales where Jewish populations were less well-integrated than they were in modern Germany. There are arguments that Hitler might have picked up the extreme anti-Jewish attitudes he promoted in *Vienna* and the discombobulated world of the late Austro-Hungarian Empire (and, indeed, that Hitler managed to sneak some of his anti-Semitism in through the backdoor behind some early political-economic success).[22] It's also the case that pogroms and other anti-Semitic mass violences and murders had been a part of the European landscape on a long-term basis; Europeans had been Jew-hating well since the Middle Ages and the violences of anti-Semitism past played out not only in German territories, but in locales from England to Russia to

---

20 See Henry Friedlander, review of *Hitler's Willing Executioners* by Daniel Jonah Goldhagen, *German Studies Review* 19, no. 3 (1996): 578–80.
21 Daniel J. Goldhagen, *Hitler's Willing Executioners: Ordinary Germans and the Holocaust* (New York: Vintage, 1997), 107.
22 See Sebastian Haffner, *The Meaning of Hitler*, trans. Ewald Osers (Cambridge, MA: Harvard University Press, 1979).

France.²³ To suggest Germany as the *sole* source of racism and anti-Semitism in Europe would be to argue for a misconception. And if the question is ultra-nationalism, we have to remember that Hitler's government was hardly the only radical-right formation in power come the 1930s.²⁴ The Nuremberg Trials may have thus represented a victory. A more "theoretical" trial, if it might be called that – a broader trial also taking longer-term causes and broader trends into account – might have pointed a finger beyond Hermann Göring and Alfred Jodl. It might have tried centuries of Western history, indicting broad forms of ethnicized nationalism and arguments that any number of "foreign" populations didn't really "belong." It might have looked critically at Christianity, and senses of "Christ-killing" Jews. Indeed, one might look at such things *today* too.²⁵ Of course, most modern natiomo-rightist parties assert that they're *not* fascist and they're not interested in repeating Nazistic pasts. Still, if you're a kid stealing cookies and someone catches you red-handed, you can absolutely say you're not (stealing cookies). That doesn't have anything to do, however, with whether or not that's true.²⁶

---

23 Jews were expulsed from England in 1290, they were savaged by the Crusades, the pogroms in the Russian Empire were not a small part of the reason for Jewish migration to the United States at the end of the nineteenth and start of the twentieth century, and France featured one of the more well-known instances of modern anti-Semitism in the form of the Dreyfus Affair. See Walter Laqueur, *The Changing Face of Anti-Semitism: From Ancient Times to the Present Day* (Oxford: Oxford University Press, 2006).
24 See again Cassells, *Fascism*.
25 It's well-documented that anti-Semitic attacks have been on the rise. However, that's in the context of not only a potential resurgence in antipathy towards Jews, but an entire problem concerning xenophobia in the West related to immigration, ethnic and religious minorities, or anyone else perceived as coming from the "outside." See Ishan Tharoor, "The Inescapable Anti-Semitism of Western Nationalists," *The Washington Post*, February 28, 2018, https://www.washingtonpost.com/news/worldviews/wp/2018/02/28/the-inescapable-anti-semitism-of-western-nationalists/?utm_term=.7c3070d02bf3.
26 One has to be careful here. Rightist formations are functioning as legitimate parties across Europe, from Scandinavia to France and Germany to Poland and Hungary. However, more than a few journalists are well-noting a spectrum between many newly "mainstream" nationalist parties and an ultra-right veering towards neo-Nazism. See, e.g., Max Holleran, "The Opportunistic Rise of Europe's Far Right," *The New Republic*, February 16, 2018, https://newrepublic.com/article/147102/opportunistic-rise-europes-far-right, or Paul Hockenos, "Poland and the Uncontrollable Fury of Europe's Far Right," *The Atlantic*, November 15, 2017, https://www.theatlantic.com/international/archive/2017/11/europe-far-right-populist-nazi-poland/524559/.

Still, justice in Courtroom 600? Was Nuremberg to be a *real* trial, where someone might be proved *innocent*? Were not the trial's results predetermined, with the question being the meaning put on events? Was Nuremberg not to be a victor's show; a chance for the Soviets, Americans, British, and French to underline Nazi evil, burnishing their qualifications as the bearers of good? Would anyone ever *possibly* agree with Göring's declaration that he was "not guilty," or that he or his compatriots were anything other than the worst of criminals engaged in drastic crimes?

I have yet to run across a scholar who sees the Nuremberg Trials as *un*problematic – which is to say apolitical. As with so many things post-War, there was simple great power positioning. No one wanted to be left out of the picture of global importance, and everyone sought a particular pride of place and veneers of legitimacy and significance. The great powers had to win the case, and it had to be seen that their systems – whatever they were – were better.[27] Especially the Western democracies were also playing to the home crowd. News of the Trials was going to be available to the public, and what if too many clear Nazis were let go? And, indeed, at issue might have been a simple tension between the task of "'objective' documentation on one hand, and the voice of 'universal opinion' on the other."[28] I.e., as some scholars have claimed, perhaps certain baselines were going to be laid down without regard to technicality – who precisely did what and under what conditions – because the larger, *gestalt* picture was that the Nazis *had* plundered, murdered, and dragged the world into war *generally*, and global opinion demanded they be held to account.

These are tough concepts. Nuremberg prosecutors were genuinely nervous. "You must put no man on trial if you are not willing to see him freed if not proven guilty," chief prosecutor Robert Jackson told Harry Truman when he was asked to lead the prosecutorial team – and, indeed, Jackson had his concerns regarding especially Göring's cross-examination (the Nazi leader was notoriously charming, and there was concern he might talk his way out of being seen as responsible for his crimes).[29] It's tough to be nervous if one *only* has sham trials, and it's telling that Jackson thought there was risk in the trial process. There were also three *acquittals* at Nuremberg – not *everyone* with associations

---

27 See, e.g., John Lewis Gaddis, *The United States and the Origins of the Cold War* (New York: Columbia University Press, 2000).

28 Herbert R. Reginbogin and Christoph J.M. Safferling, eds., *The Nuremberg Trials: International Criminal Law since 1945* (Munich: S.G. Saur, 2006), 79.

29 See Michael Kloft (director), *American Experience: The Nuremberg Trials* (United States: Public Broadcasting Service, 2006).

with the Third Reich was subject to automatic conviction; some people got off. Hans Georg Fritzsche, Franz von Papen, and Hjalmar Schacht (a functionary of the propaganda ministry, the former Chancellor, and head of the Reichsbank, respectively) *were* let off as it was unclear precisely how they *directly* contributed to the crimes in question (crimes against humanity).[30] Still, as Whitney Harris, another prosecutor at the trials, noted, "this was not a trial of Germans alone; this was a trial for humanity."[31] A statement *was* likely to be made and it would be problematic if *everyone* went scot-free. Footage from concentration camps was going to be shown, and acts of murder enumerated. Starvation and rote abuse were to be featured, as well as horrendous war crimes. That couldn't go unanswered, and it need be signaled that Nazism had no future and a new age was upon us vis-à-vis international law.

And, indeed, that leads to another story that becomes embedded in all this – one that's a primary story of our times. *Another* narrative attaches itself to the lifeworld of Nuremberg – to the experience of standing in the echo chamber of Nazi party rallies and the resolutions of international justice. That's the story of human rights *as such*. It's the story of not only crimes against humanity, or indicting Nazi war criminals, but the story of *declaring* international rights, and asserting that there were "high[er] moral precepts and political ideals" to which we had to live up.[32] It's the story of creating the Universal Declaration of Human Rights (1948) and the rights agencies of the UN, trying to normativize the idea that international standards were imperative, and finding the bodies that might institutionalize humanitarianism across the borders of states. It's the idea that, though the roots of rights ideals lay in the Enlightenment, or even a Greco-Roman past, such things weren't international justice in a truly global sense. It's the idea that really thinking human rights as *human* rights – rights in their most universal sense – was somehow a *product* of the experiences of Nazism, and that events like the Holocaust are part of their DNA. It's the sense that vis-à-vis not only Nuremberg, but further efforts around human rights, that World War II represents a kind of

---

30 Of course, one can make the argument, *à la* Goldhagen, that the entire society was guilty. However, 100% conviction rates can look like show trials and, as such, as soon as you've decided to assign *personal* blame, this means having to establish some criterial as to who's to blame and not. These are complex issues indeed. See Anna Tusa and John Tusa, *The Nuremberg Trial* (New York: Skyhorse, 2010).
31 See Koft, *American Experience*.
32 Samuel Moyn, *The Last Utopia: Human Rights in History* (Cambridge, MA: Harvard Belknap, 2010), 1.

Hegelian moment – a moment in which, out of the negativity of destruction came reflection and the construction and articulation of a bellwether concept humanity would carry forward in time.[33]

There are different theses about this. The first is that this *is* the case – that something shifted come the discovery of, if not Nazi camps, then at least the extent of them; that Nuremberg wasn't just a moment, but the beginning of a catharsis in which "Never Again!" became a rallying cry and the international community thought itself obliged to systematize humanitarian ideals. World War II was a "catalyst," one historian has proclaimed, via which the "camps," Nazi destruction, and the attempt to avoid their repetition, was on the minds of those who gathered to establish rights frameworks after the War. Now, there's evidence of this. When it was decided that there in fact needed to be a broad, declaration of international rights principles, Charles Malik, Lebanese member of the drafting committee for the Universal Declaration of Human Rights (1948 [work on the document began in 1946]), noted that the attempt to codify human rights principles "was inspired by opposition to the barbarous doctrines of Nazism and fascism."[34] The Nazis tried to establish a society based on murder and discrimination, Malik argued, and those charged to outline a new *raison d'être* for international society had that squarely in mind; they knew what happened in Dachau and Majdanek and that was enough; it would be clearly stated "no more." The Ecuadoran representative to the UN noted that, "from the ruin and destruction wrought by the Second World War" came a new spirit of humanitarianism – one which would keep alive immortal flames of "civilization, freedom and law."[35] What happened under the second half of what some have characterized as a European "civil war" (World Wars I and II) was "barbarity" and modern culture

---

33 The basis for calling this moment "Hegelian" is Hegel's notion of a supersession of the previous historical moment by way of a reflection on it, wherein one becomes conscious of it, and bases action upon it, but relegates it to the past. This is itself a destructive act; a new historical state is created by obliterating another. However, in the long, winding road towards ideas based on true reason, destructive politics themselves can also dominate in relation to perceived historical problems (e.g., Nazism was posited as a response to something, and an attempt to start anew). This process would stop, Hegel thought, with the realization of the "Absolute," or an understanding of the nature of reason itself – the end of history, as such. See Daniel Berthold-Bond, *Hegel's Grand Synthesis: A Study of Being, Thought, and History* (Albany: SUNY Press, 1989).

34 In Johannes Morsink, *The Universal Declaration of Human Rights: Origins, Drafting & Intent* (Philadelphia: University of Pennsylvania Press, 1999), 36.

35 Ibid.

needed a different charge.[36] The Soviets chimed in to suggest that "whatever discrimination still exists in the world must be destroyed" – and if Nazism didn't convince people of that, what would?[37] Indeed, if one looks at the terms under which Allied powers such as the United States *entered* the war – terms laid-out a full year *before* the Japanese bombed Pearl Harbor – the war becomes more than a matter of national defense. In his January 1941 State of the Union, Franklin Delano Roosevelt outlined a vision for global politics in which the keywords were "freedom of speech and expression," the "freedom of every person to worship God…his own way," "freedom from want," and "freedom from fear."[38] The war was pulling people into a cesspool of oppression and, if there *was* a way out of it, the global community need assure that such structures be put in place. These concepts – indeed, FDR's words specifically – sit centrally in international rights documents, closely reproduced in their wordplay.[39] The attempt to prosecute Nazi crimes at Nuremberg was part of this; it furthered the idea that an authority beyond the laws of nation-states might be invoked. Beyond indicting Nazi honchos for "crimes against humanity," however, there was an idea that "law designed to protect all individuals from…abuse" need be furthered and embedded into organizations and practices that would further spread basic rights standards.[40]

For others, however, there's a more nuanced picture. Yes, the Allies, or the War's democratic powers, were involved in a "mid-century project of human rights;" the U.S., France, and Britain had varying levels of interest in not only national rights law, but sets of ideas about freedoms and privileges people should hold on an *international* scale. However, so too did many other states, and for a variety of reasons.[41] Self-determination was on the mind of nations like Saudi Arabia, Egypt, and India, taking up the charge to speak up for countries held under imperial yokes. Economically challenged nations, such as those of

---

36 United Nations, "The Universal Declaration of Human Rights" (1948, preamble), http://www.un.org/en/universal-declaration-human-rights/index.html. Hereafter UDHR.
37 Ibid., 39.
38 In Micheline R. Ishay, *The History of Human Rights: From Ancient Times to the Globalization Era* (Berkeley: University of California Press, 2004), 213.
39 The clearest example of this in the UDHR, which then stands as the foundation for most further international rights declarations. See UDHR, preamble.
40 Steven R. Ratner, et. al, *Accountability for Human Rights Atrocities in International Law: Beyond the Nuremberg Legacy* (Oxford: Oxford University Press, 2009), xlv.
41 Susan Waltz, "Reclaiming and Rebuilding the History of the Universal Declaration of Human Rights," *Third World Quarterly* 23, no. 3 (2002): 443.

Latin America, were interested in socio-economic rights; they provided early outlines to concepts like the "right to development" and addressing the alleviation of poverty at international levels. The women's movement had influence on the momentum around global rights ideals – assuring that half of the world's population, North, East, South or West, was treated on an equal basis, and not seen as second-class citizens. The American Civil Rights Movements and organizations like the NAACP supported human rights, attaching them to issues of racial justice. As such, none of these phenomena were necessarily contingent on Nazism; they weren't matters of the Holocaust or the overrun of eastern Europe in any ostensible sense.[42] And though, yes, Nazism was on diplomats' minds as they formulated international rights documents, that was often in generalistic terms, sometimes without *specifically* namechecking the persecution of Gypsies, homosexuals, or Jews.[43] Indeed, that's a striking lack – not clearly linking the murder of *two-thirds* of a relatively sizeable ethnic population on the continent of Europe with the new-found declarations of international humanity and its intrinsic worth. Indeed, this has led some to assert that the "save-the-world" humanitarianism with which rights are often associated may have *actually* been a matter of social movements emerging in the 1960s and '70s – artifacts of the Sakharov hearings and Eastern Bloc dissidents, the anti-war movement, and a free speech counter-culture.[44] In any case, human rights discourse post-World War II was relatively diverse, and the rationale behind institutionalizing rights had more than one logic.

This can be surprising. History provides certain moments in which you'd think a single theme would arc over all others; that there'd be undeniable unity of purpose: the end of the Second World War, the end of the Cold War, the end of the First World War – these are moments in which one might think that the calamities had been so large or the slog had been so long that there would be a simple statement that "this is what all this is about." The Holocaust can't be repeated, humanity can't divide itself into dueling ideological camps constantly at each other's throats, or the world can't afford to throw itself into large-scale conflict again; one would think there are just moments in which one would say "*that's* why it's important to indicate that life isn't just a war of 'every man against

---

42 See Jean Quataert, *Advocating Dignity: Human Rights Mobilizations in Global Politics* (Philadelphia: University of Pennsylvania Press, 2010).
43 This is a point made by both Moyn and Waltz.
44 This is, in essence, the thesis advanced by Samuel Moyn in *The Last Utopia*. See David Howe, review of *The Last Utopia: Human Rights in History* by Samuel Moyn, *International Affairs* 87, no. 6 (2011): 1511–2.

every man,'" as Hobbes put it, and that there is space for idealism in international affairs.[45] One would think that humanity *would* have taken a moment of silence and, instead of taking three years to produce a Universal Declaration of Human Rights, they would have taken three months. Still, history provides unpredictabilities. It being in no small part Wilson's idea, you would have thought the United States would be among the first in line to join the League of Nations after World War I, instead of being one of the few Western hold-outs. You might have thought that there might have been an extra diplomatic effort to get Saddam Hussein out of Kuwait instead of entering into conflict precisely as the world's mid-twentieth century geopolitical tensions were beginning to relax (the end of the Cold War). You would have thought that regimes like Franco's in Spain or the years of the colonels in Greece would have been impossible post-Hitler and Mussolini. And you would think that a finger pointed at the Holocaust and saying that "that – that's what human rights are about" would have emerged from every UN representative's lips. Only it wasn't quite so. If history is human spirit "emptied…into Time," as Hegel wrote, we might see spirit's journey as a rollercoaster. It's tough to predict the moments at which we coalesce around an idea and where things will get complex, or, at the very least, involve a diversity of interests in the call for change.[46]

That's while progress came. It's while an attempt to increase the spread of liberalism, create *some* level of international order, and spread concepts of global justice and political right *had* meaning; it's while the Universal Declaration, the Convention on the Prevention and Punishment of the Crime of Genocide (1948), and rights documents such as the European Convention on Human Rights (1950) were written. It's while it's because Allied powers and individuals like Robert Jackson sat Nazi leaders down and said "this is wrong" that we have precedence to say so today. It's while, when UN representatives spoke of Nazism's "barbarities," it's hard not to know what that means. Maybe anti-colonialism and the women's movement had influence on human rights; maybe America's civil rights movements had its impact. However, any anti-genocide activist would applaud extending rights in such directions, and realizing that so much of Nazi destruction came from social exclusion may have provided the occasion for groups seeking varieties of *in*clusion to state their case. Perhaps there's something to saying that it's misleading to suggest a clear line from Nazi Ragnarök

---

45 See Thomas Hobbes, *Leviathan*, ed. Edwin Curley (Indianapolis: Hackett, 1994), 76.
46 G.W.F. Hegel, *Phenomenology of Spirit*, trans. A.V. Miller (New York: Oxford University Press, 1977), 492.

to clarion calls of human rights in the years following World War II. Maybe the line from Nazi parade grounds to Courtroom 600 or the UN Human Rights Council isn't precisely straight. Still, if Nazi crimes were *any* part of thoughts of concerning new definitions of international justice, that matters. If looking at fascist oppression and acknowledging its eliminationist tendencies brought *anyone* to say "we need to institutionalize liberty, people's legal recognition, and non-discriminatory privilege on a global plane," that has significance. *Any* way of saying "there has to have been a reason to have fought this war exceeding the rights of nations" denotes World War II as more than *realpolitik*. There's a difference between a world in which international rights conventions exist and a world in which they don't. A world in which they do leaves those concepts to refer to; a world in which such things aren't present leaves humanitarian law as a lack. The narrative axis from the Nazi's "Party Days" to Courtroom 600 and beyond has meaning. It provides at least *part* of the outline of a world in which, if one *doesn't* refer to rights concepts, one has to explain why.[47]

Still, the stories that we put together regarding our atmospheres – the things we tell ourselves about the lifeworlds we find ourselves in – at some level, refer back to those atmospheres *themselves*. They refer to the subject as he or she stands at the *lieux de mémoire*, compressed between the realities of the things they confront and the ideas we have propagated about them. There's an issue of what one is doing somewhere, and why one finds oneself at a site. One can debate academic particulars; one can talk theses and historiography. There's nonetheless a question of what *drives* one somewhere and the meaning a location has – whether that meaning involves a simplification of affairs or not.

Simply put, no one goes to the Nuremberg Palace of Justice for the coffee and there are few *tabula rasas* as one walks through Courtroom 600's doors. It would be the rare person who would run randomly across Nuremberg's Nazi party rally grounds and who wouldn't have pieced together *some* concept of what they're looking at (that it has to do with a wrong, and it represents behaviors we've tried to escape). There are issues of historical facticity and debates concerning the tales we tell. If more was involved in rights consciousness than the Holocaust, if the Nuremberg Trials weren't a naïve process, or if there are multiple perspectives on how the German nation and German culture contributed to the tragedies of the Second World War, those are things we need to know.

---

47 This thesis – the mainstreaming power of rights – is developed in Thomas Risse, Stephen C. Ropp and Kathryn Sikkink, eds., *The Power of Human Rights: International Norms and Domestic Change* (Cambridge, MA: Cambridge University Press, 1999).

We need to investigate how historical meaning is constructed and, in the same manner that the meaning of things as we have them is important, we need to have sensitivities to the nuances and, if accepted narratives are simply wrong, we need to know that too. If it turns out that Hitler wasn't pulling the strings in Nazi Germany, we'd want to know that, as we would if George Washington had but a minor part in the American Revolution. That's while there *is* a question of the meaning of things as they're had, and the narratives that orient us as we stand in the spaces of historical imagery – in the case of Nuremberg, a vortex of historical intensity in which the fate of so many seemed to be involved.

Here, we *do* have a rights issue. Here, one *might* debate whether or not 1930s and '40s Germany was gripped by a kind of madness, or if German history has involved some particularly dark tendencies. Here, one *can* debate whether or not Göring and other Nazis who marched around Nuremberg before the War had their fates pre-decided, or if their trial was a political affair. We can debate about the *kinds* of punishment the Nuremberg Trials meted out. Though yes, there were acquittals, there were also killings: judicial ones, in which the death sponsored by Hans Frank, Wilhelm Frick and others was met by death itself. Maybe there's something unfair in that – a lack of doing unto others as one would have done unto oneself. Maybe Nuremberg's justice was short-sighted, not practicing the fullest ethics for which human rights might provide (life, say, even for those convicted of genocide).[48] Still, we need be clear on what had been celebrated at Nuremberg – what was valorized on the Zeppelin Field and with the boots tramping down the Great Road. Celebrated was a "reawakening" in which the nation was to be purified by destroying others and individuality suppressed with free thought relinquished in favor of conformist wholes. Fêted was a politics of derision, a demeaning of fellow persons, and a ridiculing of things one didn't like. The Nazi's "party days" celebrated the politics of the gun; they valorized the idea that the nation should be martial, not civil, and that it should be oriented towards war as opposed to freedom and peace. The Nuremberg Trials involved asserting counter-values – proposing that, while one can't easily prescribe social

---

48 Indeed, though the death penalty is not *outlawed* via international rights conventions, it is frowned upon. The International Covenant on Civil and Political Rights, e.g., refers to "countries which have not abolished the death penalty" – a recognition that it might be maintained, yet that it isn't in the spirit of basic rights ideals. See United Nations, "International Covenant on Civil and Political Rights" (1966, article 6), https://www.ohchr.org/en/professionalinterest/pages/ccpr.aspx. See also William A. Schabas, *The Abolition of the Death Penalty in International Law* (Cambridge: Cambridge University Press, 2002).

morality, at least war-mongering and mass murder should be out. They suggested one *could* commit crimes against humanity, and not just violate the laws of war. Such ideas had momentum; regardless of whether Latin American states sought economic development, there was more than a little finger pointing at Nazism in writing the Universal Declaration, and there was acknowledgment that fascism was a threat to justice. When at Nuremberg, it's hard *not* to confront such concepts to the extent that, at the moment one engages the city further than its castles and does more than drink beers in its sometimes-in-need-of-a-bit-of-upkeep streets, that's the meaning that screams through. The sense that, vis-à-vis its modern history, we're looking at one of the most horrific abandonments of humanitarian values, is the dominant feeling for spectators standing in front of the Congress Hall. The sense that it was built for a parade of evil is what people think as they wander up the Great Road, as is the feeling that one is at a site of insanity as one stands near the rostrum at the Zeppelin Field. However, so too is the sense that one is in a room that helped resolve some of that when one goes to the *Justizpalast* and contemplates where international justice went from there.

To that extent, then, we have to ask what human rights are. To the extent that we're interested in them, we need ask what human rights are intended to *do*. We need to ask about the consequences if we *don't* have interest in rights ideals, and we need ask what it might mean if we deconstruct the concept, or if we *don't* take scenes like those in Nuremberg to be about the need for liberation and humanitarian thought. What happens if we *don't* understand the *lieux de fascisme*, as one might put it, to concern "freedom, justice and peace in the world" – and, really, if we don't assert such sites as charging us to think about that question, can we see them appealing to anything else?

Regarding the question of what happens if we stand in the Zeppelin Field and *don't* feel nudged towards rights ideals, or one steps into Courtroom 600 and doesn't get the sense that "this is a heck of a lot better than that" (say, the images associated with the Congress Hall), I'd say we're indicating one of two things: either we don't care – moral discourse doesn't affect us much – or we're willing to let such things happen again. We are either indicating oblivion (and, with the massive amount of education on the Third Reich and the Holocaust, I wonder about the degree to which that's possible) or that we're there to *celebrate* the site's ideals (a revolting concept). Now, not everyone's a political philosopher. The messages of *lieux de mémoire* may be hard to articulate or feel somehow vague. Maybe we'd have a hard time writing a five-page essay on the meaning of the party rally grounds or Courtroom 600, or we're not ready to hold a lecture at the public library on the issue. However, if senses of oppression and compassion for brutal experiences aren't things we're able to feel, we need ask ourselves about our values, our educational systems, and the knowledge our societies are organized around. We need to ask into what *is* being lectured about in the public library and, if that at least *partially* concerns what our fellow human beings go through, why the message isn't getting through. Indeed, as much as it's ok to let the dominant story *be* the story – say, that the Nazi past simply represents something "out of order" – that's the reason for telling an *alternative* tale: to think more closely about experience and consider the meanings *we'd* like it to have. Let's put aside anyone who would be interested in Nazism rising again or goes in for discrimination. We may have a cultural crisis if many of us can go to the Zeppelin Field and it's absent much effect.

That, however, revolves around what rights should do. It revolves around what humanitarianism should accomplish. It concerns what liberation should be about, as well as the institutionalization of international law. *If* we want the Congress Hall, Great Road, and Zeppelin Field to say "rights problems!", and Courtroom 600 should say, "here's how to deal with it!", what are we looking for, and what do we think people deserve? Why was Robert Jackson's expounding important and what's the nature of Roosevelt's four freedoms? What might *we* do that the Nazis didn't – or, phrased differently, what did the Nazis do that we *don't* want to do, and what's the *point* of preserving things like "freedom of speech and belief" and "freedom from fear?"[49]

I'd pose this as a matter of emancipation. I'd pose it as a matter of reflection and being who one is. I'd pose it as a matter of thinking as one wants, having a dash of creativity in one's life, and exercising a degree of sovereignty over oneself. I'd pose it as a bit of autonomy – living with some level of possession of the self. Now, I'm not sure whether Rousseau was right when he suggested that to "renounce one's liberty is to renounce one's humanity."[50] Humanity may extend partly from *not* telling others what their humanity *is* – and one may not want to be told oneself. I also don't know if existence need be an "act of rebellion," as Camus put it; perhaps we can have existences where not every moment is an existential meditation or reflection on the authenticity of the self. If we don't preserve *some* space for freedom, however, we are condemning ourselves to no sovereignty and the risk of *always* being told who we are. If some space isn't carved out to be "us," we relinquish ourselves as the source of authority and leave space for the idea that we might *not* be equal with everyone else. Even if one *wanted*

---

49 See UDHR, preamble.
50 Jean-Jacques Rousseau, *The Social Contract and the First and Second Discourses*, ed. Susan Dunn (New Haven: Yale University Press, 2002), 159.

a society of brownshirts and Strength-through-Joy (the Nazi cultural organization engaged in popular brainwashing), we'd never know that unless the space was preserved for free thought. We'd never know that's what people wanted unless they were not only asked, but had the space to reflect. And, honestly, while Goldhagen was onto something – that *someone* put Jews, Gypsies, communists, Slavs, homosexuals and other "undesirables" to death – I'd say that's the largest hole in his thesis: that after Hitler came to power, Germany saw the institutionalized end of dissent. That makes it hard to say if Nazism reflected what German's wanted, or if it's rather what they got.

Finally, though, if we take sites like Nuremberg to ultimately concern justice, we have few ways to discuss the issue except through human rights. I get it: do human rights simply rise like a phoenix from the ashes of the Second World War – a kind of negative, "my God, what have we done?" reaction of humanity to itself? Evidence provides more subtlety; the soup of human rights was cooked by many different chefs. It seems like many had Nazis, the Holocaust, and Hitler's horrors in mind – however, also, many not (or at least not only that). Still, it might be partly Nuremberg's legacy, both through the party rallies and the trials, that when we *say* a historical scene has to do with justice on a larger scale, it's rights ideals to which we largely appeal. Again, a lot of moments have played into rights' popularity: World War II, 1960s counter-culture and the Vietnam War, issues surrounding dissidents and free speech activists in the Eastern Bloc, and perhaps the end of the Cold War itself. Nazism, the Holocaust, and the violence of World War II isn't absent the scene, however, and that has decided meaning.

I'd thus leave off with this. The number of sites, or "sites of memory," in which narratives play out regarding tragedy, and specifically tragedy organized around Germany and the Second World War, is extensive. If one is in Berlin and goes to the parliament, or *Bundestag*, one is confronted with something similar. The building – largely disused after Germany disbanded parliament come the '30s – was bombed and destroyed over the course of the war. Some sense of the damage has been left in place; it's possible to see where the cupola was crushed – that in a building which now serves as the nation's capital. That represents the tragedy of the war; it's the abyss into which Germany pulled the world via Nazi ideals. It's all the bombs that were dropped not only in thousands of places around Europe, but around the world. Today, however, that cupola has been replaced with a glass dome in which, again, one can *see* where bombs fell and damage was done. However, the rising glass also provides an indication of hope as one looks onto the floor of a democratic legislature, concerned with law, privilege, and the people's business. It's the building of something good and a reconstruction of not only Germans', but *everyone's*, rights. Out of the pit of Nazism came an alteration – a course adjustment, a remaking, and a putting things into a better place. It's not dissimilar to the line one might draw from the party rally grounds to Courtroom 600: the worst of the worst leading to something better.

That's while Nuremberg provides a particular compression. There's an intensity to its scenery, and a sense of weight on one's chest. As one goes through the town, one *feels* bookended by history and squashed in by the past. One feels the enormity of what went on in the city – that for better and worse. On one hand, the worse: the party rally grounds are *massive*; you can't ignore what Hitler's henchmen tried to do. They sought to put their thumb on people and ground them into inconsequence. The whole thing sits there – a seething, monstrous wreck. Of course, the Palace of Justice isn't bombastic like the rally grounds. It's the better end of things: the attempt to speak to a higher law and take the world in a new direction. That's also monumental, however: turning back evil and trying to tear a new page for world history while trying to ball up and toss out the old. It's significant, Nuremberg; the *lieux de mémoire* on turbo-charge.

That pressure, though – the intensity – pushes something out. It makes something crystalline; it crushes a debate into an object of diamond clarity. This is that "special path" or not, something happened in Germany. A regime *was* built on the simple act of murder, and as widespread as European anti-Semitism was, no one quite saw racist views so thoroughly through to their conclusion as the Nazis did. Justice in reaction to that regime was hard to keep objective. No one was out to make the Nazis look good, and it would have been problematic for the Allies if Göring wound up vacationing in the Antilles. Still, the evidence was overwhelming: the camps, piles of corpses, and the egregious abuses of civil rights. The Holocaust-to-human-rights story has its facile nature; in fact, it might take away from what rights accomplish if their foundations are whittled down to *only* fascism and the Second World War. That might be what Nuremberg hands us, however, regardless of anything else– that history's message is "Never Again!", and, that the purpose of putting people in such pressure cookers of memory is to make sure that message is heard loud and clear.

Khashoggi
A Tragedy and a Wrong
(October 22, 2018)

Abstract: *The journalist Jamal Khashoggi appears to have met a violent death among suspicious circumstances – that due to his dissent against the Saudi regime. There's suspicion that the government itself had Khashoggi killed – a shocking idea. Khashoggi's death is a tragedy in the first degree. It particularly stings, however, because Khashoggi, as do all serious commentators and journalists, organized his life around the principles lying at the heart of human rights: free thought, the open exchange of ideas, and the free expression of the self.*

The Jamal Khashoggi case has been in the news a lot over the past few weeks, and it's a tragedy – a tragedy and a wrong. The outlines of the case have been complex. Firstly, there is the figure of Khashoggi himself. In general, the man has been posed as a "dissident journalist," and largely that's so. However, his positions have been subtle, and painting him with a single brush may not be totally correct. There's no doubt that Khashoggi advocated for a much freer press and a radically greater level of self-expression than is often allowed in Saudi Arabia, his native country – the government of the House of Saud, for example, ranking ninth from the bottom on The Economist Intelligence Unit's Democracy Index.¹

"Newspapers" @ Purple Anvil / shutterstock.com 598583138

Khashoggi himself, however, imagined himself as a Saudi *patriot*, and watching him make a presentation at the Arab Center in Washington D.C. in 2017, one hears him proclaim that he "called for [essentially] everything Mohammad bin Salman is doing

---

1   The Economist Intelligence Unit, "Democracy Index 2017: Free Speech under Attack" (2017), https://www.eiu.com/topic/democracy-index.

right now."[2] I.e., Khashoggi saw *himself* as behind what, until his murder, looked like a legitimate attempt at regime reform and an attempt to make the Saudi state look a *bit* more modern.[3] Khashoggi also largely identified Iran as perhaps the region's greatest threat – Iran being the great Mid-East power outside of Saudi Arabia and in a contest with the Saudis for supremacy throughout the area – and he was *quite* willing to serve as a spokesman for Saudi culture, helping outsiders navigate the ins and outs of the country's politics as well as understand the nation's historical turns. Still, the overtones of Khashoggi's final editorial are clear. Published posthumously in *The Washington Post*, Khashoggi proclaimed that "[in the Arab world], we suffer from poverty, mismanagement and poor education. Through the creation of an independent international forum, isolated from the influence of nationalist governments spreading hate through propaganda, ordinary people in the Arab world would be able to address the structural problems their societies face." There needed to be more "oas[es] that continue to embody the spirit of the Arab Spring," Khashoggi contended, and authoritarianism was still rife in the region extending from North Africa to the hinterlands of Iran.[4] It was partly for this reason that Khashoggi moved to the U.S. He sought the open air of democracy and the constitutional-guaranteed ability to write and speak more or less as he'd like.[5]

So, what happened? Explanations have been coming hard and fast. Khashoggi was in Turkey, where he apparently had a fiancée. The two wanted to marry, which involved some paperwork, which Khashoggi went to the Saudi consulate to get – there is security footage that shows him entering consulate premises, at which point, all was fine. It wasn't fine for long, however, as Khashoggi apparently never came out. There are reports that a fifteen-man hit squad showed up in Istanbul to get him – something which *also* appears true as there's video of

---

2   Arab Center Washington DC, "Shake Up in Riyadh: Regional and International Implications," November 17, 2017, https://www.youtube.com/watch?v=IPn4LqEKkak&t=1923s.
3   See Deutsche Welle, "Saudi Arabia: Prince Says Women Should Decide Whether to Wear Robes, Face Veils," March 19, 2018, https://www.dw.com/en/saudi-arabia-prince-says-women-should-decide-whether-to-wear-robes-face-veils/a-43043071.
4   Jamal Khashoggi, "What the Arab World Needs Most is Free Expression," *The Washington Post*, October 17, 2018, https://www.washingtonpost.com/opinions/global-opinions/jamal-khashoggi-what-the-arab-world-needs-most-is-free-expression/2018/10/17/adfc8c44-d21d-11e8-8c22-fa2ef74bd6d6_story.html?utm_term=.616d8549dc05.
5   See Alison Tahmizian Meuse, "Who is Jamal Khashoggi?" *Asia Times*, October 10, 2018, https://www.asiatimes.com/2018/10/article/who-is-jamal-khashoggi//.

some pretty suspicious characters showing up at Atatürk International Airport and, because they bug the Saudi embassy, Turkish security seems to be sitting on audiotape in which one can hear Khashoggi being killed. The Saudis say some sort of conflagration took place; that the operation wasn't sanctioned by the government. Could be; bureaucracies are complex, and one can't always know who ordered what. Still, no government culpability is *also* hard to imagine as, more than a dozen guys showing up on consular grounds and beating someone to a pulp? How could such a thing take place without *some* kind of official knowing *something*, or someone having signed off on *some* document – or, at the very least, having looked away?[6]

It's hard to know what to say about the whole affair. The reaction of the Americans, particularly that of Donald Trump, has gotten the lion's share of the attention. It's been like every time Trump has been asked to call out authoritarians or strongmen: he's only done so with the greatest reluctance and a lot of hemming and hawing over what others see as clear moral ground. Saudi Arabia's *de facto* leader (bin Salman), tweeted Trump, "has totally denied what took place in their Turkish Consulate" (Trump loves to capitalize things that, grammatically, one isn't supposed to).[7] "Here we go again," the President bemoaned; *à la* Brett Kavanaugh, over-zealous liberals were looking to condemn anyone they saw as a villain without due process.[8] Maybe he's right. Kavanaugh was never convicted and, for that matter, bin Salman hasn't been either. Still, how hard is it to say that one is concerned with dignity and that one's primary thought is with *free* thought – that as opposed to weapons deals or insisting that "it's not *our* job to uphold the standards of international law"?[9] It echoes Trump's handling of

---

6 I simply note that consular ground is official ground. I also note that it's pure speculation as to *who* within the Saudi government knew about the plot to kill Khashoggi. That there was a plot, though, seems clear. Again, a hit squad showed up in Istanbul, and it included men from Saudi security. And, again, one simply can't ignore where it took place. Either everyone in the Saudi consulate went home, or someone in government employ was in the know. See Martin Chulov and Bethan McKernan, "Jamal Khashoggi: Details of Alleged Saudi Hit Squad Emerge," *The Guardian*, October 10, 2018, https://www.theguardian.com/world/2018/oct/10/alleged-saudi-hit-squad-linked-to-jamal-khashoggi-disappearance.
7 Ben Hubbard, Rick Gladstone and Mark Landler, "Trump Jumps to the Defense of Saudi Arabia in Khashoggi Case," *The New York Times*, October 16, 2018, https://www.nytimes.com/2018/10/16/world/middleeast/pompeo-saudi-arabia-turkey.html.
8 Ibid.
9 See Landler, "In Extraordinary Statement, Trump Stands with Saudis Despite Khashoggi Killing," *The New York Times*, November 20, 2018, https://www.nytimes.

Russia and North Korea. I haven't problems with better relations with traditional rivals or undoing the vestiges of Cold War. Journalists and dissidents *have been* subject to severe crackdowns under Putin's eighteen years of rule, however, and, *North Korea*? The man the Americans are elevating on the world stage has had rival family members executed with *anti-aircraft guns*, to say nothing of the tens of thousands who languish in the country's gulags.[10]

Then there *is* Saudi Arabia. There was clear excitement with the arrival of bin Salman in power. Technically, the Crown Prince isn't head of state; that honor goes to his father, King Salman bin Abdulaziz al Saud. Day to day operations have been handed to MBS, however, and to much fanfare, among the Prince's first acts were allowing Saudi citizens to go to movie theaters again, making "morality police" less present in town squares, and (most famously) allowing women to drive. These were meaningful reforms, and there *are* senses in which they represented a variety of "Saudi Spring."[11] Still, as *The Economist* reported in June – well before the Khashoggi incident – bin Salman had been going hard after political enemies, the number of dissidents in Saudi jails was going *up*, and the country was using impressive amounts of funds to prosecute its brutal war in Yemen (a war largely fought with American arms).[12] It raises the question as to whether bin Salman was really interested in *civil rights*, or if he calculated-out but a few splashy moves to paper-over the same old authoritarian line. Sure; go

---

    com/2018/11/20/world/middleeast/trump-saudi-khashoggi.html; Louis Rene Beres, "Trump's Defense of Saudi Arabia after Khashoggi Murder Violates Law and Justice," *Jurist*, November 24, 2018, https://www.jurist.org/commentary/2018/11/louis-beres-khashoggi-murder/.

10 See Justin McCurry, "North Korea Executes Officials with Anti-Aircraft Gun in New Purge – Report," *The Guardian*, August 30, 2016, https://www.theguardian.com/world/2016/aug/30/north-korea-reportedly-executes-officials-anti-aircraft-gun-purge.

11 See David Ignatius, "Are Saudi Arabia's Reforms for Real? A Recent Visit Says Yes," *The Washington Post*, March 1, 2018, https://www.washingtonpost.com/opinions/global-opinions/are-saudi-arabias-reforms-for-real-a-recent-visit-says-yes/2018/03/01/a11a4ca8-1d9d-11e8-9de1-147dd2df3829_story.html?utm_term=.2ce7121820b2; Thomas L. Friedman, "Saudi Arabia's Arab Spring, At Last," *The New York Times*, November 23, 2017, https://www.nytimes.com/2017/11/23/opinion/saudi-prince-mbs-arab-spring.html.

12 Declan Walsh and Erin Schmitt, "Arm Sales to Saudis Leave American Fingerprints on Yemen's Carnage," *The New York Times*, December 18, 2018, https://www.nytimes.com/2018/12/25/world/middleeast/yemen-us-saudi-civilian-war.html.

see *Black Panther* in Riyadh. It may be dangerous to criticize the Crown Prince, however, as the man may have a hit squad.[13]

With that said, though, it's nonetheless clear that that's what the issue is: human rights. At play is *some* set of universal standards to which global politics is supposed to be held, and *some* sense of moral rectitude on a more or less global plane – and rectitude not just as a matter of philosophy, but as a matter of policy and law. Now, this is tricky. The number of places in which it's been noted that human rights standards are really artifacts of Western liberalism is innumerable, and I myself have noted that one of the things that makes Saudi Arabia interesting is that it asks us to consider what to do when, as one regime representative put it, someone proposes an alternate "-ism." What happens when someone holds out a substitute for mainstream ideologies and asserts that secular progressivisms aren't the *only* guideposts societies might follow? Who gets to decide what the "right" rights standards are – that *regardless* of whether the government or religious authorities in the Saudi Kingdom represent the Saudi people's will?[14]

Now, I'll just say I see the first point as unlikely. I *don't* see bin Salman as out to defend Saudi Wahhabism, and I *don't* see him as the spokesperson for an alternate "worldview" – that except to the extent that it might be politically expedient. I don't perceive bin Salman as a religious warrior, and I don't see him as concerned with Arab "authenticity." No doubt: one can wonder why it's ideas with roots in the European Enlightenment that always need hold sway, and it's important to ask why, every time a major event plays out on the world stage, the first question is the reaction of the Europeans and Americans. We can surely discuss legacies of intellectual colonialism and, we can absolutely note that Saudi Arabia was lodging objections to dimensions of human rights thought as they were being formulated in the UN in the 1940s.[15] I'm not sure those concerned *free speech*, however (largely, they didn't), and I'm not sure that's why Khashoggi

---

13 The Guardian, "Saudi Arabia's First Cinema in over 35 Years Opens with *Black Panther*," April 20, 2018, https://www.theguardian.com/world/2018/apr/20/saudi-arabias-first-cinema-in-over-35-years-opens-with-black-panther.

14 See Ben Dorfman, "What to Do with the Kingdom?: Rights and Cultural Life" in *13 Acts of Academic Journalism and Historical Commentary on Human Rights: Opinions, Interventions and the Torsions of Politics* (Frankfurt am Main: Peter Lang, 2017), 109–24.

15 See Johannes Morsink, *The Universal Declaration of Human Rights: Origins, Drafting & Intent* (Philadelphia: University of Pennsylvania Press, 1999), 21–7. Saudi Arabia abstained from ratification of the Universal Declaration – one of a small handful of

would disappear on *consular* grounds. I'm not sure that's why the Saudis are launching an "investigation" into the Khashoggi incident, nor why the Saudi government is saying it has "no idea" what happened. I don't know if that really explains bin Salman's press junkets, or his seeming interest in gussying-up the Saudi image.[16] There have been debates in Saudi society about the House of Saud glad-handing Presidents from Eisenhower to various Bushes to Trump. Many also wonder if the decision to allow hundreds of thousands of troops on Saudi soil in the first Gulf War contributed to 9/11.[17] It doesn't seem like *that's* what's going on here, though. The whole thing *looks* like a free speech issue and, specifically, a regime saying "a few reforms, ok; but now you've spoken more than freely enough."

And, indeed, what *of* the Saudi people's will? What *of* the popular voice? Is that to be *discounted*? Do we need say that we have to accept the mores of what one political philosopher has called "decent hierarchical peoples" and that we can extend *no* expectations of political liberalism as long as people are clothed and fed? Indeed, can "hierarchical peoples" behave in *authoritarian* ways – and can authoritarianism extend to the killing of citizens beyond *national borders* (and here, of course, "can" means "should")?[18]

---

    states to do so (with the exception of South Africa, the others were the Communist Bloc). Partly, this was on cultural grounds; there were concerns that the formulation of UN rights was too "western." As such, though, freedom of speech doesn't seem to have been the primary issue. The right to choose one's religion and marrying *across* religions was (though, admittedly, religious freedom involves free speech issues). See also Makau Matua, *Human Rights: A Political and Cultural Critique* (Philadelphia: University of Pennsylvania Press, 2002).

16 Reuters, "Saudi Team Arrives in Istanbul for Khashoggi Investigation: Sources," October 12, 2018, https://www.reuters.com/article/us-saudi-politics-dissident-turkey/saudi-team-arrives-in-turkey-for-khashoggi-investigation-sources-idUSKCN1MM12A; Mike O'Sullivan, "Saudi Prince Wraps Up Charm Offensive Tour," *VOA New*, April 13, 2018, https://www.voanews.com/a/saudi-crown-prince-tour-charm-offensive/4347201.html.

17 See Rachel Bronson, *Thicker Than Oil: America's Uneasy Partnership with Saudi Arabia* (Oxford: Oxford University Press, 2008); Dorfman, "What to Do with the Kingdom?"; Bruce Riedel, *Kings and Presidents: Saudi Arabia and the United States since FDR* (Washington DC: Brookings Institution, 2019).

18 See John Rawls, *The Law of Peoples* (Cambridge, MA: Harvard University Press, 1999). Of course, consulates aren't foreign territory. Still, going after someone in an embassy abroad is a daring move; one sure to stir up controversy.

I have to say "no." Firstly, the notion of accepting that not everyone might be as democratic as everyone else is contingent upon the society in question *meeting* socio-economic standards. All *in fact* have to be properly clothed and fed, and all need be provided an education and held from destitution. Everyone should be able to see a doctor, and everybody need be assured a roof over their heads. In Saudi Arabia, that's not a given. I.e., for all its oil wealth, the country has a well-documented poverty problem and, never mind gender issues, the country has problems in terms of making sure all its *children* are fed (that to say nothing of serious problems of wealth *disparity*).[19] Moreover, one has to ask if that's really enough. Can we *really* say, "hey, you've got food on your plate; pipe down now, and stop asking for change"? *Are* demonstrations featuring the Shi'a minority supposed to be fired on with live rounds, and are dissidents supposed to disappear in Saudi prisons – or worse yet, be executed for expressing an opinion? Those are pretty low standards – and, as some have argued, if that's all we're looking for, we're not looking for much.[20]

Here, human rights matter. Here, international norms have consequence. In this context, ideas of better deportment carry water, and, on such terrain, demands that we *not* just provide sufficient food and shelter carry some weight. Now, socio-economic rights *are* human rights, and those must be addressed. Let someone starve and there's nothing to discuss as regards free thought or speech.[21] Indeed, freedom can also be realized in a lot of ways. Rights belong to "peoples," and collectivities should be able to express themselves. There deserves to be a level of national self-expression as such things are somehow matters of

---

19 See Kevin Sullivan, "Saudi Arabia's Riches Conceal a Growing Problem of Poverty," *The Guardian*, January 1, 2013, https://www.theguardian.com/world/2013/jan/01/saudi-arabia-riyadh-poverty-inequality; Sherifa Zuhur, *Saudi Arabia* (Santa Barbara: ABC-Clio, 2011) 252. By the wealth disparity issue, I mean that there *may* be a moral obligation in which portions of society are enormously wealthy – be it in the U.S. or in the Gulf – to really assure the availability of a middle-class life to a nation's people and assure that the extremes of wealth don't grow too far apart. See Samuel Moyn, *Not Enough: Human Rights in an Unequal World* (Cambridge, MA: Harvard University Press, 2018).
20 See C.L. Ten, *Theories of Rights* (Farnham: Ashgate, 2006), 420. See also Toby Matthiesen, "A Saudi Spring?: The Shi'a Movement in the Eastern Province 2011–2012," *Middle East Journal* 66, no. 4 (2012): 628–59. I will also simply turn readers to the Human Rights Watch World Report section on Saudi Arabia, "Saudi Arabia: Events of 2018," https://www.hrw.org/world-report/2019/country-chapters/saudi-arabia.
21 See Philips Alston and Katarina Tomaševski, eds., *The Right to Food* (The Hague: Martinus Nijhoff, 1984).

free though.²² Still, expressing interest in an Islamic Republic or Lutheran state church only makes sense if one can consider what one wants *oneself*, and if one is allowed decide that it's in relation to such entities that one wants to *live*. Culture has to come from *individuals*, and not predetermined ideas of who the people "are."²³ The philosopher Jean-Jacques Rousseau once suggested that it might be that to "renounce one's freedom is to renounce one's humanity."²⁴ To not maintain a modicum of critical perspective and not assure systems in which others can do the same is to give up the essence of who one is. The rationale behind this is simple: some of us might *want* to think and say something, and more to the point, all of us may maintain the capacity to do so. If a government or authority speaks on behalf of people who haven't expressed themselves, they can't claim to speak on behalf of the people *themselves*. Such things might be examples of "might makes right;" they may be examples of rulers "imposing" their will. I'm not sure it's even that, though. Ruling without reference to democratic process is ruling in reference to nothing – no agreement, no opinion, no cultural self, and no evidence for one's claims. It's a Nietzschean "will to power" in the worst of its nihilistic sense.²⁵ As John Locke put it, perhaps security means "divest[ing]

---

22 Human rights themselves note that "all peoples have the right of self-determination. By virtue of that right they freely determine their political status and freely pursue their economic, social and cultural development." See United Nations, "International Covenant on Civil and Political Rights" (1966, article 1), https://www.ohchr.org/en/professionalinterest/pages/ccpr.aspx. Hereafter ICCPR. See also Avishai Margalit and Joseph Raz, "National Self-Determination," *The Journal of Philosophy* 87, no. 9 (1990): 439–61.

23 See Yael Tamir, *Liberal Nationalism* (Princeton: Princeton University Press, 1993). It should also simply be noted, however, that cultural rights have to be reconciled with the right to self-expression; a primary right noted in nearly every major international human rights document. See, e.g., ICCPR, article 19, United Nations, "The Universal Declaration of Human Rights" (1948, article 19), https://www.un.org/en/universal-declaration-human-rights/index.html. Hereafter UDHR.

24 Jean-Jacques Rousseau, *The Social Contract*, trans. Maurice Cranston (New York: Penguin, 1968), 55,

25 There are a lot of interpretations of Nietzsche's politics. It is nonetheless problematic when he writes things like the "great man…is colder, harder, less hesitating, and without fear of opinion," and that the "same conditions that hasten the evolution of the herd also hasten the evolution of the leader animal." I understand that such statements may have been a critique of modern conformity, or perhaps an attempt to be post-political. Nonetheless, it gives a sense of justifying might and hierarchy as principles for social organization, or at least social *value* – something just not in the spirit of human rights. See Friedrich Nietzsche, *The Will to Power*, ed. Walter Kaufman

ourselves" of our "natural liberty."[26] Maybe we need to give something up to get something back. That shouldn't be such that we have *no* input into what security means, however, and it's not such that citizens who are supposed to *contribute* to the social contract should suddenly become its victims. As much as human rights look after many things – food, shelter, housing, education, access to a doctor – that might be their heart: the right to autonomous reflection and the possibility of intellectual choice.

To that extent, then, when I think of Khashoggi – when I think of the murder of a man who said many things, yes, but also simply asked for the right to think and say out loud – I think about that: basic rights. I think not only of the notion of the right to life – the idea that someone shouldn't be just flat-out *killed* – but I think of the notion of what it is that human rights should be *about*. I think of the idea of maintaining not just "bare life," as it's been put, but maintaining life that has a *purpose*; a life in which we have the ability to leave our thumbprint on the world.[27] I think of lives in which we *don't* relinquish our humanity, and in which we think about the ways in which others might be free too. One never wants to "academicize" a tragedy. Murder and the abuse of power aren't to be related to by quoting philosophers. A few remarks about democracy aren't hardcore advocacy, and wagging one's finger around about free speech doesn't qualify one for the Nobel Prize. Liberal ideals nonetheless encapsulate a significant part of who Khashoggi was, and they formed the foundations of his work for popular voice. They describe the arc of a life of a writer and a journalist who tried to chronicle his world. As human rights put it, Khashoggi sought the "full development" of the human "personality;" he looked for the "due recognition" of the cognizance we inevitably have.[28] He sought to underline "reason and conscience" as life's foundations, and he asked for dialog in place of rule by threat.[29] Supposedly, on the tape held by Turkish security, you can hear Khashoggi's bones cracking and evidence of the worst corporeal abuse. You can hear the dismemberment of another human being and a fellow person crying out in pain. Such

---

(New York: Vintage, 1968), 501, 505; see also David Owen, *Nietzsche, Politics, and Modernity* (London: Sage, 1995).

26 John Locke, *Second Treatise of Government*, ed. Richard Cox (Wheeling: Harlan Davidson, 1982), 58.
27 I borrow here from the vocabulary of Giorgio Agamben in *Homo Sacer: Sovereign Power and Bare Life*, trans. Daniel Heller-Roazen (Stanford: Stanford University Press, 1998).
28 UDHR, article 29.
29 Ibid., article 1.

things are tragedies and wrongs when done to anyone – tragedies playing out a thousand times a day. What *makes* such things tragedies, however, is the snuffing out of voice; it's the murder of *esprit*, *Geist*, and reflection – the things that make us "us," and which define our individual and collective lives. Boy, I can't wait until we stop abusing each other on those levels. It will be interesting to see what happens on the day that *all* governments throw open the doors of democracy and we're *all* allowed to participate in building the societies in which we live. Our worlds should never belong to the privileged few, and people like Khashoggi should certainly never have to pay for exercises of power with either their spiritual or physical lives.

Political and Social Change

Edited by Martin Bak Jørgensen and Óscar García Agustín

Volume 1   Martin Bak Jørgensen / Óscar García Agustín (eds.): Politics of Dissent. 2015.

Volume 2   Laura Bang Lindegaard: Congestion. Rationalising Automobility in the Face of Climate Change. 2015.

Volume 3   Ben Dorfman (ed.): Dissent! Refracted. Histories, Aesthetics and Cultures of Dissent. 2016.

Volume 4   Aleksandra Ålund / Carl-Ulrik Schierup / Anders Neergaard (eds.): Reimagineering the Nation. Essays on Twenty-First-Century Sweden. 2017.

Volume 5   Mette Toft Nielsen / Peter Hervik: Women in post-revolutionary Egypt. Can Behaviour Be Controlled? 2017.

Volume 6   Ben Dorfman: 13 Acts of Academic Journalism and Historical Commentary on Human Rights. Opinions, Interventions and the Torsions of Politics. 2017.

Volume 7   Maren Lytje: On the Justice and Justification of Just War. How Does Life Dwell in the State? 2018.

Volume 8   Ben Dorfman: Rights under Trial, Rights Reflections. 13 Further Acts of Academic Journalism and Historical Commentary on Human Rights. 2020.

www.peterlang.com